HOSTILE CLIMATE

Jon Pepper

NORTH COVE PRESS
New York

Hostile Climate
Copyright © 2024 by Jon Pepper. All rights reserved.

No part of this book may be reproduced in any form or by any electronic or mechanical means, including information storage and retrieval systems, without permission in writing from the author. The only exception is by a reviewer, who may quote short excerpts in a review.

Cover design by Diane Pepper
Copy editing by Nicky Guerriero
Production and finished art by Erik Christopher

ISBN (paperback edition): 9798991111508

This book is a work of fiction. Names, characters, places, and incidents either are products of the author's imagination or are used fictitiously. Any resemblance to actual persons, living or dead, events, or locals is entirely coincidental.

More information is available at www.jonpepperbooks.com.

INTRODUCTION

The story you are about to read is fictional, but it is inspired by true events.

In the days around Christmas of 2022, Winter Storm Elliott blanketed the eastern two-thirds of the United States, killing more than a hundred people and knocking out power for six million more. It was the fifth time in eleven years that cold weather threatened the stability of the nation's grid.

Ten months later, a 167-page report on the disaster was issued by the Federal Energy Regulatory Commission and the North American Electric Reliability Corporation. It noted that the pressure inside all of New York City's major gas lines dropped to dangerously low levels during the storm. Had the power provider to America's largest city not been able to activate its liquified natural gas (LNG) capacities and the cold snap had not been broken, heat would have been lost for the entire winter, and the disaster would have become a catastrophe with many more fatalities.

"For the natural gas local distribution system to return system outages to normal operations, workers must go house-to-house and individually light every pilot light," the report noted. The power company "would have taken months to restore service, even with mutual assistance from other utilities, had it experienced a complete loss of its system."

The report made several recommendations to avoid another close call in the future, including a study on creating more natural gas infrastructure. Its findings were largely ignored by the news media, which focused instead on tying every hot day, wildfire, hurricane, and flood to a supposed "climate crisis" engulfing the world.

The *Wall Street Journal* noted the report in an editorial, which piqued my interest and inspired me to look further into the issue. What I found was that the rush by politicians, activists, foundations, government, and media to shut off the use of fossil fuels without adequate replacements was not only causing higher energy costs and inconvenience for the public. It was endangering lives in a way that very few people knew about.

JP
New York, 2024

"It's true! It's true! The crown has made it clear.
The climate must be perfect all the year."
—King Arthur in Camelot, by Alan Jay Lerner & Frederick Loewe

PART ONE

Earth Daze

1. A PUNCH AT LUNCH

Earth Day brought New York City dazzling sunshine, low humidity, and warmer-than-average temperatures, all of which were dutifully reported by the hand-wringing news media as signs the planet would soon die in a climate cataclysm.

The impending-doom scenario didn't faze Lindsey Harper Crowe, who barely noticed the weather. She was more concerned about the imminent danger posed to her company's power plant on New York's East River. Failure to win the governor's approval for the last mile of her natural gas Peace Pipeline through a Brooklyn neighborhood threatened disaster for the plant and its millions of customers.

Lindsey stepped from her black Cadillac Escalade on Fifth Avenue and entered the posh, polished, and fabulously expensive restaurant Harry Cipriani, where she was ushered to a corner table along the windows to await Governor Frank Cardini. Running a perfectly lacquered fingernail down the screen of her phone, she flipped through a long series of emails, dispensing most of them into a digital trash can.

Lindsey glanced over to the bar, where her public relations counselor, frequent companion, and occasional paramour Marty McGarry appeared far more relaxed than she was. He was sipping a Peroni beer, gesturing, and making the bartender laugh.

Short blasts from a siren outside diverted Lindsey's gaze to the windows behind her. She pulled back the curtain to see a caravan of black cars and State Police cruisers sweep to the curb, heralding the arrival of a potentate. A security agent with a coiled earpiece sprang from the front seat of a black Tesla and raced around the vehicle to open the rear door for the proudly fit governor. He bounced out of the car with the spring of a jack-in-the box, buttoning his form-fitting suitcoat before lightly smoothing back his curly hair. Cardini glanced about to see if any admirers were aware of the celebrity in their midst, then offered a wave and a smile to a handful of puzzled gapers before heading through the door.

Lindsey turned off her phone and rose to greet the governor, who offered air kisses on each cheek and an overpowering whiff of his cologne-marinated neck. He settled into a chair next to her and surveyed the room of moneyed and beautiful people for donors he might wish to acknowledge. Anyone who caught his eye nodded. Some smiled, even if they wondered, *"Who's he?"*

"Think I see a few of my peeps around here," Frank said as he scooched himself in.

Lindsey bowed her head to get in his line of vision. "Thank God. I'd hate for this to be a wasted trip."

"Ah, c'mon," he said, with a dismissive wave. "Always good to see you, Linz."

Lindsey had recently abandoned all her principles in favor of political expediency by sending Cardini the largest donation she'd ever made to a candidate for office. Odious as he was, she still preferred him to his opponent in the upcoming primary: the dogged climate crusader Felicity Redfeather. The state Attorney General, Redfeather was known derisively as "Two Blue Eyes" for her dubious claim that she was a descendant of Native Americans. Even so, Lindsey sent a perfunctory donation to Redfeather, too, in the hope it would serve as protection money against her political prosecutions.

"Always good to see you, too, Frank," Lindsey said, almost as if she meant it.

A waiter arrived to announce a list of specials, which didn't impress the governor. He shrugged and casually discarded his menu atop his place setting. "Best Italian food in town is still my mother's house in Queens."

"I'm sorry," she said. "Would you have rather gone somewhere else?"

"Like my mother's?" he asked with a laugh. "She'd probably love it."

"We could have had lunch in my office downtown."

"Nah. This is fine," he said with a shrug. "It's just that it's... what? Two bucks a noodle?"

She reached over and lightly touched his forearm. "Governor, please. This one's on me."

He shook his head. "No, no, no. Gotta go Dutch," he replied. "Papers are on my ass, watchin' everything I do. I can't take a breath without the *New York Post* demanding to know where I got it."

Lindsey nodded her head toward the window, where Mona DeLisi, the governor's comely press secretary, was standing near the curb, talking on the phone. "Is that why she's here? Shoo away the media?"

The governor blushed. "Ah... no," he said. "That's for a little something we got going later on."

The governor ripped off a crust of bread and studied it as if it were a rare gem before breaking it in chunks and dipping it in olive oil. The conversation turned to updates on their families: her notorious daughter, Missy, and her expanding role at Crowe Power's fusion subsidiary; her son, Chase, currently heading Crowe Power of Aruba; and her terrible, no-good, consistently awful ex-husband Robbie, running his Crowe Foundation for the Greater Good downtown. The governor opined briefly on his former live-in girlfriend, Jayne, who had very publicly dumped him for a hockey player ten years her junior, and his daughter, Oriana, who had graduated from SUNY and—surprise—landed a lucrative job as a state lobbyist in Albany. "I'm so proud of her," he gushed.

Lindsey nodded. "Always good to see your kids stand on their own two feet."

Cardini acknowledged her comment with an embarrassed smile. He could have said the same thing about her kids. "Let's face it," he said. "They all took the express elevator to the top."

Lindsey nodded. "True."

With their pasta finished, the governor offered an unappetizing dish. "A little birdie tells me Two Blue Eyes is coming after you."

"Have at it," Lindsey said with a shrug. She and her company had been a political pinata for years, with successive waves of ambitious politicos taking whacks at Crowe Power for its heavy use of fossil fuels, which the city's poohbahs had decreed should go away. Numerous lawsuits against the company had resulted in large legal bills, but no guilty verdicts. "I've got nothing to hide."

The governor folded his hands on the tabletop and leaned close. "It doesn't matter if you do or you don't. You've seen what her fishing expeditions can do. She can hook anybody if she really wants to. Next thing you know—*plop!*—you're in the boat, and she's slicing out your guts in a newspaper."

"The *Daily Reaper*, no doubt," Lindsey said. "I'll worry about when she makes a move."

Frank checked his watch. "I'd worry about it now," he said.

Lindsey was alarmed. "Today?"

"As we speak."

"Couldn't you call her off?" Lindsey asked. "You're her boss, right?"

The governor laughed mirthlessly. "You want me to hand Two Blue Eyes a campaign issue to beat me over the head? Let her say I'm in the pocket of those greedy bastards at the Crowe Power Company? I don't think so. She's already calling me a tool of big business."

Lindsey gulped. She could see where this was going, and it wasn't good. "What does all this mean for the Peace Pipeline?"

"I think you know."

She sucked in her breath and glared at him. She would not make this easy. "Tell me."

"Denied," he said flatly, picking basil from a bicuspid with a fingernail.

She fell back in her seat and shook her head. "On what grounds?"

"Take your pick," he said. "Impact on water quality. Inconsistent with our state's goal of net zero for carbon dioxide emissions by whenever. I think my guys settled on environmental justice. That's always a good one. Your pipeline was going to run through a black and brown community in Brooklyn."

"That's one mile out of forty," she said, exasperated.

The governor shrugged. "It doesn't matter if it's ten feet long. You know, there could be a disproportionate impact on minorities." His eyes went big as if he were about to burst out laughing.

"Which ones?" Lindsey asked.

"I don't know. Minorities. Does it matter?"

"Specifics would be helpful. Everyone I see out there protesting is a white liberal from the Upper West Side worried about climate change. I seriously doubt whether they really care that the street in front of a housing project an hour away might be dug up for a month or two."

"Look," he said, holding up the palms of his hands, "all I know is it plays well with a key demographic."

Lindsey eyed the governor. "Are you really that cynical?" she asked. "You do know the black and brown people in that neighborhood are the ones most likely to suffer if we have a blackout because our power plant doesn't get enough natural gas. That area is chockablock with drafty public housing with poor insulation and crappy windows. If their heat goes out, they're in a world of hurt. And without that pipeline to provide extra gas in a pinch, the chances of a major power outage are better than fifty-fifty. We've barely avoided catastrophe every other winter for the past ten years. If we can't secure more supply, we could easily have a disaster on our hands."

"You have your idea of disaster," he said blandly. "I have mine."

"Losing an election?"

"Top of my list," he said, staring at her and blinking slowly.

Lindsey, flustered, shook her head. In a one-party state, the relatively moderate Cardini was her best shot at a favorable decision. "Have you read the regulators' report about the storm last winter?" she asked. "Both the grid and our gas system nearly went down."

"I don't read reports," he said. "I read the papers and I read the polls. And they say Two Blue Eyes is gaining on me."

"Governor, please," she said, gripping his forearm. "I hate to use this word, but I *beg* you. This isn't just about my company. Unless we prepare now with more reliable supplies of gas, we can't guarantee the system won't go down in the future. And if that happens during a cold snap, you are going to have a genuine climate apocalypse, not the BS kind they talk about now where the temperature might go up a degree or two in fifty years. I'm talking about a real crisis where the temperature drops forty degrees in a few hours and people can't turn on the heat or the lights. And when that happens, who do you think people are going to blame?"

The governor's eyes sparkled. "You."

Lindsey spat, "Don't be so sure."

"Are you kidding? I'll make sure it happens."

"I can't believe this..."

The governor's expression hardened. "Do you know what comes before winter?"

She ground her teeth and awaited his answer.

"*Summer!*" the governor said heatedly, sticking his index finger onto the tabletop for emphasis. "If I don't get through the primary this summer, winter is cancelled for me. Understood? I may as well pack my pickleball racket and head to Florida with the rest of the people fleeing this state."

Lindsey sat back and dabbed the corner of her mouth with her linen napkin. "My mistake, governor," Lindsey said. "I honestly thought you had at least a little concern for the people who remain here."

Frank bristled. "You know, Lindsey, this is just about more than I can take," he declared. "All your little jabs and innuendos are starting to piss me off. Your solution to avert a catastrophe is to import more fossil fuels? Are you kidding me? What kind of backward shit is that? The gas you want to ship into the city was fracked in Pennsylvania. You know that? *Fracked!*"

She stared at him in puzzlement. "So what?"

"'Fracked' sounds like 'fucked,'" Cardini said, scratching his neck, "which is what I would be if I approved your Peace Pipeline."

Lindsey could no longer conceal her contempt. Reason and money hadn't moved him. It was obvious there was no changing his mind. "I see," she said. "So, if someone said to you that you don't know what the frack you're doing, you might take offense."

The governor crossed his arms and raised his chin in indignation. "I probably would."

"Or if they said this is one of the stupidest fracking decisions you ever made?"

He glared at her, his temperature rising, his face reddening. "I definitely would."

The maître d' approached and whispered to Lindsey. "I am so sorry to disturb you, Ms. Crowe, but there is an urgent phone call for you in the bar."

Lindsey shot an alarmed glance at the governor, who suddenly looked as innocent as an altar boy. She rose from the table, leaned over so only he could hear, stuck a breadstick in his water glass, and said, "Frack you, Frank."

She turned and stepped over to the bar, where Marty looked up from his phone. She arched an eyebrow in his direction, shook her head, and continued to the corner, where the bartender handed her the house phone. She put the receiver to her left ear, plugged her right ear with a fingertip to block the ambient noise, and turned toward the windows overlooking the carriage station at the southeast corner of Central Park.

Her assistant, Winnie, was on the line from her office, sounding very rattled.

"Lindsey, there's something terrible going on," she said, her voice trembling. "The state police are here. They're boxing up files and taking them out of the office."

"Files? Why?"

"I have no idea."

Lindsey struggled to calm herself. The attack from Two Blue Eyes was clearly on. "Did you alert Digby Pierrepont?" she asked, referring to the company's general counsel and her former brother-in-law.

"He's right here," Winnie said.

"Put him on, please." She heard Winnie hand over her phone.

"Not your normal day in the office," Digby said drily.

"How can they do this?" Lindsey asked.

Digby said, "AG got a warrant from a friendly judge."

"What are they looking for?"

"Files about climate change. What did you know and when did you know it?"

Lindsey staggered backward. "Is that criminal?"

"In this state, possibly," Digby said.

"Hold the fort. I'm on my way back."

Lindsey hung up and looked at Marty, who was walking quickly to the table where she had been eating. He retrieved her phone and handbag and returned with a furrowed brow. "The governor's gone?" she asked.

Marty nodded toward the window. Outside, Frank stood amid a throng of lights and cameras, while his press secretary handed out printed statements to the media. Apparently, he was not about to let his rival

Felicity Redfeather steal the campaign spotlight. He would one-up her with news of his own. Lindsey felt her phone vibrate and looked down.

BREAKING NEWS ALERT
Governor Kills Crowe Power's Peace Pipeline
Activists Claim Another Win in the Fight Against Climate Change

So that's why Mona DeLisi was hanging around. Lindsey looked out the window to see three more State Police cruisers pull up with lights flashing, drawing even more attention to the governor's curbside press conference. Clearly, he was intent on making a splash. "Can you do anything about that?" she asked Marty.

He studied the scene out the window. "Not at the moment." He grasped Lindsey by the upper arm and walked her toward a glass door at the rear of the restaurant that led into the Sherry-Netherland Hotel and an exit on a side street. "I'll call for the car."

2. ROAD TO RUE IN

Stuck at a dead stop in bumper-to-bumper traffic on the southbound FDR near the Brooklyn Bridge, Lindsey's driver Andrei searched the map on his phone for a route to Crowe Power headquarters. He shook his head in frustration. "It's solid red, Ms. Crowe," he said. "Something's blocking the road and we're a mile past the exit."

Lindsey craned her neck to see around the wall of red taillights ahead of them. A few drivers were getting out of their vehicles and walking between lanes. Horns were honking, and loud angry voices could be heard.

"Of all days," Lindsey sighed. She put her hand on Andrei's headrest. "Hate to press you, Andrei. But I need to get back."

"I know, I know, I know," Andrei said. "I'm sorry."

Marty, typing in his phone, asked Lindsey, "How's this for a statement to the media? 'We are deeply disappointed by the governor's decision to deny the completion of the much-needed Peace Pipeline,' said... blank.' Who do I attribute that to?"

"Lucy Rutherford," Lindsey replied.

Marty continued typing as he talked. "...said Lucy Rutherford, Chief Executive Officer of the Crowe Power Company. 'A robust gas supply is critical for maintaining a functioning system of heat and electricity in our region, especially in times of peak demand, such as hot summer days and cold winter nights.'" He looked over to Lindsey. "What else?"

"What else, what?" she asked.

"What else do you want me to say?"

"I don't know," she said, annoyed. "Honestly, I never thought we'd be in this position."

He looked at her blankly. "I honestly don't know why you'd think that. When did reason ever enter a conversation about climate in this town? You'd better work up a Plan B." Marty returned to his phone and began reading aloud as he wrote. "Rutherford said, 'the company would consider options… that best serve our valued customers.' Sound good?"

"No. It sounds awful. But it's the best we've got," she said. "Send it to Lucy for her blessing and get it to Kristen Gilroy. She can send it out to the media."

"Got it."

Lindsey looked around Andrei at the traffic jam ahead. "This is ridiculous."

Marty unsnapped his seatbelt. "Let me find out what's going on," he said as he pulled on the door handle.

Lindsey grabbed his arm. "Don't do that. What if the traffic starts up again?"

Marty looked at her skeptically. "Fat chance."

He walked up an incline past yellow cabs, Uber drivers, and commuters, then over the crest of the highway to find the flashing lights of police cars, ambulances, and fire trucks. Halfway down the slope, a dozen solemn-looking young people wearing fluorescent orange vests sat on the pavement, their hands glued to the road. Behind them, a handful of protesters held signs:

<u>EVERY</u> DAY IS EARTH DAY
CLIMATE EMERGENCY!
BAN FOSSIL FUELS *NOW!*

Police officers stood by helplessly as seething drivers demanded action to clear the road. An irate delivery truck driver emerged from his cab to attempt to handle the job himself, but he was intercepted by a trio of cops who backed him up.

There was a part of Marty that wanted to march down the hill and join the truck driver in removing the protesters. Alas, the vigorous, virile Marty that could easily dispatch a wimpy NYU student was thirty years, twenty pounds, and a thousand cheeseburgers ago. The older, fatter, and more breathless Marty realized it would be struggle enough to climb back up the road to the car.

He returned to the Escalade and opened Lindsey's door. "We could be stuck out here for hours," he told her.

"Should we walk back?"

"It's a long way in heels," he replied.

"I didn't notice you wearing them."

"Haha," he said drily. "I'm thinking of you, obviously."

She smiled. "No worries. I've got a pair of flats in here someplace." She reached around behind her, retrieved her walking shoes, and slipped them on. "Let's hoof it. I've got to get back to see what's going on at the office."

Marty helped her out of the vehicle and looked around for a pathway back to Broad Street. He saw an exit sign half a mile ahead. "I think I see a way out of this mess."

As they walked along the shoulder of the elevated road past the protest, Marty wondered what the activists would do if they realized that Lindsey Harper Crowe, empress of an evil energy empire, was within their reach. Booing, hissing, and shouting threats would hardly suffice in demonstrating their righteous rage. Perhaps they'd glue themselves to her ankles. Marty clutched Lindsey by the upper arm and tried to move her quickly past the throng, but she stopped in her tracks and gazed at the protesters.

"Look at that," she marveled.

"I saw it already. Let's *go*."

She shook him off and remained in place. "This is a perfect demonstration of what's ahead for us."

Marty was incredulous. "What are you talking about?"

"It shows exactly what will happen if these people get their way. Cars won't move. People won't go to work. Everyone will be angry. And all these protesters will still be honked off because there's always another grievance around the corner they can use to attract attention."

Marty tugged gently on her arm and Lindsey started walking again. "I thought of giving them a piece of my mind, you know."

"Why didn't you?" Lindsey asked.

"I might have to back it up with a piece of my body."

She glanced sideways at his physique. "You made the right decision."

They trudged along the road, with the northbound FDR and Brooklyn skyline on their left and a sheer wall of high-rise hotels, office buildings, and apartments in New York's Financial District on their right. With the sun beating down on them, Marty was breaking a sweat for the first time in months.

"So, tell me," Marty said, as he huffed and puffed, "do days like this ever make you want to quit? Just hand over the keys to someone else and head off to Aspen or Napa Valley or Martha's Vineyard? You certainly have the means to live a very good life somewhere else."

She nodded vigorously. "Absolutely."

Marty was surprised by her vehemence. "Why don't you?"

"I've got a job."

Marty scoffed. "It's not like you need it. Your pay is what? A dollar a year?"

Lindsey shrugged. "It's not about the pay, Marty. It's about the purpose. It's about something to do." She chuckled. "I read a story the other day about a steelworker who hit the lottery and still showed up at the mill the next week and punched the clock. Why did he do that?"

"I have no idea."

"I do," she said. "It gave him something important to do. He was making something real, something useful. And he did it with people he liked. I totally get that. What am I gonna do if I leave Crowe Power? Hang out by the pool with the parents of those entitled brats sitting in the road? You know, I did that when I was married to Robbie. I was sloshed every day by two o'clock."

Marty shrugged. "If I had your money, I'd be sloshed by one."

"No, you wouldn't," she said. "You're like me. We both need a challenge."

"You've got one now," Marty said. "How are you liking it so far?"

She sighed. "Honestly? It's a bit more than I bargained for."

They stepped off the FDR just as traffic resumed, and were met by Tom Michaels, the former Secret Service agent who ran Crowe Power's security operation, along with his second-in-command, Morris Jenkins. "We've got an extremely hostile situation," Tom said. "You're not safe out here alone."

Lindsey protested, "I've got Marty with me."

Tom looked Marty up and down. "Right."

Marty huffed. "Thanks, Tom."

"No offense, sir," he said. "Let's go."

Tom led the way up Broad Street toward Crowe Power Company headquarters, a white terra-cotta skyscraper built in the 1920s. As they crossed Beaver Street, they could see a crowd of protesters marching in their direction, chanting, *"Lindsey Harper Crowe! What did you know? Lindsey Harper Crowe! What did you know?"*

Lindsey, alarmed, asked, "Know about what?"

"Climate change," Tom said. "Two Blue Eyes held a campaign rally in front of the National Museum of the American Indian. I'm told you were mentioned many times."

"Nicely, I'm sure," she said.

"Not exactly," Tom replied. He looked over his shoulder at the demonstrators moving their way. "Let's get you off the street."

As they picked up their pace, Lindsey was relieved to find a half-dozen police officers patrolling the front of her building. She nodded thanks to them as Morris held the door for her and Marty to enter the ornate lobby. Tom directed the security guards behind the front desk to watch the street as he opened the swing gate next to the turnstile and summoned the executive elevator.

"I'll keep an eye on things down here," Tom said. "Call if you need me upstairs."

On the twenty-fourth-floor, Lindsey and Marty walked through a wood-paneled corridor known as the Hall of Fam, a gallery of spotlit portraits of nearly all the company's leaders, who had built Crowe Power into one of the world's most successful energy companies, with power plants, refineries, and pipelines on six continents. A notable omission from the gallery was former chief executive Walker B. Hope, who had led Crowe Power to record earnings, despite the destructive meddling of then-chair Robbie Crowe. While Robbie had not consented to a portrait of Walker on account of his inferior lineage, Robbie made the wall for the same reason he got his job in the first place: his DNA.

Lindsey and Marty stepped into her corner suite, where a bronze bust of the pioneering industrialist Homer Crowe presided over the reception area. Lindsey paused and inhaled deeply to calm herself, but her mind continued to race. Just two years earlier, she had been celebrated for Crowe Power's technical breakthrough in the development of fusion energy, which showed great promise for replacing fossil fuels. How had she become such a pariah so fast? In the space of just three hours, she'd had a critical pipeline denied, a police raid on her office, a traffic-stopping protest, and a march on her headquarters.

She gripped the door handle to her inner office and looked at Marty. "Who's after us?"

Marty shrugged. "Who's not? It's the silly season for politicians."

She shook her head. "It has to be more than that. Candidates don't dream these things up on their own. Something else is at play here."

"Like what?"

"That's what I need you to help me find out."

3. EXERCISING POOR JUDGMENT

Two Blue Eyes' splashy raid on the Crowe Power offices took the pole position on New York's cable TV news, nosing out Governor Cardini's denial of the Crowe pipeline in Brooklyn, which finished a close second. The attorney general had teared up at the emotionally charged press conference in front of the National Museum of the American Indian as she promised she would not rest until she had achieved environmental justice for "our peoples," though she stopped short of saying which peoples she was talking about.

Robbie Crowe watched the news with glee as he walked on a treadmill at the Equinox gym in the Brookfield Place in Lower Manhattan. He quickened his steps, energized to see his ex-wife Lindsey portrayed as a vile combination of Marie Antoinette, Imelda Marcos, and Ma Barker.

On TV, Redfeather declared, "Billionaire Lindsey Harper Crowe ignored warnings of Earthly peril to pursue profits and damn the consequences, especially for communities of color." For Robbie to then watch Lindsey get smacked down on the Peace Pipeline by Governor Cardini doubled his fun. After shoving him out of his rightful chairmanship at Crowe as the first-born male of his generation, Lindsey was finding out the hard way that running the company was not as easy as he made it look.

"I bet you none of that would have happened if you were still in charge," said a female voice.

Robbie turned to see a sleek Asian woman in workout gear with a towel around her neck nodding toward the TV. He gladly slowed his pace. "Do I know you?"

She offered a gleaming smile. "No, but I'd like to know you," she said. "I'm Li Zhang."

Well, aren't you, though! Robbie stepped off the treadmill and tried not to stare at her stunning good looks. "Nice to meet you," he said, offering his hand.

"I'm a big fan of your work," she said, grasping his hand in both of hers. She held it a moment longer than Robbie expected while she looked meaningfully into his eyes. If she had worked out, it did not show. Her makeup was perfect, and every hair was in place.

"Thank you for saying so," he said. The fifth-generation descendant of Homer Crowe grabbed a towel off the counter and dabbed his barely perspiring forehead. He tried to recall any work he'd done that someone might have noticed. He hadn't kept up much of a public profile since he left Crowe Power, other than to sign an op-ed for the *Daily Reaper* on the importance of giving back, deliver a speech at FRED Fest on making the world a vaguely better place, and accept an award as a great humanitarian, which he demonstrated with a donation back to the awarding body, whatever it was.

Li took one step back. "I hope I'm not interrupting anything," she said. "Do you have a minute?"

"I think so," Robbie assured her, suddenly appearing anxious. "Do you know the time?"

"A little after two," she said. "Am I keeping you from something?"

"I'm kinda between meetings." They were spaced a week apart, but that seemed like an unnecessary detail to share. "I can probably squeeze in a little break here."

They walked toward a seating area overlooking the 9/11 Memorial across the street and sat on stools at a high table. "I am so excited to run into you," she said. "My organization does a lot of work with the Planetistas, and everyone in the group raves about how willing you were to talk to them when you were chairman of Crowe Power. You were the only corporate leader they picketed who seemed genuinely eager to find common ground."

Robbie blushed as he remembered how he'd waded through protesters outside headquarters in pursuit of his primary objective at the time: to snuggle up to a Planetistas activist named Natalia who had worked as a barista at Café Che, the coffee shop across the street from Crowe Power headquarters. Known as Commie Coffee for its celebration of socialist fads and fashions, Café Che served as an informal gathering place for the activist group. Despite his wealth, or maybe because of the very different circles in which he travelled, Robbie was weirdly attracted to the café's bohemian bonhomie. "I haven't been there in some time," Robbie allowed. "They probably don't remember me."

"Don't be so modest!" Li put her hand on top of his. "You are a legend there. People used to say, 'if every company had the kind of vision that Robbie Crowe had, we wouldn't have all these big businesses pushing the little people out of the way. We'd have a much better world. Cleaner. Greener. More equitable. And maybe we'd have no big businesses at all!"

Robbie swooned. *This chick gets it!* Maybe not all the details exactly, but she clearly dug his act, and she was so freaking sexy! "Well, you know, I've always thought we have to look beyond the day-to-day and take the long view. That only comes through dialogue," he said solemnly. He gazed deeply into her eyes and leaned in close enough to catch a whiff of jasmine. "I believe you have to know what's in someone's head," he said, as he put an index finger on his temple. "And in their heart," he continued, as he tapped his chest. *And if that works,* he thought, *you might get in their pants!*

Li Zhang read his mind and smiled. *This is even easier than expected!* "You are so right," she said. "In China, we have a saying: 'We help each other in the same boat and move forward hand in hand.'"

Wow. That was some fucked-up metaphor! It made no sense whatsoever! Still, Robbie started to consider all the ways he could work hand in hand with Li Zhang, and get in a boat if he had to, and hold hands, and maybe do some skinny dipping in the Yangtze River. Was the Kama Sutra Chinese? Or was that some Indian deal? "You mentioned an organization," he said. "Do you work around here?"

She nodded toward the ceiling. "Upstairs. I'm the Executive Director of the Center for Unity and Cooperation," she said. "We work to advance a worldwide agenda on win-win solutions for trade and commerce."

"I see."

"We believe the old ways—of one country imposing its imperial will on all others and selfishly exploiting all the planet's resources—don't work anymore. It's not healthy for our planet or our people. We need a balanced approach that shares the wealth."

Robbie could not tell what she was selling, but he was buying. "I couldn't agree more," he said. "That's always been a part of my vision for the planet. The only question for me—and it's really just a detail—is... how do you do that, exactly?"

"Well, in our case," she said, "we offer financial assistance to organizations that work on global goals irrespective of borders. We help them educate the public about issues they should care about if they want to build strong countries."

"Like the United States?"

"Oh, not so much."

"What then?"

"More like China."

"Ah."

"We think the best way to build world peace is to create economic security and equity for all," Li said. "I believe these are very much the same principles as the Crowe Institute for the Greater Good."

They are? Robbie couldn't remember what their principles were for handing out money. Mostly, he gave it to the best-looking women who came to his office with a half-decent pitch. He tried to recall the citation on his most recent award as "Human of the Year," or whatever it was, but the sponsoring group was hazy. Was it the Carbon Free Coalition? The Decarceration Committee? He remembered they promoted some kind of Utopian wet dream that he could care less about, but he went along because he needed another plaque for the foundation's lobby, and the director was a total babe. "I'm sure there are areas where we'd align perfectly."

She gazed at him admiringly. "We'd love to have you in our corner. Just think what we could accomplish together…" She fluttered her eyes. "It would be such an honor to work with a great leader of your stature."

Robbie felt a little drool at the corner of his mouth and dabbed it with his towel. "You've definitely got something there I'd like to explore."

"Same," she said. "I'd love to know more about your incredible career. As I recall, you were one of the very few leaders in the energy industry willing to talk about climate change. I remember you said at FRED Fest that the planet could no longer afford business as usual." She nodded toward the TV. "But look at where they are now. Even your old company has gone backwards."

"Well, you know, that's why I got into the business in the first place, to drive change," he said. "I tried like hell to change Crowe Power." He winced. "Nobody wanted to hear it. Everyone thought I was some sort of communist. Ultimately, I believe that's what cost me my job. My philosophy."

"That's true leadership."

Robbie didn't need a staff report to advise this budding relationship with Li Zhang was most definitely trending toward a roll in the hay. "We do whatever we can," he said.

She stood. "Drop me a note when you can," she said. "I want to know everything there is to know about you." She stepped closer to him, handed him her card, and leaned over, giving him a bird's-eye view of her northern assets. "I *need* to know more."

Robbie studied the card. "Do I call you Li or Zhang or Li Zhang?"

She chuckled. "Call me for a drink and I'll let you know."

He purred, "Count on it."

4. SUITE SMELL OF EXCESS

Lindsey and Marty found Lindsey's office in disarray and her staff in distress. The overwhelming speed and power with which the State Police stormed the premises had proven deeply unsettling to the normally unflappable Winnie, long accustomed to presiding over a calm, orderly office. She appeared near tears as she stood next to a file cabinet that had been ransacked.

"I am so sorry, Lindsey," Winnie said, shaking her head. "I didn't know what to do. There were so many police. And they came in so fast…"

Lindsey patted her gently on the back. "This is not on you, Winnie. I'm sure you did the right thing." She stepped back to lock eyes with her. "They wanted to upset us. Let's not give them the satisfaction."

Lindsey nodded to Digby, who followed her and Marty into her office and closed the door. She dropped her handbag on her desk and walked to a tufted leather sofa, where she flopped down, put her head back on the cushion, folded her hands on her lap, and closed her eyes. Marty and Digby took adjacent wingback chairs.

"I'm sick to my stomach," Lindsey said.

"Something from lunch?" Digby asked.

She opened one eye. "A meatball didn't agree with me."

Digby said, "When does he ever?"

Lindsey sat up. "Here's what I don't get. What's the point of buying a politician if they don't do what you want?" she asked. "'Frank Cardini is bad enough. And now we have Felicity Redfeather rummaging through my drawers?"

Marty said, "From what I understand, she might like that."

"Wouldn't do a thing for me," Lindsey said, with a dismissive wave. "How many offices did she hit?"

"Five, including yours," Digby replied, peering through his owlish glasses.

Lindsey shook her head. "What's the end game here, Digby? Do they want to put me in jail?"

Digby scratched the back of his long neck. "Thankfully, no. I think they've given up on pursuing criminal charges, which obviously hasn't worked out for them in the past. Their only real option is a civil suit."

Lindsey sat up. "For what?"

"Fraud, possibly. They've used that to go after other people they don't like."

"Oh, come on!" Lindsey said. "Who did we defraud?"

"I don't know. They might claim it was shareholders."

She waved that away. "How did we do that?"

"By not admitting the climate was changing and that our products and services were responsible," Digby replied. "They could say that failure to disclose what we knew about a topic nobody seems to understand poses an unacceptable risk to shareholders."

Lindsey laughed. "Except that it hasn't," she said, standing. "Our stock's at a five-year high."

Marty, looking at his phone, said, "Not anymore. We're down 8 percent on today's news."

Lindsey walked to the window overlooking the ships, ferries, tugboats, and freighters plying the waters of New York Harbor, then turned back to the room. "Can either of you tell me this: why would a dyed-in-the-wool communist sympathizer like Felicity Redfeather ever give a crap about corporate shareholders—especially ours? Is she suddenly feeling compassion for people who buy stock in energy companies?"

"Obviously, she's a lot more concerned about her opponent in the primary," Digby said, following her to the window. "If she's going to beat Frank Cardini, she needs to energize her base, which hates fossil fuels. We're the last company she can target in New York. Everyone else has merged, moved, or gone out of business. Exxon. Mobil. Esso. Texaco. Conoco. Shell's U.S. headquarters. All gone."

"Can you blame them?" Lindsey asked. "I'd split, too, if I could. How exposed are we?"

"Impossible to say," said Digby. "Our lawyers at Glickman Edwards say any report, memo, or presentation they find in our files could be used against us. It could come from the lowest levels of the company or the highest. It doesn't matter. All it takes is one person to write a note to a manager claiming our products lead to global warming. They could use that as proof that people at the top knew something—or should have known something—and did nothing about it. It could have happened five, ten, or twenty years ago."

"I wasn't at the company then," she said.

"That doesn't matter. They'll still say you should have known something about such an important topic."

"Important to them," Lindsey snapped.

"And to the entire legal community in this part of the country," Digby said. "The judge who signed off on the warrant is regarded as a political operative. Melvin Hardiman. He came out of retirement to do Two Blue Eyes' bidding to try Roland Platt on fraud charges based on a bookkeeping error. Facts didn't matter much for him, and they won't matter much for you. Neither will the law, which Hardiman's been known to bend and twist beyond recognition."

Marty sighed. "I hesitate to tell you this."

Lindsey, pacing, stopped in her tracks. "What?"

"I'm invited to a Felicity Redfeather fundraiser tomorrow night."

Lindsey laughed. "Stop! Don't they know the company you keep?"

Marty shrugged. "I worked with her spokesperson in a previous life. Nancy Lanci. She's a true believer. She's been trying to convince me for years that we need systemic change, whatever that is. I barely have enough energy to change my socks."

Lindsey said. "You must go to that event."

Marty shook his head gravely. "I was afraid you were going to say that."

"Marty, *please*," Lindsey said. "Find out who's in the room. Maybe that will tell us who else we're up against besides Felicity Redfeather."

Marty arched an eyebrow. "It's a hefty price."

"How much?"

"Ten thousand dollars to join Felicity's Powwow."

"What's that?"

"Her circle of donors."

"*Powwow?* Seriously?" Lindsey said, scrunching her face. "Isn't that considered offensive or racist or something?"

"I think the rule is, it's okay to say if you're indigenous. Two Blue Eyes claims to be part Indian."

Lindsey scoffed. "Right. And I'm a mermaid. She just *looks* like the whitest person on Earth."

"Okay. So she's a Pretendian," Marty said. "Obviously, it works for her."

"Well, I don't," Lindsey asserted.

"Not yet," Digby added. "She wins a case against us, we might all be working for her."

Lindsey rose and walked to the door. "Buy the ticket and I'll make up for it somehow, Marty. But go. I insist."

5. PARTY FAVORS

Marty couldn't help wondering why Schuyler Hornblower, swashbuckling head of SolarPlexis, needed such lavish taxpayer subsidies to finance his solar power ventures in the Hudson Valley. With a duplex overlooking Central Park, a highly successful private equity firm, and a reputation for indulging expensively exotic tastes, he had an impressive track record of generating his own capital. Then again, Marty surmised as he waited in line to enter Schuyler's apartment for the *Meet Felicity Redfeather* event, why risk your own loot when you can offload the risk entirely onto the public? Surely whatever subsidies he was getting dwarfed his political donations.

"Grand to meet you," Schuyler said. He reached out from his black silk kimono to offer a vice-like handshake and nodded his head, garnished on top with a tightly knotted silvery bun with what looked like a chopstick rammed through it. The host appraised Marty's country club wardrobe of blue blazer and camel slacks with unconcealed disdain. "Call me Sky."

"Call me underdressed," Marty conceded. Was this a costume party? The only thing missing to complete Sky's look was a scabbard and a samurai sword—and perhaps a swing from the chandelier. "I'm Marty McGarry."

"Isn't that nice," Sky said with a smile that suggested it wasn't. "Please make yourself at home."

Marty stepped into the two-story living room with an ornate carved ceiling, procured a glass of champagne from a server's passing tray, and scanned the room for his friend, Nancy Lanci. He didn't see her, but he recognized plenty of boldface names from TV, movies, and music. Based on his Page Six perusals, Marty could make out the rapper couple Cheezy Beezy and his baby mama PonyFace, the activist actor Brad Steele, and the decrepit ninety-year-old rocker Junior Lewis, of Junior Lewis and the Teeny Boppers. Over by a giant aquarium was Morty Winkledink, the high-powered chairman of First Call Finance. Wendy Ward, the new editor of *Vogue*, charmed a gathering of young women with a stylish ensemble she had sewed herself. And Bob Smythe, the exceedingly wealthy Silicon Valley software mogul and chief investor in BlowCo, the wind power firm, was surrounded by a trough of politicos wondering how much cash might fall out of his pockets if they held him up by the ankles and shook him vigorously. No wonder Frank Cardini was nervous about the upcoming primary. This was a wealthy crowd with far-reaching influence. Interesting that Felicity Redfeather's campaign slogan was *People Not Profit*, when profits were what made this evening possible. Despite her reputation as a dull, humorless scold, Two Blue Eyes must have at least some sense of hilarity.

"Would you like a Sesame Toasted Mealworm?" asked an earnest young server.

Marty turned to view a sterling silver plate of crusty worms with toothpicks stuck in their guts. Their fried carcasses surrounded a sauce dish of brown goo.

Marty regarded the offering and shook his head sadly. "Wouldn't you know it? Mealworms for lunch."

The server scrunched her face in sympathy. "Too bad. These are super yummy."

"No doubt," Marty replied. "Especially if you're a trout."

"If you're…?"

Marty tried another tack. "Have you actually tried one?" he asked.

"No," she said uncertainly. "But I hear good things. Would you prefer Crispy Crickets?"

"I don't know," Marty said, patting his tummy. "Is that all you're serving? Bugs?"

Her expression suggested pity for this creaky dinosaur. "Sky feels very strongly that insects are where humans should get all their protein because it's so much better for the planet. Bugs require less land, less water, and less fuel for transportation. Compared to, like, beef, they have a much smaller carbon footprint."

"Of course they do," Marty said. "Just look at how tiny their feet are."

The server eyed him suspiciously. *Was that a joke?* She turned away and Marty focused his attention on a commotion at the front door, where cameras were flashing. The candidate had arrived with her entourage, including his former colleague, Nancy Lanci. A crush of suitors rushed the candidate, eager to show they were present. At stake was a treasure trove of government goodies for those lucky braves and squaws who bought their way into Felicity's Powwow. They could obtain future access to the governor's office, tax benefits from the state treasury, a nod and a wink from regulators, and bragging rights about a social connection to a rising star. *I saw Felicity Redfeather at a party last night and Felicity said…* No wonder they were all pushing their way in like piglets scrounging for teats.

Sky Hornblower nudged his way into Felicity's pack to rescue the candidate with a glass of white wine, then led her out of the scrum toward the picture windows in the living room overlooking Central Park. Marty, meanwhile, worked his way through the crowd to say hello to his former manager of sustainability communications.

"Marty!" Nancy exclaimed, as she lightly hugged him. "So glad you could make it. Have you met Felicity?"

"Not sure I can break through," Marty said. "She's pretty popular."

"You've got to meet her," Nancy insisted. "She's such a… I don't even know how to describe her."

"Indian?" Marty asked.

Nancy nodded. "Well, yeah, she's that, for sure."

Marty glanced at the petite woman standing near the window with blond pigtails, wireless granny glasses, delicate features, and translucent skin as white as a snowflake. "I must admit. She doesn't really look the part," Marty said, tilting his head. "Maybe if I squint…"

Nancy clutched his arm. "No, she's seriously Indian. That's how she got her name."

"Two Blue Eyes?"

"Redfeather," Nancy said. "She's Sioux or Chippewa or… what's that Jeep?"

"Cherokee?"

"That's it. She's part Jeep."

Marty blinked. "I think you mean Cherokee?"

"Oh. Right." Nancy slapped herself on the cheek. "She's like one hundred-twenty-eighth Cherokee, or something. But the actual percentage doesn't really matter. It's really how you identify. Know what I mean?"

"I think so. I like to identify as fit."

She smiled sympathetically. "It's whatever you believe! I had one of those tests done and—can you believe it?—I'm part Jamaican."

Marty regarded her pale visage and nearly broke out laughing. "I went to a wedding there once," he said. "Does that make me Jamaican, too?"

"I don't judge, Marty," she assured him. "All I know is this Indian deal is more of a spiritual thing with her. She wants to, you know, get back to the way things were before all these colonialists showed up." She looked Marty up and down before adding, "Like you."

He scoffed. "You may find this hard to believe. But I'm not 400 years old. I just look that way."

She nodded in solemn agreement. "Yeah. Well…"

"Tell me," Marty said. "Wasn't her heritage kind of how she made her way to the top? The gig at Harvard and all those board seats? She's supposedly a woman of color. But she looks more like a woman who needs to be colored in. Something about her makes me want to reach for a crayon. Maybe burnt sienna. From a communications perspective, I have to imagine that's a bit of a challenge for you."

Nancy shrugged. "Oddly enough, reporters never ask. I guess everyone knows it's the thing these days. Besides, they're sick of Frank Cardini and the old patrimony. They want something fresh and new. And Felicity's got this total Earth Mother aura that really resonates with the press. They all know we must treat the planet with respect, or nothing can survive. Not even rocks."

"Rocks? Really? They're in danger, too?" Marty said, shaking his head. "Hadn't heard that one."

"Oh yeah," she said confidently. "I just saw a study. Climate change is killing rocks. Can you believe it?"

"Wow," Marty uttered. "I didn't even know they were alive."

Nancy gripped his forearm. "They have souls," she assured him.

Their conversation was interrupted by Sky, who was loudly tapping a silver spoon on his glass of cold sake to command everyone's attention.

"Gotta go," Nancy said. Sotto voce, she added, "I'd stay away from the Poo Poo Platter."

"Oh no," Marty said.

Nancy arched an eyebrow. "Oh yes."

She departed as Sky cleared his throat. "Welcome everyone," he shouted, as the room quieted down. "I want to thank you all for coming to what I can assure you will be a *most* stimulating evening. We've been waiting a long time for a leader to come along with such a bold new vision. But I have known Felicity for what seems like forever. It's been—what?" he asked as he turned to her.

"Three weeks," she said flatly.

"Right," Sky continued, "three of the most incredible weeks of my life. There's so much I've learned! It doesn't take long to be around Felicity Redfeather before you're simply blown away by this woman." He paused, alarmed. "Is it okay to say that?"

Felicity looked puzzled for a moment. "Yes," she said. "I'm still a woman."

"Right-o," he continued. "Bottom line is that I am gobsmacked by Felicity and what she represents. Fearlessness. Vision. Integrity. And absolute authenticity. That is why I'm so honored to host this gathering and introduce her to you, my dear, dear friends, so that we may help support this growing grassroots movement."

Marty looked around to see if he could detect anything about this event that suggested grassroots, other than the bowl of sludgy green punch on the sideboard. This crowd was incredibly well-heeled, and apparently intended to stay that way by currying favor with the powers-that-may-be.

"So, without further ado, *they-dees* and *gentle-thems*, Felicity Redfeather!"

Felicity stepped forward to applause that was muted not for lack of enthusiasm, but because most people were holding a drink, or a plate of bugs, or both. Marty maneuvered around the perimeter of the crowd, looking for a better angle on the would-be governor. As he brought out his phone to record her remarks, he bumped into an Asian woman. He was about to say hello when Felicity began her remarks.

"Thank you so much, Sky," Felicity said. "And thank you all for coming tonight. As my great-great-great grandmother would say, '*Asusdi awaduli.*'"

The crowd cheered as Marty ran her comment through the AI application on his phone for translation.

Cherokee language (Tsalagi):
I want some gravy.

Okay. So, it was gibberish, like most of her speeches. Regardless of Nancy Lanci's view, it was clear to anyone not in the tank for Felicity that she had advanced her career by making unlikely claims that were uncontested by the press, academia, or corporate America. She had been rewarded with a tenured professorship at Harvard Law School and high-paying positions on numerous corporate boards seeking a show of diversity. Her bio seemed ridiculous on its face—especially *her* face, with a button nose as its centerpiece. Yet her contentions about great-great-great grandma Gitchee Gummi—or whatever her name was— had been repeated so often, they were apparently beyond question. Still, her demeanor suggested a smoldering indignant anger, as if she'd had her own lands stolen from her and she had been mistreated her entire life.

"I am honored to have this historic opportunity to become the first woman of color to lead this state toward a new ideal of justice," Felicity said with a straight face.

Much to Marty's astonishment, nobody laughed, choked, or threw a Bumblebee Fritter. They were both feet in on Two Blue Eyes.

"Haven't we had enough of the old standards of so-called merit?" Felicity asked. "That's an obsolete construct that has no meaning in the world we imagine for our future. I want to create new avenues of advancement for all peoples, based on their lived experiences, their heritage, and their unique truths. And we'll begin by dismantling this oppressive system of white male privilege that dominates our state."

More cheering rang out. Marty looked around him to see all the men's eyes— mostly blue and green—glistening with love and appreciation. Surely, she was talking about *other* white males, not the dudes who had paid handsomely for admission into Felicity's big teepee. *Out with the old privilege! In with the new!* All they had to do was pay their way in through a different ticket taker! This could be a seamless transition! They wouldn't even have to move!

"Some people dismiss the society I envision as some unachievable nirvana. But they are wrong, and I can prove it. And you know how? *Because it's already been done, people!* Yes, we can live like the ancient tribes that once roamed this land before it was stolen from them. If we show more respect for our Mother Earth, she will show more respect for us, and she will not punish our ways with ever-fiercer storms and heat and wildfire. Over time, we can reduce our population to a sustainable level, we can reduce our draw on the earth's resources, and we can live in harmony with all of her creation." She stretched the palms of her hands to the heavens.

Shouts of "Yes!" and "Alright!" and the rapid clinking of forks on hors d'oeuvres plates, muffled only by the remains of fricasseed insects, rang out from the assembly. Marty couldn't help wondering whether they really understood what they were rooting for. Didn't she just say she wanted to reduce the population? Who was on her list for removal? Anyone here?

"Under my leadership, our state is going to lead the world in repairing our climate," she said. "And we're going to start by demanding that energy companies behave responsibly, or they will lose their license to do business in our state. One way or another, these rogue companies must yield to the collective control of people whose top priority is the planet—not profit!"

More huzzahs were sounded, more wine was poured, more fetid green punch ladled. The mood was becoming ecstatic. They were whipping themselves into a frenzy, fueled by French Fried Fire Ants.

"Where's Bob Smythe?" Felicity asked, scanning the crowd. "Ah. There he is! Bob, come up here and join me." She paused briefly as the BlowCo majordomo lightly jogged his way to the front and stood next to the candidate. Felicity smiled and put an arm around her patron. "Now I want you all to take a moment to look behind us," Felicity said, gesturing with her free hand toward the park. "When I'm elected governor, that's where we're going to put the first wind turbine farm in Manhattan. Right there in Central Park! And it will be enough to power three entire blocks!"

Marty looked around at the crowd. Were they seriously going along with this lunacy? He pulled out his phone and found the city had *120,000* city blocks. And this monstrosity that would destroy a chunk of the city's most revered park would cover *three*?

"It's time we stopped situating industrial projects in poor communities. It's time we started spreading them out into every neighborhood," Felicity continued. "Sixty million people visit our city every year. This project will show them all that New York is unsurpassed in its commitment to the planet. Because this, my friends, is what truly virtuous leadership looks like!"

While most people applauded politely, Sky looked like he was going to throw up. Windmills outside his window? Right in the middle of his magnificent view? He may as well look over a landfill! This shit was supposed to go upstate, not here! What was she thinking? As Felicity concluded her remarks, he sidled up to her and said, "Felicity. Could we have a word?"

Marty turned to leave but was stopped by a photographer. "Can I get a shot of you two?"

Two? Marty looked around to see the Asian woman he noticed earlier. She was standing next to him, smiling at the photographer. After the photo was taken, the woman introduced herself to Marty.

"I'm Li Zhang."

"Marty McGarry."

"I know you," Li said, with a big smile. "You work with Lindsey Harper Crowe."

"You know Lindsey?"

Li laughed. "Not so much. I know Robbie Crowe," she said.

Marty regarded her red minidress, which looked like it could fall off without too much prodding. "Somehow, I'm not surprised."

"Such a nice man," Li said. "So smart!"

Marty nodded, thinking. *And I'll bet you're a lot smarter than he is.*

6. A LAYER OF LAWYERS

A receptionist for the uptown law firm of Glickman, Edwards & Stein ushered Lindsey, Marty, and Digby into a large conference room, triggering dismal memories for Lindsey. Here was where she had worked through the details of her divorce from Robbie. With the help of partner Bentley Edwards and his massive team of lawyers, Lindsey executed Robbie's ouster as chairman of the Crowe Power Company and took the job herself. Now looking out over Sixth Avenue as she awaited Bentley's arrival, she couldn't help wondering whether that was such a great idea after all. She turned to Marty.

"So tell me: How was Felicity's war dance last night? Worth the price of admission?"

"It was for me," he said. "I didn't pay."

"What did you get for my ten grand?"

"We ate bugs."

"Ten thousand dollars' worth?"

"I had to eat really fast."

She smiled and shook her head. "Who's on Team Felicity?"

"The usual suspects behind world domination schemes: wealthy do-gooders, commies, hedge funders, virtue-seekers, venture capitalists, campus radicals," Marty said. "Sprinkle in some yuan and rubles laundered through tax-exempt foundations, and you've got yourself a winning combination."

"We better hope not," Lindsey said with a shudder. "God forbid she gets more power."

A door opened behind them and Lindsey felt Bentley's air kiss on her cheek. "Lindsey, my dear," he said.

"Thank you for responding on such short notice, Bentley," Lindsey replied.

"Of course," he said.

"It appears we have ourselves another situation," she said.

Bentley nodded gravely as he gently patted her shoulder. "I'm afraid so."

Digby and Marty sat on either side of Lindsey, who took a chair in the middle of the table. Bentley sat opposite and folded his hands on the tabletop. Lindsey looked around at all the vacant chairs, usually filled with lawyers billing 2,000 dollars an hour for her meetings.

"Are we waiting on others?" she asked.

"Not at this point," Bentley said quietly. "Given the rather significant opposition you face, I thought it prudent to keep this within a small circle for now. We'll grow our team very selectively, and only when we need to. As you know, there are many people in this city whose sympathies lie with the climate overlords, even in this office."

Lindsey cocked her head and studied her lawyer. "What about you, Bentley? Do you have a belief one way or another?"

He shrugged. "I believe everyone has the right to fair legal representation. That's as far as it goes. When in doubt, we think of John Adams defending the British soldiers after the Boston Massacre."

"Except I didn't kill anybody," Lindsey protested.

"Not according to Felicity's supporters," Bentley replied. "They say millions of people have been killed by climate change."

Lindsey scoffed, "Perhaps they could name one."

"You're getting rather picky," Bentley said drolly.

A young woman in a conservative suit entered the room with a laptop and took the chair next to Bentley. She shook her head so that her long hair fell into place. "This is Amy Jackson Kroll, who's been working out of the capital," Bentley said. "I've brought her up from D.C. to help with cases like this."

"You have more than one?"

"Dozens," Bentley said. "Attorneys general across the country are looking for opportunities to sue energy companies over climate change. They want to drive them out of business to clear a path for the 'green tech' companies that fund their campaigns. That may not do anything for climate change, but it will certainly make some very rich people a whole lot richer."

"What does Felicity Redfeather want out of this?"

"The governor's office. Our sources in the AG's office tell us that she wants to win a settlement from you before the primary and use it as a campaign prop."

Lindsey sighed. "What would a settlement entail?"

"We're not certain," he said. "But you should prepare yourself for an offer that will exact a significant penalty for using fossil fuels in the great green State of New York, as well as a clearly defined road to redemption for you and your company."

"I'm beginning to think that road is I-95 South."

"More likely an agreement to end fossil fuel use by 2035."

"And still provide reliable energy to New York City? Not possible."

"Details don't concern her. Trophies do."

"Well, it doesn't really matter what she wants," Lindsey said. "It can't be done."

"Felicity Redfeather is not one to negotiate."

"Fine. I'm not inclined to settle," Lindsey said.

Bentley held up his hand. "Let's not draw a line in the sand just yet," he said. "If her case were to proceed to trial, a guilty verdict would allow her to confiscate your entire business portfolio in New York."

Lindsey slapped the table. "What? How is that even possible?"

"Look at what she did to Roland Platt," Bentley said. "You may recall she seized all his properties in New York. High-rises. Condominium complexes. Hotels and resorts. All were placed in receivership. And all because she was afraid he would file to run for governor before she did."

Lindsey put her hand on her chest. "I'm not running for office."

"She is," Bentley said. "And you make a useful whipping girl. She can cancel your business permits and take everything you've got in this state—without compensation. That would mean your headquarters building, your pipelines, and your East River Powerhouse. A big win over Big Energy would be a big feather in her cap."

"If not her big headdress," Marty noted.

"Indeed," Bentley acknowledged with an arched brow.

"On what possible basis could she take my property?" Lindsey wondered.

"Fraud. As I mentioned to Digby, it doesn't take much to charge misrepresentation in business," Bentley said. "Under the New York statute she used against Platt, the flimsiest pretext will do. A memo. A white paper. A text message. Anything, really. With a sympathetic judge—which she already has in her pocket—the odds of success for the plaintiff are very high indeed."

Bentley nodded to Amy, who peered over her laptop, her face illuminated by the glow of the screen. "She could argue you failed to alert the public of the role your products play in climate change," she said. "The good news, to the extent there is any, is that such a charge is impossible to prove. Nobody can say with precision how much the climate has changed from one period to another. Nor can they tell you the exact cause or causes. Even if they could, there's no way to quantify how much Crowe Power was responsible. All they have is speculation."

"What's the bad news?" Lindsey asked.

"That line of defense is unlikely to find a receptive audience in New York," Amy said. "Justice Melvin Hardiman is assigned to this case, and he is likely to play judge, jury, and executioner. He found Platt guilty without a trial and he could very well do that to you, too."

Lindsey got up and walked to the windowsill. "I get that Felicity's a zealot. What about ordinary folks, the people who just want to live a decent life and have the lights work when they want? Wouldn't some of them side with us?"

Bentley chuckled. "An amusing thought, I suppose."

"Is there no sympathy for a good corporate citizen?" Lindsey paced as she spoke. "My company employs thousands of people. We provide reliable products and services. We pay billions in taxes. We're trying very hard to develop new sources of energy, like fusion, because we know demand is going through the roof and we're going to need all the energy we can get."

Amy said. "None of that matters to Felicity. She's trying to save the planet. And you're standing in the way, representing white privilege. In her mind, you have no right to your position, your power, or your money. Your ill-gotten gains must be redistributed, and you must be humiliated in the process."

"How is my white privilege different from the people at Felicity's fundraiser last night?"

"That's a question that answers itself," Bentley said.

Amy added, "They were at Felicity's fundraiser."

"And I wasn't," Lindsey said glumly.

"Precisely."

Lindsey slumped on the windowsill. "What do you recommend I do?"

Bentley stood up and joined her at the windows. He placed a gentle hand on hers. "I think this is a good time for you to consider a way out before this goes too far."

"Which is what?" Lindsey asked.

"Play ball," Bentley said.

Lindsey slumped.

Amy said, "Most big companies have learned it's easier and cheaper to simply go along. They know that 'controlling our climate' is a delusion, but they also realize it's embedded too deeply in our culture to fight. It doesn't matter that predictions about a climate catastrophe have been wrong for fifty years. Money has so corrupted science, journalism, academia, politics, and digital information that the public is under the impression they must do whatever the authorities say to fight this scourge."

Lindsey looked puzzled. "Suppose I agree. How would I make peace with them?"

Amy ticked down her list. "You have to distance yourself from your industry. Resign from any organization that fights the Fenwick administration on climate regulations, such as the Safe & Reliable Energy Coalition. Sign on to the administration's Corporate Climate Manifesto to declare your commitment to a greener future. Adopt the United Nations' Sustainable Development Goals and back it up with an advertising campaign. Agree to—"

"Stop," Lindsey said. "That's a complete waste of money."

"I could go on," Amy said.

"Please don't," Lindsey said.

Amy slammed her laptop shut.

"Sorry, Amy. I know you're trying to help," Lindsey said. "But it's all feel-good nonsense. It doesn't help customers. It doesn't help investors. It certainly doesn't help me. If I capitulate, I'll be seen as an easy mark. And that will only lead to more and more demands. We've been down this road before. It never ends."

Bentley chimed in. "I think what Amy's suggesting is that you stay alive to fight another day. If you let them take you to court and you lose there, you could lose everywhere. California, Colorado, and Massachusetts will come after you next."

"I'm sorry, Bentley. I think the fight is in front of us right now," Lindsey said. "And I'm just not going to bend a knee. Once these climate bullies get you on the ground, they keep you there. Look what they did to the auto companies. They tore up their business models for what? I can't do that. This city will go dark."

The air went out of the room for a moment as everyone went back to their corners.

At last Bentley broke the silence. "We're here to serve you and we'll do whatever you want us to. But I would caution you. The atmosphere is charged. And it's getting more dangerous by the day. All the resources are on the side of your opponents." He locked eyes with Lindsey. "Be careful out there."

7. BRIDGE GAME

Four blue State Police cars with flashing lights converged on Lindsey's Escalade as it entered the ramp to the 59th Street Bridge and directed it to the shoulder of the road. Officers hustled out of their squad cars and swarmed the vehicle. A trooper ordered Lindsey's driver, Andrei, out of the vehicle and a police sergeant tapped on the rear passenger window.

Lindsey's heart pounded as she lowered the glass. "What is it?"

The sergeant leaned in. "We have a warrant to collect mobile phones from Lindsey Harper Crowe," he said, glancing around the cabin before fixing on Lindsey. "Is that you?"

"Yes, it is," Lindsey said, her heart racing.

He stuck a hand through the window. "Hand over your phones, please."

"Why? What possible—"

The sergeant cut her off and handed a warrant through the window. "You can argue with the judge," he barked. "Not with me."

Lindsey passed the warrant to Digby, sitting in the front passenger seat. "What do I do?" she asked.

Digby sighed as he read the paper. "Warrant was initiated by state Attorney General Felicity Redfeather and signed off by New York Supreme Court Justice Marvin Hardiman." He turned to Lindsey. "This is not optional."

Lindsey's hands trembled as she fumbled around in her handbag for the phone she kept for business and another for personal use. "This is nothing but harassment," she muttered. She plucked out one phone and handed it blindly to the sergeant, then dug around for the other. "Did New York run out of real criminals to go after? What does Redfeather expect to get out of my phones?"

"Felicity publicity," said Marty, who sat next to her. He pointed a thumb out the back window, where a trio of TV news trucks had caught up with them and parked. Reporters and camera operators scrambled around Lindsey's vehicle for the best angle.

Lindsey looked over her shoulder. "Oh, for God's sake! This is ridiculous," she said.

"Please hand me the other phone," the police sergeant said impatiently.

"I'm *looking* for it," Lindsey huffed as she dug deeper.

"Ma'am, right *now*."

"You can't have it until I find it," Lindsey said, through gritted teeth.

"Alright," the cop said, standing up straight. "I'm going to need you to step out of the car."

Lindsey glared at him. "Why? So you can get a better shot of me for the TV cameras? No thank you."

"This is not a request, ma'am," the cop said as he grasped the door handle.

"Fine. Arrest me," she said hotly. "I'm not getting out."

Digby leaned over from the front seat to intervene. "Sergeant, I'm Digby Pierrepont, Ms. Crowe's attorney," he said. "Could you please give her a moment? Obviously, this was not something she expected, and she was not prepared."

The cop seethed but backed up a step as Lindsey finally found her second phone, the one she kept for personal matters. She handed it through the window and the sergeant snatched it out of her hand.

"Thank you, ma'am," the cop said, touching the brim of his cap.

"When will I get those back?" Lindsey called.

"When we're through with 'em."

Marty watched the cop walk away, holding the phones up for his colleagues and—not coincidentally—the news media.

Lindsey turned to Digby. "What are they going to do with my phones?"

"They'll copy everything you've got on there," he replied.

"All my contacts? My texts?"

"Everything," Digby said.

"I've got some very private information on there." She flashed a glance at Marty. "I feel violated."

"That's the point," Marty said. "Two Blue Eyes wants you to know who's in charge. It's not you."

Outside the car, the police officers conferred among themselves. The sergeant handed Andrei's driver's license back to him while TV cameras captured the roadside drama and took shots of Lindsey's vehicle as if it were Bonnie and Clyde's getaway car.

Lindsey sank deeper into the backseat as Andrei reentered the car and buckled himself in up front. "Let's get the hell out of here," he said angrily.

Andrei pulled away from the shoulder and proceeded to the bridge, looking in his rearview mirror to watch the police return to their vehicles and turn off their flashers. The show was over, for now.

Lindsey looked at Digby with pleading eyes. "How long does this go on?"

Digby shrugged. "Until the primary, at least."

8. POWER TRIP

Andrei exited the 59th Street Bridge in Queens and snaked through a maze of streets to the East River Powerhouse, a campus walled off from its industrial neighborhood by tall fences topped with concertina wire. Signs near the electronic gate warned against the cameras on the powerhouse property and advised visitors of the plant's continuous surveillance. That didn't faze the perma-picketers, who wore Covid masks and sunglasses to disguise their identities as they marched, holding signs, in slow circles around the public sidewalk.

CROWE POISONS COMMUNITIES
We can't breathe!
LNG=DEATH!

Security personnel cleared a space to allow Lindsey's car through. Andrei drove carefully through the picketers, who glowered at the car, yelled obscenities, and pulled down their masks to spit on the windows. The gates closed behind the car as Andrei pulled up to the employee entrance. He parked behind a Chevrolet Tahoe that had, a short time earlier, ferried across other members of the Crowe Leadership Team.

Plant superintendent Dexter Tatum sprang open the door to greet Lindsey, Marty, and Digby. With blue jeans, steel-toed boots, and a hardhat over his thickly muscled physique, Dexter projected toughness, strength, and a no-nonsense demeanor.

"Exciting day, Dexter?" Lindsey asked as she passed through the portal.

He broke into a broad grin. "Every day is electrifying."

He led the way down a corridor to the powerhouse control room, the command center of Crowe's New York energy system. Despite her growing sense of anxiety over her own fate, Lindsey was relieved to see the powerhouse in good hands. Dexter was considered the best in the business, notorious for managing a high-pressure operation with a clear head and calm nerves. Leading a team of Navy SEALs in Iraq had proved useful experience for running a tight ship on the East River.

Dexter walked Lindsey, Marty, and Digby to the back of the control room, where they could get the big picture: a forty-foot-wide wall of digital screens with monitors, data charts, and colorful maps covering all the issues Dexter needed to track. In front of the screen was an array of desks, each with an operator watching smaller monitors arranged in wide half-circles. Other than their eyes and fingers, the people working behind the monitors barely moved. Their minds, however, were in constant motion.

"What are we looking at?" Lindsey asked.

"They're keeping an eye on weather forecasts, tracking power demand and generation, and making adjustments to balance the load," Dexter replied. "At all times, I want to know: Do we have enough juice? Do we need more gas to keep pressure in the lines? There are a thousand variables, and this team needs to be on top of them all."

Lindsey studied the people quietly doing their work, then looked at Dexter. "Thank God these people are on the job," she said. "Unsung heroes."

Dexter nodded. "You got that right. Nobody thinks about this crew when they turn on their TVs or charge their phones. But without 'em, it's lights out in NYC. These people are the best of the best. And do you know why?"

"You trained them," she said.

"I *tested* them," he corrected. "You have to know that every person in here has the psychological capacity to make split-second decisions under pressure. Can they keep their head when things are moving fast? Would they freak out when the heat is on—or off? All it takes is one person to fall apart at crunch time and boom! The system goes down with them. It's like air traffic control. One slip-up and you get a crash."

Dexter led the group up a metal staircase to a second-floor conference room, where Crowe's Chief Executive Lucy Rutherford, Chief Financial Officer Armani Jones, and Chief Information Officer Faraz Rahman rose to greet them.

"Where have you been?" Lucy asked.

"We stopped to chat with the police," Lindsey replied.

"Lucky you," Lucy said.

"Not really," Lindsey said flatly.

They settled around the conference table, facing a projection screen. "Thanks for hosting us today, Dexter," Lindsey said. "Lucy, this is your meeting. Why don't you start?"

"Thanks, Lindsey," Lucy said. She punched a button on her computer and a chart with a straight line that broke upward like the blade on a hockey stick came up on the screen. "As you all know, we're expecting a sharp rise in demand for electricity from our customers in the years ahead. AI, cloud computing, and manufacturing facilities for microchips require massive amounts of energy. Add in government mandates for electric vehicles, ovens, and heating systems and we have a huge challenge ahead of us. At the same time, the government has made it nearly impossible to get enough supply. That's because of their climate rules and regulations."

She touched another button, and the screen showed a flat line that gradually moved downward. "They outlawed coal, which is cheap, portable, and widely used by our adversaries, such as China. They've nearly finished phasing out fuel oil for heating, which is practically non-existent in New York City. They won't allow nuclear, which would meet their mandates on carbon emissions but freaks them out. I guess they think it means mushroom clouds."

"What about renewables?" Armani asked.

"The most reliable renewable source in this state is hydropower," Lucy said. "Think Niagara Falls. But we can only get so much power from water. The activists pretend offshore wind and onshore solar farms will somehow replace coal and gas, but we know that's not possible—and they must know it, too. For one thing, power that depends on sunshine and wind is unreliable and always requires a backup. For another, you've seen more and more of these proposals for wind or solar fail—either because of local opposition or bad economics."

"Where does that leave us?" Lindsey asked.

"Natural gas," Lucy said. "It's how we generate the biggest chunk of our electricity. It's also how we heat homes. But we can't get enough. The governor just denied—for the sixth time—our permit for a natural gas pipeline."

Lucy punched another button and brought up a chart that showed the energy supply and demand lines moving in opposite directions. "This is where we stand." As everyone studied the chart, she added, "On an average day, we can get by.

People will hit their switches and the lights will come on. Their air conditioners and heating systems will work. Unfortunately, not every day is average. The highest demand for energy comes when supplies are hardest to get."

"When is that?" Lindsey asked.

"A winter storm," Lucy said. "Dexter, let me turn it over to you."

Dexter grabbed a clicker and stood up next to the screen. "It wasn't too long ago that we came this far—" he held his thumb and index finger a quarter inch apart, "from catastrophe."

"Winter Storm Elliott?" Lindsey prompted.

"Exactly," Dexter said. He hit his clicker, which put a map of the eastern two-thirds of the United States on the screen. He gave a broad outline of what occurred: a bomb cyclone, characterized by a rapid drop in barometric pressure, had generated blizzards, record snowfalls, high winds, and frigid temperatures over an area two-thousand miles wide. The storm had killed more than a hundred people. Forty-one had died in and around Buffalo as Elliott dumped more than four feet of snow in five days.

"We had a massive spike in natural gas demand at the exact same time production plummeted. Well heads froze in Ohio, Pennsylvania, and West Virginia. Mechanical and electrical equipment broke down everywhere." He showed a photo of wellheads covered with icicles. "Our guys couldn't fix the problems because there was so much ice on the roads. We were having one hell of a time keeping enough pressure in the lines."

Dexter hit a button on his computer screen and the map filled up with red, blue, and orange dots across thirty-six states from Texas to Minnesota and Florida to Maine. "These are all the unplanned wellhead outages that occurred. The Marcellus Shale, where we typically get our gas, was down anywhere from twenty-three to fifty-four percent. There wasn't nearly enough natural gas to handle demand for residential heating and electricity generation."

Armani Jones asked innocently, "I hate to sound naïve, given what you said earlier. But what about... renewables? Could they help at all?"

Dexter shook his head. "No. Sorry, ma'am. Solar and wind are only three percent of our electrical generation on a good day. On bad days like we had there? Forget about it. Wind turbines freeze up. Solar panels get covered in snow. They're useless."

Lindsey asked, "So what did you do?"

Dexter looked up at the screen. "Normally, in a situation where we're running low, we import gas from other parts of the country. But we found out the hard way that's not always a solution. That's because they're killing permits for pipelines all over the eastern United States. Climate activists insist we don't need them because they only look at daily averages, not spikes, like this storm.

"Elliott was so damn big—" He swept his hand across the screen, "they had the same problem in other states that we were having here. Everyone was ripping through their reserves. And that still wasn't enough." Without natural gas to both provide heat and generate electricity, Dexter said, the entire power system started to wobble, and blackouts occurred for the first time ever in North Carolina and Tennessee. "And that's not even the worst of it."

"I hate to ask," Lindsey said.

"If the gas lines go down, they'll stay down for months," Dexter said. "Millions of people in New York City could go the entire winter without heat." He let that concept hang in the air as everyone considered the ramifications.

Lindsey looked puzzled. "Why would it be out so long?"

"Bringing the gas system back up isn't a matter of flipping a switch," Dexter said. "We'd need to bring in an army of utility workers—provided they're available from other states—to go door to door, building to building, and shut off every single gas valve to make sure there's nothing coming out. Every point of service for gas lines would have to be cleared before we fire up the pilot lights or you could get explosions. That takes two or three months, easily. And those months could be January and February."

Lindsey leaned forward and focused on Dexter. "How did you avert disaster?"

Dexter's face grew tense as he recalled the harrowing moment. "It came down to the three most dreaded letters in the English language—at least as far as climate activists are concerned."

"L-N-G," Lucy said.

Dexter nodded. "Liquefied natural gas," he said. "LNG is methane that's converted from a gas to a liquid for transport and storage. We have a storage facility here on campus and we get a shipment every November in case we need it on a rainy day—or, more likely, a snowy one. When Elliott came blowing through here, we needed it—badly."

Lindsey stood up. "How badly?" she asked.

"We were minutes from losing the whole system—heat, electricity, everything. We vaporized all the LNG we had and that still wasn't enough. If the weather hadn't warmed up, we'd have been out of luck. Then we'd have had a real climate apocalypse—not the kind the politicians talk about, where the temperature might rise a degree or two in a hundred years. When Winter Storm Uri hit Texas, people lost power for four days in freezing temperatures. Eight hundred people died. They came within four minutes and thirty-seven seconds of seeing their entire system go down."

"Don't the activists understand the danger posed by these storms?" Armani asked.

Dexter laughed. "Oh, hell no! They blame Crowe Power for causing the storms. Apparently, we've got some mystical powers."

Lindsey sighed. "Alright. We've got a massive problem here. What do we do? It sounds like the only option is to get more LNG capability."

"We have an application into the state to expand and upgrade our facility," Digby said.

"What are the odds we get that approved?" Lindsey asked.

"Ten-to-one against," Digby said. "There's way too much pressure from the activists. And they have tons of money behind them. As we've seen, they've got Frank Cardini by the balls."

"Two Blue Eyes, too?" Lindsey asked.

"I don't know what she's got down there," Dexter said.

Lindsey rubbed her forehead. "What do we do?"

Dexter folded his arms across his massive chest. "I know what I'm going to do. We get another storm like Elliott, or like Uri, or like another half-dozen storms we've had in recent years, it's gonna be every person for themselves. I hate to say it, but I recommend you all get yourself a go bag."

Lindsey's hands fell to the sides of her chair. "And go where?"

"Wherever you can find shelter," Dexter said.

"Where would you go, Dexter?" Lindsey asked.

HOSTILE CLIMATE

"I've got me a cabin in the mountains north of the city. I can live off the grid up there," he said. "I've got my own wind and solar power, a diesel generator, well water, an outhouse, and a pot-belly furnace. If it gets to be survival of the fittest, I plan to be extremely fit." He looked around the table. "But there isn't room enough for all of you."

9. PHONEY NEWS

The confiscation of Lindsey's phones played like the capture of the Unabomber across all the local news channels as speculation mounted over the dastardly secrets they might contain.

What did Lindsey Harper Crowe know about menacing changes to the world's climate that she wasn't telling? Who was in on her conspiracy to roast the Earth? How long did Lindsey and her gang think they could get away with robbing the nation's children and grandchildren of their future?

"Busy news day today as North Korea sent a missile within fifty miles of Los Angeles. Rating agencies warned that the United States could default on its debt. And China launched a Death Star armed with lasers that could vaporize Chicago," said anchorman Lawrence Ascott. "But first, our top story this afternoon: the continuing threat posed by our ever-worsening climate. Energy maven Lindsey Harper Crowe faces possible charges tonight after police swarmed her car on the FDR and seized her phones."

"That's right," co-anchor Mitzi Chong gravely intoned. "State Attorney General Felicity Redfeather issued a statement saying the phones were taken because they could contain evidence suggesting Crowe and her company knew about her products' impacts on climate change but did not tell the public. This on the day when scientists issued more worrisome reports that climate change could cause earthquakes, decrease sexual activity among rabbits, and corrode your aluminum siding."

Ascott added with a raised eyebrow, "The company issued a statement late this afternoon saying it has acted responsibly at all times and has always put the interests of its customers first."

Marty switched off the TV and poured himself a coffee in the pantry as Lindsey emerged from her private bathroom, looking pale and stressed.

"Well?" she said.

Marty turned. "Well, what?"

She nodded toward the TV. "What's the verdict?"

"You're Public Enemy Number One," Marty said, "and there isn't a close second. Not even a Chinese Death Star is as threatening to our future as Lindsey Harper Crowe."

"Great," she muttered.

"Aside from fires in the Bronx, shootings in Brooklyn and stabbings on the subway, life was apparently pretty good before you came along and mucked it all up," Marty said.

She flopped into a chair at her conference table. "I am so sick of this crap."

Marty sighed as he took a seat across from her. "It's not sick of you. You better get used to it."

She looked exasperated. "Why, Marty? This is wrong—on every level."

He sympathized. "I get it. If it feels like everyone's against you, it's largely because they are. This climate narrative is so embedded in the public psyche I can't even hire a PR firm to help, and these are people who will take money from anybody. And I know because I'm one of them."

"It's that bad?"

"Nobody wants to sully their reputation by being associated with a deeply unfashionable cause."

Lindsey seethed. "Like me."

"Like anyone associated with climate change," Marty said. "They give awards in the PR industry for firms that advance the hysteria in the most creative ways possible." He reached across the table and squeezed her hand. "Sorry. I really am."

"Isn't there a way to break through? How do we get people to understand what's going on here? What they're telling people isn't real. It's science fiction."

Marty checked his watch. "I'm going to see Hollis Blackwell at the *Daily Reaper* in an hour. Most of the corporate media follow their lead. If I can move them a bit, that would help. But don't expect a miracle." He leaned forward. "They're deeply invested in their narrative. And they're widely applauded for it. They won a Pulitzer Prize last year for their climate coverage that, as far as I can tell, was completely fabricated."

She slumped in her chair. "The so-called paper of record?"

"A broken record," Marty said. "They partnered with a leftist paper in the U.K., Bartleby College, and several foundations to produce a ten-part report on 'solutions' to climate change. Number one on their list was to prepare for scarcity. The *Reaper* has decided we shouldn't expect to have energy any time we want it in the future if we're going to beat climate change. So, get ready, folks. Lower your expectations—and your thermostats. Only use enough energy that's sufficient to keep living. Nothing more."

"Hardship is one thing," Lindsey said. "Do they have any understanding of how dangerous their ideas are? Maybe you could get the *Reaper* reporters to meet with Dexter over at the Powerhouse. What he said was chilling."

"I intend to make that pitch, but I doubt they'll catch it," Marty replied. "In their world, climate change explains everything." He paused, thinking. "Maybe that explains the rash on my ass."

Lindsey laughed. "I don't think I've seen that."

"Trust me. You don't want to."

"You make them sound like simpletons."

Marty shrugged. "That's not my doing."

They both sat in silence a moment, considering their plight. Finally, Marty said, "This isn't a battle about our business or even about you. It's a cultural war, one this industry has already lost. Even the biggest companies are conceding that. Look at their commercials. All they do is beg for mercy. 'Look at us! We're planet-loving people just like you, working hard to address climate change! We're creating energy from the office fish tank! It's enough to power a pencil sharpener for a day and a half.'"

"Of course they say that! Who wants to go through this?" Lindsey stood up and walked over to her desk and picked up a folder. "We're developing new kinds of energy, too—arguably more than anybody else. I'd put our fusion initiative ahead of every other company out there." She put the folder back down. "But fusion isn't ready yet. And, aside from nuclear fission, neither is any of this other stuff they pretend can replace fossil fuels."

Marty stood. "I'll make the case as best I can."

As he turned toward the door, the security man Tom Michaels knocked on the frame. "Two things, Ms. Crowe. First, I've got these for you." He walked into the room and handed back her phones. "And, if you don't mind, I'd like to go with you to your five o'clock meeting."

Lindsey shook her head. "I don't think that's necessary, Tom," she said. "I'm only going to the library. How dangerous could that be?"

Tom pressed. "Nothing is safe for you right now. Threats against you on social media and on our switchboard are up considerably over the past few days."

"Oh, c'mon. You can't take that seriously," Lindsey said.

"Actually, I do, and you should, too. All it takes is one nut who wants to be a hero," Tom replied. "You should have me or someone on my team with you whenever you go out in public—at least for the time being."

10. MENACE TO POLITE SOCIETY

Lindsey's bid to go incognito on her trip to Midtown required oversized sunglasses and a floppy hat. She cast a sidelong glance for trouble as she exited her car on Fifth Avenue and walked up the steps to the New York Public Library. Tom positioned himself in front of her and his deputy Morris walked behind. She passed Patience and Fortitude, the iconic marble lions guarding the entrance, and noted those were qualities she could use right now.

Tom and Morris escorted her through a bag check at the front door and up the stairs to a private meeting room. There, a small sign welcomed Literacy Foundation donors to a reception to meet the organization's new president, Winton Hinkle.

"I should be reasonably safe from here," Lindsey told Tom. She handed him her glasses and hat, and he said he'd wait for her.

The cold temperature in the room was no match for the icy reception of tight smiles, stiffened postures, and swiveling backs, until she felt a tap on her shoulder and heard a familiar voice. "*Sooo* glad you're here."

Lindsey turned to see Bits, her longtime friend and former sister-in-law. They embraced lightly. "You don't know how relieved I am to see you," Lindsey said. "At least there's one person here who will talk to me."

"So you think," Bits sniffed.

"Oh, c'mon," Lindsey said, with a playful slap. "Can you at least stand next to me? I'm in a rather lonely place right now."

Bits dismissed the idea with a wave of her hand. "Don't worry. If your last check cleared, the people who run the foundation will still talk to you," she said. "Maude Chambers fakes an orgasm better than Meg Ryan."

Lindsey laughed. "I don't kid myself: that's the only reason she keeps me on the board. It's also the reason I came. I don't know what these people are doing with our money anymore. Based on their newsletters, I'd say they forgot their mission."

On cue, Lindsey and Bits turned to see the always elegant civic doyenne Maude Chambers, the Literacy Foundation's chairperson. She was making the rounds with a meticulous looking gentleman in a gray pinstriped suit with a red bow tie and pocket square to match, his hair combed and lacquered severely to one side.

"Bits. Lindsey. I'd like you to meet Winton Hinkle, our new president," Maude said proudly, as he took turns shaking their hands. "Winton comes to us from the Hackford-Harrison in Boston, where he managed their fine educational programs. I'm sure you've heard of them."

"I thought Hackford-Harrison was a funeral home," Bits said drily.

"It is, in a way," Winton said grandly. "We buried the old methods of teaching literacy."

"Ah," Bits said. "Based on test scores, it appears the old methods were cremated in New York years ago."

Winton nodded thoughtfully. "Rightly so. I'm no fan of tests to measure success. Anyone can teach to pass a test."

"Not in our schools," Lindsey noted.

Maude tut-tutted. "Winton says—and I quite agree—we need to teach our children how to think *critically*," she said. "That's far more important. It's not their reading comprehension that is the issue—

"*Way* overrated, in my view," Winton interjected.

"...It's more what the children comprehend," Maude continued. "There's so much misinformation floating around. I don't know how they can distinguish fact from fiction."

"I'm having trouble with that myself," Bits conceded.

Winton put an index finger to his lips. "Something that worked very well for us in Boston could work very well here, too, I believe," he said. "We created a consortium of partners from government, academia, news media, social media, and search engines to create a curriculum comprised of verified facts regarding pressing issues such as climate change."

Maude butted in. "Isn't that marvelous?"

"Depends on the supposed facts they approve," Lindsey said. "How do you decide what's right and what's wrong?"

"First and foremost, of course, we follow the science," Winton said.

"And if there's disagreement on the science?" Lindsey asked.

Winton raised his imperious chin and looked down his nose. "If you follow the issue of climate change at all, Lindsey, I'm sure you know there is no disagreement at all among scientists. They overwhelmingly agree that the climate is changing and that humans are the primary cause. *Res judicata,*" Winton said. "Nearly sixty percent of the general population in the United States agrees with them too."

Lindsey nodded. "Is that how you measure truth? Majority rule?"

He regarded her with feigned puzzlement. "I don't follow," he said.

"Sorry. Let me state it more plainly," Lindsey said. "If you studied the issue from many angles as I do, you would realize the science on climate change is far from settled. Many people would like us to think the research is behind us so that we can move on to adopting their far-fetched solutions. I've not heard of one yet that I would recommend."

Winton looked at Maude with an expression that suggested: *Kook alert!* "Lindsey, darling," Maude said soothingly, "I know there are a few people out there who just can't quite get with the program, especially in your business. But surely, you are not among them. You've been such a staunch advocate for our children. Don't you want them to grow up armed with knowledge about issues that could dramatically affect their future?"

"I do, which is why this bothers me," Lindsey said. "Marinating our children in questionable science doesn't promote literacy. It supports indoctrination. The issue is far more complex than they're letting on."

"But that is my point!" Winton exclaimed. "We can't possibly expect young minds to sort through data and formulas and so on."

"Especially when they're not learning math," Bits said.

"Precisely," Winton allowed. "We have to interpret for them and offer the best guidance possible from certified experts."

"Such as?"

"Like Dr. Spanky MacFarlane, whom I'd really love to join our board," Winton said. "If we reach our children early enough, they will understand they can change the world. They'll make more informed choices about our democracy, better decisions in the voting booth, and support more sensible policies to govern our way of life. What good would it do for them to go against the grain on an issue as fundamental to our existence as climate change?"

"A powerful concept, wouldn't you agree?" Maude asked.

"Very," Lindsey allowed. She threw her head back and drained her drink.

Maude, whose late husband had made his fortune selling sub-prime mortgages, continued. "It's quite apparent—and Winton, please stop me if you disagree—that we're moving into a post-capitalist world. There's simply no way for civil society to achieve its goals if it's every person for themself. Solving issues like climate change requires a top-down approach."

"Why is that?" Bits asked.

"Because there's no time to lose!"

"I see. And you're the top?"

"If I were, I would say 'let's stop glorifying conspicuous consumption,'" Maude continued. "People need to know that they're just going to have to do without certain things." As her speech became more animated, a hundred thousand dollars' worth of jangling jewelry punctuated each point. "I say—and Winton, I know you agree with me here—"

"Oh yes," he said, without waiting to find out what it was.

"—that it's our duty to inform our young people how they can live a more responsible life than their parents."

Winton looked at Lindsey and Bits. "How long have you ladies been involved with the Literacy Foundation?"

Lindsey said, "My company has supported the foundation for about twenty years." She turned to Bits. "That is, until today."

"What do you mean?" Maude asked.

"I don't mean to be rude," Lindsey said, "but it appears it's time to direct my resources elsewhere."

Maude reached out and touched her arm. "Lindsey, dear. I hope you're not serious. You know how very grateful we are for your support."

Winton leaned in. "If you don't mind my asking: what's the name of your business?"

"The Crowe Power Company," Lindsey said.

Winton blanched. "Oh."

"Yeah," Lindsey said. "Oh."

"I'm a shareholder there myself," Bits added. "My great-great-grandfather was Homer Crowe. You may have heard of him?"

Winton cleared his throat. "Well, well, well," he said. "There's much to atone for there. I know that many other scions of energy fortunes have come around to a more enlightened way of thinking. They know these old energy companies can't go on willy-nilly. Everyone must adjust to the new realities of our planet."

Lindsey ground her teeth. "You think I need to atone?" she asked. She stepped forward. "How would you like me to turn off your lights?"

A ruffled Winton stepped backward and reflexively adjusted his bow tie. "I meant no offense."

"I did," she said. She turned to Bits. "Are you ready?"

Bits nodded, took Lindsey's arm, and they walked out. "I thought you were going to kick that twerp's ass."

"And break a nail?" Lindsey replied. "He wasn't worth it."

"I get it," Bits said. "Why waste a perfectly good mani on an idiot like that?" She squeezed Lindsey's arm. "And, by the way, screw those sudsy spritzers they were serving. A million dollars a year for a club soda and a squirt of champagne? I could use a real drink. Let's go around the corner."

"My security people won't let me."

"It's that bad?" Bits asked.

She looked around for Tom. "You have no idea."

11. DON'T FEAR THE REAPER

As a long-time practitioner of public relations, Marty had historically been compensated well for defending reputations that didn't deserve it.

He had shooed away swarms of media flies from CEOs who stunk at their jobs. He had explained disastrous quarterly performances by directing attention to the bold, bright future that always beckoned just around the corner. He had even convinced one nosy scribe that the inebriated woman seen canoodling with his boss at the Polo Lounge was in fact his wife, who had recently dyed her hair, lost weight, and had an impressive boob job. Afterward, Marty delivered the bad news to his boss: stay away from the boozy floozy in public. In return for such sensible advice, Marty was fired.

Lindsey was the first company leader Marty had worked with whom he truly respected as a leader and as a human being, yet she was the hardest to defend. The new generation of reporters, schooled in disciplines such as "environmental journalism," was wed to political narratives that put her squarely in their crosshairs. Climate change was a conviction that had driven them into the business in the first place. Armies of reporters had trained to become advocates of changing the world. On their side was truth, justice, intelligence, and a sizable sense of moral authority. On the other side were mopes, dopes, and deplorables.

If reporters didn't truly believe they were saving the world by connecting every thunderstorm, wildfire, or unusually hot day to climate change, they knew enough to recite their lines to keep their standing in the newsroom. The narrative went that an indulgent and decadent West, in a century-long grip of capitalist excess, was destroying the earth through its continued use of fossil fuels. That unleashed the "toxin" of carbon dioxide, formerly regarded as an essential life-giving gas.

"Mr. Blackwell will be with you shortly," an editorial assistant said to Marty after he entered the reception area of the lush green atrium that ran through the center of the *Daily Reaper*'s headquarters. "Please have a seat."

Marty remained standing as he perused the *Reaper*'s massive collection of journalism prizes framed on the wall, featured in display cases, and running in a continuous stream on a giant TV screen. He was struck by the number of awards for series, stories, and columns that he remembered as thinly disguised propaganda. One unintentionally hilarious display case featured a titanium hockey stick, awarded to the *Reaper* for its explanation of the climatists' favored hockey stick graph, a supposed representation of global temperatures over the past thousand years that was used in climate reports by the United Nations. The graph was so named because its shape resembled a hockey stick laying on its side. The handle represented a gradual decline in temperatures until the late 1800s, when the blade suddenly shot up to indicate the world's imminent demise. It was a ludicrous exaggeration on its face, oversimplified and thoroughly debunked by underpublicized scientists. Yet the *Reaper* found it very credible indeed, thanks in part to the assurances of proponents such as Dr. George "Spanky" MacFarlane, the media's favorite climate change enthusiast, and his dour band of climate grifters.

Despite the implausible coverage, Marty understood why the *Reaper* was so gaudily honored: the organizations that bestowed the awards were universities, foundations, and other non-profits that had become the *Reaper*'s business partners, financing journalism that comported with the views of their donors. As part of the non-profits' comprehensive approach to providing a full spectrum of climate initiatives, they also funded research into climate change, climate activists, and political campaigns, as well as corrupted journalism. The quaint newspaper, TV, and radio model of old had funded news organizations through disinterested advertisers such as local retailers, car dealers, realtors, and home remodelers. Much of the modern digital media system was shaped and financed by global philanthropists from Silicon Valley with a very specific agenda in mind. After making the largest fortunes the world had ever known, they traveled to conferences around the world in private jets to discuss new ways to herd the West's unruly cats into more virtuous and profitable corrals that they had constructed through public policy. The fact that the moguls just happened to be investors in Earth-saving ventures was not to be mentioned in the media they financed. Rather, their motives were portrayed as conscientious investment instead of grubby profit-making. Marty couldn't help noting that Mom and Pop had been supplanted by Big Brother.

"Martin," said Hollis Blackwell.

Marty turned to see the paper's patrician editor, clad in gabardine slacks and a cashmere sweater. "You win any more awards, Hollis, and you're going to need to build more walls."

"That's a problem I'm happy to have," Hollis said. "Come on in."

Hollis led his way through a half-populated newsroom to a conference room on the corner of the building looking east toward Times Square. "Would you like some coffee or water?"

"No thank you. I'm fine," Marty said, taking a chair.

Hollis leaned back in his seat and clasped his hands behind his head. "What's on your mind? Your message suggested you're taking issue with our coverage of Lindsey Harper Crowe. She's your client, I take it?"

Marty nodded. "She is. And, yes, you guessed right. She's a good person who I think you're treating unfairly. We've provided statements in her defense; you've only run selective snippets that distort the meaning of what she said. We've offered important context that doesn't make the cut at all. And, unfortunately, your stories not only mislead your readers, they carry a great deal of weight with the rest of the media. They follow your lead."

Hollis nodded thoughtfully, then shrugged. "I understand your discomfort, given who pays your bills—"

"It's not just that," Marty interjected.

"Right, right," Hollis said with a dismissive wave. "It never is for PR people, is it?"

Marty ignored the shot. "It's a question of fairness and balance."

Hollis scoffed. "Balance? Wake up and smell the latte, Marty. Those days are long gone."

Marty's jaw dropped. "You admit it?"

"Of course I do," Hollis said. "The antiquated notion that you simply throw out a few facts and let the public decide for themselves went out with Edward R. Murrow. The people in our newsroom strongly believe that it's wrong to present both sides of an issue in equal measure, if both sides don't have equal credibility," Hollis said. "And on the issue of climate change, bothsidesism won't wash. On one side, you have the overwhelming number of scientists who concur that the science is settled. On the other side, you have a handful of crackpots and whack-a-doos in tinfoil hats. That's a false equivalence."

Marty seethed but kept his cool. "I can see how one might reach that conclusion reading the *Reaper*," Marty said. "But that's simply not true. The computer models that have predicted disaster for the past fifty years have been proven wrong time and again. And the skeptical scientists you dismiss are highly credentialed researchers who are doing their jobs, which are to continue looking for answers on an incredibly complex topic. Meanwhile, you're selling nonsensical solutions to a manufactured crisis. The fact that you keep pushing that ridiculous hockey stick graph suggests somebody ought to be tossed in the penalty box."

"You should be happy we're doing what we do," Hollis insisted.

"Why is that?"

"Because we're making the case politely," Hollis claimed. "There are many in the climate movement who think it's well past the time of reasoning and gentle persuasion. It's time to force compliance in a way that some might say would be — how shall I put it? — uncomfortable."

"That sounds like a threat."

"Take it as you like. I'm only telling you what you need to know."

"Wow. I guess I should thank you for that."

Hollis slapped the table. "You know, Marty, this is all amusing conversation. It's interesting to know there are people like you still out there, pounding the pavement for good ol' fossil fuels. But everything you say suggests you're in denial and that makes it difficult to take you seriously. If we're going to save our planet, we simply have to move on. We're facing an existential crisis, you know." He started to get up.

"I absolutely agree," Marty said.

Hollis sat back down. "You do?"

"Absolutely," he said. "It's just not the existential crisis you imagine."

"You don't say," Hollis said with a barely concealed sneer. He looked at his watch. "I have a moment for some entertainment. Please enlighten me."

"The solutions you advocate for addressing climate change are not only ridiculous, they're futile. Rationing food and energy. Forcing people out of gasoline-powered cars. Banning natural gas heating in new buildings when we can barely generate enough electricity now. Sucking carbon out of the atmosphere with giant vacuum cleaners. All of that will have little or no impact on climate change. Worse, it will endanger lives today—not fifty or a hundred years from now," Marty said.

"Sounds like you've been drinking your client's Kool-Aid, Marty."

"You want an example?"

"If you have one," Hollis scoffed.

"Take the Peace Pipeline that Frank Cardini just killed. Its death was extolled by the *Reaper* as a much-needed victory in the war against climate change. You quoted giddy activists who claimed environmental justice. But that pipeline was designed to provide natural gas in times of extreme winter cold when consumer demand was at its peak. Without it, Crowe Power's plant—and this town—are living dangerously."

"Says who? You?" Hollis said, with a sarcastic chuckle. "I'm supposed to believe a corporate flack?"

Marty pulled a report from his satchel and tossed it on the table. Then he stabbed a finger on it. "Believe these people. When federal regulators issued this report on Winter Storm Elliott, you never even mentioned it. As far as the *Reaper* goes, it doesn't exist. Nothing to see here, folks! Yet this tells you exactly how close we came to a massive disaster. And one of the key issues was the unavailability of natural gas. The Peace Pipeline was Crowe's answer to provide more backup. LNG is another, but the activists are threatening those plans, too. God help us if we have a storm like that again."

Hollis picked up the report and casually thumbed through it. "If you think we're going to argue for more fossil fuel capacity in our country, guess again," Hollis said. "And we're certainly not going to confuse our readers with information that distracts them from the core issue, which is the action we need right now to fight climate change. Ms. Crowe's reckoning is long overdue—as it is for the entire fossil fuels industry. The days of polluting our world with carbon dioxide are thankfully drawing to a close. And so is this conversation."

Hollis rose. "Your client will have her day in court, Marty. Probably sooner than you think." He started to walk out, then turned back. "Our sources tell us Felicity Redfeather is bringing charges against your client tomorrow. You might want to prepare another statement."

"Would you print it?" Marty asked.

"That depends," he said with a shrug. "If she finally admits her culpability in our overheated world, we'll make sure everyone knows it."

12. SLAPPY HOUR

Tom Michaels reluctantly approved of Lindsey grabbing a drink with Bits under one condition: *stay close to the car*. With militant climate change agitators amping up their pressure, Lindsey needed to keep her public exposure to a minimum and plan for a quick retreat if necessary. Under the radical City Council's newly enacted Good Cause clause, thugs accused of assaulting climate polluters were released without bail, issued an apology, and given a fifty-dollar gift card for the inconvenience of being arrested.

Tom, Morris, and two other security people accompanied Lindsey and Bits around the corner from the library to 42nd Street, where they attempted to blend into the throng unnoticed.

"I feel like a celebrity," Bits cooed as she hugged Lindsey's arm.

Lindsey scoffed. "You like this?"

"I could get used to it," Bits said as they walked through the thicket of pedestrians, bicycles, mopeds, and hawkers. "I wouldn't mind having Tom follow me around all day."

"It's not as much fun as you might think," Lindsey said. "He's a constant reminder that I'm in danger."

They found a table under sycamore trees in a distant corner of the Bryant Park Café. It was as far away as they could get from the boisterous crowd of happy hour drinkers gathered around the bar and as close as they could get to her getaway car idling on 42nd Street. Lindsey continued to wear her sunglasses and hat, even though the sun had fallen well below the Midtown skyscrapers.

Bits eyed her. "You know that's a ridiculous getup, right?"

Lindsey muttered, "It worked for Holly Golightly."

"It's not quite *Breakfast at Tiffany's*," Bits replied. "You look like you're in the Witness Protection Program."

"I kind of am," Lindsey said, taking a calming sip of white wine. "I'm getting death threats every day."

"Do you think anyone would really come after you?"

"We suspect they're more bark than bite," Lindsey said. "But I have taken up kickboxing in case Tom's not around when I need him."

"You packing heat?"

Lindsey laughed. "You don't think I'm hot enough already?"

"With that hat? I'm thinking you might need more ammo." Bits nodded toward the park, where a flushed Marty was alternately walking and jogging toward them. "He doesn't look very happy."

Lindsey sat up with a start. "What's the matter?"

Marty grabbed a chair and sat down, trying to catch his breath. "AG…" he huffed, "is filing a lawsuit… against you… tomorrow."

"For what?" Lindsey asked.

"…Fraud."

Lindsey shuddered. "How do you know?"

"Hollis Blackwell told me," Marty said, mopping his brow with a cocktail napkin. "The *Reaper*'s practically an arm of the Redfeather campaign, so you know his sources are good."

"Oh, crap," Lindsey muttered.

"That's not all," Marty said. "I saw a bunch of protesters holding signs with your name on them." He shook his head. "Looked like the Planetistas. They're heading in this direction."

"How would they know I'm here?" Lindsey asked. She looked over Marty's shoulder to see the activists marching her way from 40th Street. Some held up signs with Lindsey's picture in a red circle with a line through it. Others carried banners: "CLIMATE JUSTICE 4 ALL," "STOP CO_2 POLLUTION," and "CLEAN ENERGY IS A RIGHT!" A few allied causes were thrown in, too, with signs supporting intifada, transgenderism in sports, defunding police, and rights for practitioners of bestiality. As they got closer, Lindsey could hear them chanting, *"Hey, hey, ho, ho, Lindsey Crowe has got to go!"*

"Take that literally," Marty said urgently. "You've got to get out of here."

Lindsey looked around her. "Where's Tom?"

Marty nodded behind her. "He's coming now." Tom was walking swiftly in their direction and talking on his phone. He hung up and addressed Lindsey sharply. "Wrap this up," he commanded. "Planetistas are coming. Climate Rangers, too."

"Who?" Lindsey asked.

"You don't want to find out."

Behind Tom, a column of marchers wearing round helmets that resembled melting globes carried hockey sticks over their shoulders like rifles. They marched in unison, like storm troopers on parade, as pedestrians hustled out of their way.

The ragtag Planetistas, dressed in barista fatigues, moved toward them from the other direction. They overturned tables in the cafe, climbed on top of chairs, and harassed people in the crowd. One crazed woman shouted through a megaphone. "Party while the planet dies! You're all selfish fucking *PIGS!*"

With demonstrators approaching from both the north and south, and the library blocking a path to the east, the only escape route was west through the park.

"Let's go!" Tom barked. Lindsey and Bits jumped to their feet. To his security agents, Tom commanded, "Diamond formation."

With Morris Jenkins in front, Tom in back, and two agents on the side, the group moved as quickly as they could without attracting further attention. They cut through strolling couples, panhandlers, commuters heading to the subway, and nannies pushing strollers. Tom issued orders on his phone. "Meet us on Sixth Avenue at 41st near the fountain."

Halfway through the park, they heard a voice shriek behind them, "There she is!"

Tom shouted, *"Move!"*

Morris yelled, "Let's *go!*" He, the agents, Lindsey, and Bits ran toward Sixth Avenue. Tom brought up the rear. They reached the street just as two black SUVs screeched to a stop in front of them and the Climate Rangers closed in from behind. Agents opened the back door of the first vehicle and shoved Lindsey and Bits inside as the first of the Climate Rangers to reach the group raised his hockey stick over his head to take a swing.

Tom caught the handle as it came down, twisted it out of the Climate Ranger's hands, and used the stick to cross-check him into a light post, where he crumpled to the ground. "Penalty for high-sticking," Tom said to him.

The lead SUV lurched from the curb with its passenger door open as Tom jumped into the passenger seat and slammed the door shut. Morris and the other two agents climbed into the second vehicle to follow. The Climate Rangers clobbered Morris's vehicle with their sticks as it pulled away from the curb and accelerated up Sixth Avenue.

Breathless, Lindsey and Bits struggled to calm themselves.

"Oh my God!" Bits said, putting her hand over her racing heart. "This is what your life is like?"

"Not as much fun as you thought, eh?" Lindsey said. After looking around, she leaned forward and touched the back of Tom's seat. "Where's Marty? I thought he was with us."

"I sent some guys over to get him out of the bar," Tom replied.

"He stayed for another *drink?*"

"No," Tom said. "He wanted to pay the bill."

"Ah, Marty. He'd do that." She patted Tom's headrest. "Who are the Climate Rangers? I've never heard of them."

"We believe it's a front group."

"For whom?"

"A local branch of the communist party," Tom said. "This climate mania has them crawling out of their hidey-holes. Any cause will do as long as it leads to disruption and chaos."

Lindsey asked, "How did they find me?"

Tom turned to her. "They probably tracked you through your phones."

Lindsey shook her head in disgust. "You mean the same phones that were in Felicity Redfeather's custody?"

Tom turned to face her. "In case you didn't know it, they're all working together. Felicity. Protesters. The press. Better give your phones back to me."

She hurriedly fished both her phones from her handbag and handed them over.

"Take them," she said, dusting off her hands as if they were dirty. "I don't want them anymore. They're only causing trouble."

Tom gave her a different phone. "Use this for now."

"A burner?"

"You really are a gangster," Bits said.

"Don't be so impressed," Lindsey said.

"I'll have new phones delivered to your home within the hour," Tom advised her. "I'm also calling in more private security agents. We need boots on the ground."

"Jackboots?" Lindsey asked.

"Whatever it takes."

Lindsey anxiously settled back into her seat. "I'm worried about Marty. I hope he didn't get clobbered by those crazies."

"Odds are low they would recognize him," Tom reassured her. "He's not a public figure."

Bits, studying her phone, added, "He is now." She held up her phone, which had a "BREAKING NEWS" alert from the *Daily Reaper*.

Lindsey, alarmed, asked, "What is it?"

Bits handed over her phone.

Text Messages Reveal Lindsey Harper Crowe in Love Nest with Advisor Marty McGarry

"They got this from my phone?" Lindsey asked in horror, as she scanned the story. "Did the attorney general's office leak this?"

"Like I said," Tom replied. "Her fingerprints are all over this stuff."

Bits leaned over to Lindsey. "That's not the big question." She said, out of earshot from Tom, "Are you two doin' it?"

"No, no, no," Lindsey guffawed. "Well... maybe a few times. Moments of desperation, I suppose."

"How desperate were you?"

"I'm talking about him, not me."

"Oh stop." Bits laughed. "You really are getting it from all angles, aren't you?"

Lindsey raised an eyebrow. "Only when I have time."

13. THE COMMIE VIBE

The long line of people standing on the carpeted steps to the entrance of the hopelessly crowded Bemelmans Bar on the Upper East Side was no impediment to a man of stature like Robbie Crowe. He merely caught the eye of the maître d', who subtly nodded in his direction. Robbie and Li Zhang were instantly whisked past the nobodies to a cozy banquette in one of the corners where celebrities lived.

"Lovely," Li remarked as she looked around her. Ludwig Bemelmans' murals from the 1940s adorned the walls, affording the room a warm glow. All the tables were taken, and a pianist in the middle of the room tickled tunes by Gershwin. "Do you come here often?"

"I've been coming here since I was a child," Robbie said. "My grandmother used to bring me here for Shirley Temples."

"How sweet," Li cooed. "Your grandmother liked Shirley Temples?"

"No. I did," Robbie said. "She liked to slam back a few vodka rocks. Doubles. She was usually hammered by noon." He paused, remembering. "People think it's easy being rich. It's not. I think she was very lonely. Grandpa was always at work, or at the track, or entertaining his special lady friends at the Plaza Hotel."

Robbie ordered martinis, which arrived perfectly chilled with miniature iced decanters on the side. They sipped their drinks before Li leaned in close to Robbie. "I want to hear about your amazing career."

"Really?"

"Yes!" she insisted. "I'm fascinated by all your achievements. How did you get started at Crowe Power?"

Her wide-eyed gaze indicated he had found a receptive audience for the heroic L. Robertson Crowe III Story, an up-by-the-bootstraps tale that he launched with gusto. "My first job at Crowe was at a refinery in Aruba. But it didn't take long before they realized I wasn't some run-of-the-mill mechanic or a desk jockey. I was more of a big-picture guy."

"Ah! The big picture!"

"Oh yeah," Robbie said with a sniff. "That's what got me promoted so quickly. I don't like to brag, of course, but they knew I had some serious brain power."

"Oh my God," she purred as she sipped her drink. "That's incredible."

Robbie nodded. *Yeah, it was!* "They moved me to the city and put me basically in charge of corporate strategy. I mean, I had a boss and everything, but everyone was still looking at me like, 'what do you think we should do?' That's when I saw a report come out from the UN's International Panel on Climate Change, and I thought, 'Whoa! This is really happening. The world is frying, and we could be the cause.' Honestly, it freaked me out."

Li propped her chin on her fist, hanging on every word. *My hero!* "What did you do?"

"I had my assistants summarize the report and I sent it right to the top of the company."

"The *CEO?*"

"Yep. Marked the envelope, 'Urgent,' in huge red letters," Robbie said defiantly. "I thought, 'screw the chain of command.' And then I pretty much marched right up there to the corner office and demanded we take action immediately."

"That's incredible! What did you say?"

"I said, 'Dad, we can't do business like this anymore,'" Robbie said. "And he looked at me, like, 'what?' And I said, we're emitting greenhouse gases that could be warming the planet. We have to move away from fossil fuels and find new ways to generate energy."

"That was so brave. How did he respond?"

Robbie paused, thinking. "Pretty sure he said he had to go to lunch."

"Did you talk about it later?"

"Well... we were supposed to." He scratched the back of head. "I don't think we ever did."

"Ah," Li said. "Such a shame! What kind of new technologies did you have in mind?"

"Well... you know..." Robbie cleared his throat. "That's always the question, isn't it? But, even if you don't have the exact right answer, you have to keep trying. That's why I bought Greeneron when I was chairman at Crowe Power. They had something like eighteen green technologies. I just knew that somewhere in there was a better way. Weird, but it wasn't until after I left that people at the company finally got off their ass to make some progress in fusion—which I basically got started. Not that they've ever thanked me." He sank in self-pity until a whiff of Li's jasmine perfume revived him and brought him back to the present. He leaned in closer to his tantalizing companion.

"How's your drink?" he asked.

"Oooh, it's good." She took a sip and licked her upper lip. "I usually like a dirty martini."

Robbie leered. "Really? How dirty?"

She leaned close and whispered. "Wouldn't you like to know?"

Robbie gulped. He wanted to call for the check, but he didn't even know this woman. He had to at least go through the motions. "So, tell me about you."

"There is so little to tell," she said, suddenly shy. "Especially compared to a big-picture man like you."

"Where are you from originally?"

"I was born in a village near Chengdu," she said. "It's in the Sichuan province of China."

"Oh yeah. I know where it is," Robbie replied. "We took the kids there when they were little."

"Ah, yes," she said with a chuckle. "I bet you were there to see the pandas."

"Exactly," Robbie said. "The thing I remember most was, there was this massive white marble statue of Mao Tse-tung in the middle of the city. Is it still there?"

"Of course."

"That's kind of amazing," Robbie said. "In New York, we take down statues of Thomas Jefferson for owning slaves. But they still have a giant statue of Mao in Chengdu even though he killed forty million people."

Li shook her head. "I don't think it was that many."

"No?"

"It was just thirty-nine million."

"Still," Robbie said. "That's kind of a lot."

Li's expression grew somber. "Our Communist Party admits Chairman Mao made a few mistakes," she acknowledged, "but they were made with the best intentions."

"That counts, for sure," Robbie said with a shrug. "I mean, he meant well, right?"

Li nodded. "Absolutely! He always had the people in mind. He was a big-picture guy—like you. While his ideas didn't always work, we had unity and cooperation, which was a beautiful thing," she said.

"You can't overstate that," Robbie allowed. "Although, cooperation was kind of forced, wasn't it?"

She shook her head. "The Chinese people knew it was us against the world. Everyone had to do their part, and we did ours. During the Great Leap Forward, my grandfather melted down all the metals in our house—knives, tools, pots, and pans—to help our chairman meet his goal of national steel production. Everyone in our neighborhood did the same. As they did in villages all over China."

"Your family made *steel*? At *home?*" Robbie asked, incredulously. "That's crazy."

"It turned out to be pig iron, and they couldn't really do anything with it and we lost all our implements in the process, but the effort was important," she said. "The people were together. They sacrificed to help one another. We need more of that now, not less. Don't you agree?"

"Of course!"

"This is not my native country, but I see so much waste here. If we're going to save the planet, Americans need to reduce their consumption."

"Absolutely," Robbie said, as the waiter delivered another round of drinks and a three-bowl snack stand with nuts, crackers and wasabi peas. When the waiter left, Robbie leaned close and studied her. "I'm curious about something."

"Yes?"

He asked, "Are you a communist?"

She glanced around her before speaking. "Would it bother you if I were?"

Robbie shrugged. "I don't know. On the one hand, communism has never worked. It's killed a hundred million people at least. And it doesn't seem to offer the freedoms that I think are kind of important." He spoke in a near whisper. "But I've gotta admit: I really dig the commie vibe."

She smiled seductively. "You do?"

"Yeah," Robbie admitted. "It's like when I go to Café Che, with all its posters of Che Guevara. It makes revolution feel so hip. It's not some grubby proletarian uprising. The people behind the counter just seem so above it all, like they're thinking bigger thoughts than the rest of us, even when they're just wiping down latte machines. I sometimes give a twenty-dollar tip on a six-dollar coffee and they shrug. Like, 'Yeah, okay. Cool, dude. Whatever.' Money means nothing to them. I'd stand there in my Saville Row suit, and they'd wear fatigues, and I felt like I was the one who was out of style."

Li pulled on Robbie's upper arm, so that he leaned in closer to her. In a whisper, she said, "This commie wears Prada."

Robbie swooned. "That's awesome."

"She also wears Agent Provocateur."

Robbie gulped. "I don't know what that is."

"If you'd like to join me upstairs, I can show you. But don't blink," Li whispered. "I won't be wearing it for long."

14. OVERSEXED TEXTS

Andrei dropped off Bits at her apartment building on Park Avenue before delivering Lindsey to her townhouse on East 67th Street. Lindsey arrived at the same time as the local media, which produced a battery of cameras and a *pop-pop-pop* of flashing lights. Tom and his agents cordoned off reporters, who shouted questions over one another as Lindsey exited the car.

"Hey, Lindsey. Couldn't you do better than Marty McGarry?"

"Is Marty McGarry the reason you divorced Robbie?"

"Will you sell the company?"

"Do you expect criminal charges?"

Lindsey ignored their inquiries and slipped inside the townhouse. She handed her bag to her valet Alfred and stepped into the foyer, where she was surprised to find Marty, looking sheepish.

"I was just reading about you," she said, smoothing back her hair.

"Really sorry about that," he said, shoving his hands in his pockets.

"Why? It's not your fault," she said. "You didn't leak it. And you didn't take our messages out of context. The media did that."

"Still... I violated one of my cardinal rules: don't write down anything that you'd be embarrassed to read on the front page of the *Daily Reaper*." He shrugged. "Here we are."

She consoled him with a pat on his arm as the housekeeper, Lisette, approached. "Ms. Crowe, you have a call on the house line. Attorney General Redfeather?"

"Thank you, Lisette," she said. "Ask her to hold, will you please? I'll take it in my office upstairs." To Marty, she said, "Listen in with me, will you?"

Marty looked at the steps of the grand staircase and considered the additional four flights of stairs beyond that to her office. "As long as we can take the elevator," he said. "I ran here from Bryant Park."

"Of course," Lindsey said with a smile.

They took the elevator to her fifth-floor office, appointed with enough classic art works to fill a small museum. Lindsey walked behind the desk that had once belonged to her grandfather Maxwell Harper, the Chicago department store tycoon.

Marty said, "Assume she's recording this. I'll do the same." He showed the audio recorder on his phone. "Remember: she could leak anything you say."

Lindsey nodded and pushed the button on her speaker phone. "This is Lindsey. May I help you?"

"Lindsey, this is Attorney General Felicity Redfeather."

"Yes?"

"I want you to know I'm planning to file a lawsuit against you tomorrow," Felicity said.

"So I've heard," Lindsey said. "On what possible grounds?"

"You have defrauded the public by denying climate change was occurring even though you knew it was true," Felicity claimed.

"You don't say," Lindsey replied. "How did you arrive at that conclusion?"

"Between your internal files and our highly credible witnesses, we have clear and compelling evidence that I believe will be easy to prove in court," Felicity said. "That is, if it should get that far."

"What do you mean by that?"

"You could avoid a trial—and all the unwelcome attention it would bring you—by settling this matter."

"What do you have in mind?"

"An admission of guilt and a fine of three billion dollars to compensate the people of our state for the damage you have caused to our climate," Felicity said. "If you agree, I will hold off filing the suit until we work through the details. My office will prepare and record a joint video statement that would be distributed to the press and the public."

Lindsey hit mute, and looked at Marty. "That sounds like a freaking hostage video!" Lindsey hit mute again to return to Felicity. "I'm having difficulty understanding your proposal. Why on Earth do you think I would do something like that?"

"This is your chance at redemption, Ms. Crowe," Felicity said. "A public cleansing of your sins would give you a clean slate and allow you to start over. And it would spare you further public humiliation."

Lindsey processed the proposal. "That sounds suspiciously like extortion, Ms. Redfeather."

"For the record, I have made no threats whatsoever," Felicity said.

Marty mouthed: *She's definitely recording this...*

Lindsey nodded. "What record? I thought this was a private conversation."

"You've heard my offer," Felicity said tersely.

"Right," Lindsey replied. "Just so I'm clear: it's not enough that you raided my office, seized my phones, leaked text messages to the press, and coordinated with radical activists to bully and harass me. Is that the sort of humiliation you're talking about? I can only assume you're threatening more of the same."

There was silence on the other end of the line. "I am not going to entertain your reckless accusations or your insults, Ms. Crowe. You have my offer. Take it or leave it."

Seeing Lindsey's face flush red, Marty leaned over the desk and punched the mute button. "Remember: you're being recorded."

Lindsey nodded and composed herself. "Understood," she said before hitting the button again. "Here's my offer to you, Ms. Redfeather. Take your deal and shove it."

Marty's face fell. He mouthed: "Don't say that!"

Lindsey hit the button to hang up, collapsed into her chair, and glared at Marty. "Why not? Enough of this crap."

Marty threw up his hands. "I guess you forgot that part about being careful with what you say."

"You know what? I hope they leak it. Go ahead!" Lindsey replied hotly. "I said exactly what I wanted to say."

Marty heard a ding on his phone and looked to see another BREAKING NEWS ALERT, this one from Buzzniss.com. As he picked it up, Lindsey asked, "That was fast. Did they leak it already?"

"No. It's something else," Marty said. "Oh, shit." The story featured a spy photo of Marty in his Paulie Walnuts track suit walking out of a Commie Coffee shop on the Upper West Side.

BARGAIN BIN
BOY TOY
Lindsey Harper Crowe's plaything
is a rumpled and paunchy PR man.
Hot Tub invited to her hot tub.

Marty scoffed, then handed the phone to Lindsey. "I take exception to this."

Lindsey looked at it. "This is great!" she said with a laugh. "What's your beef?"

"I am *not* rumpled," he complained.

She bit her lip. "You kinda are."

"It hasn't seemed to bother you."

"You clean up when you have to," she said. "That's good enough for me." She patted the desk and made a pouty face. "C'mon. Sit down."

Marty sighed and sat on the edge of her desk. "I'm sorry to cause you this embarrassment. Clearly, they're making a lot of assumptions."

"I haven't even seen the texts they're talking about," she said. "What do they say?"

Marty took the phone back, punched a couple of buttons, and read aloud. "You write, 'Meet me at six? Usual place?' I reply, 'I'll get there early. Between the sheets?' You say, 'Lay it on me!'"

Lindsey looked puzzled. "What was that about?" she asked.

"We were meeting at Nougatine. That was the drink I ordered for you."

"Oh! That's right," she said with a shrug. "Could be interpreted another way, I suppose."

"Ya think?" Marty said. "Here's another. You wrote, 'Can you come over and play?' I said, 'You bet. I've developed some astonishing new techniques.'"

"I don't remember that, either."

"Pickleball."

She laughed. "Oh my God. This is so ridiculous."

Marty paused as he read the next one. "This is a text from you to me: 'Can't wait to see you tonight. I have a surprise for you in the hot tub.'" He looked up. "They might have us there."

"Ah, right. I do remember that one," Lindsey said. She smiled at the memory. "The smoking gun."

Marty put the phone down. "I think it was more steaming than smoking."

Lindsey nodded. "But you know something? That might be the best idea I've heard all day. Granted, it's a low bar."

"What idea?"

"A little splash around?" She cocked her head as she regarded him. "I could use a little play time with my—" she waggled her eyebrows suggestively, "hot tub."

Marty brightened. "I'll get some wine."

"Sounds like a plan," she said. "Just don't write it down."

15. CHINESE TAKEOUT

Li Zhang emerged from the bathroom of her suite wearing a robe emblazoned with the Carlyle Hotel logo. She found Robbie sitting on the bed, the house phone pressed to his ear. She sat down next to him and planted a soft kiss on his neck. "What are you doing?"

"Ordering room service," he said. "I'm getting hungry."

She took the phone out of his hands and put it down. "We're going out."

Robbie looked at her and shrugged. "Where?"

She smiled. "Nothing too fancy. But I have an idea."

"What are you thinking?"

"I'll surprise you."

Robbie, mesmerized, watched Li get dressed, which entailed shimmying into a thong, pulling a minidress over her head, and strapping on her heels. When she finished, he picked up his phone and summoned his driver to the hotel entrance on 76th Street. Within minutes, they were climbing into the back of a sleek white Tesla, and Li directed the driver to a nondescript storefront on 45th Street. Robbie didn't realize where they were going until they got out of the car.

"Oh no," he said as he looked up at the sign over the door. It was the Great Chengdu Noodle Bowl—site of an infamous encounter Robbie had initiated years earlier with a disgruntled shareholder. "I don't think so."

"C'mon!" Li said. "I'm hungry for a taste of home." She pulled him close. "Besides, I know these people. They love you here."

They stepped inside the brightly lit restaurant, featuring a long white counter where workers assembled dishes, and a colorful overhead sign showing photos of the eatery's best-selling entrees and appetizers. Li nodded toward a wall, where a yellowing copy of the *New York Post* was framed. There on the cover was a stunned-looking Robbie. He was slumped on a stool, his face dripping with sauce from his bowl of Bang Bang Noodles, picking chives out of his ears. The headline said:

FOOD FIGHT!
Robbie Crowe in Bang Bang brawl
Noodle Boy goes limp in attack
"Waiter, there's a face in my soup!"

"Not my finest hour," Robbie grumbled.

Li playfully slapped his shoulder and said something in Mandarin to Wang, the man taking their order. Wang appeared confused at first, before he took a second look at Robbie, then at the wall. He broke into laughter and shouted in Chinese to everyone in his kitchen. Suddenly, there was a great hubbub, and all the workers came to the counter and erupted in applause for their celebrity diner.

"It is a great honor to have you back!" Wang said with a bow. "Order anything you like. It is on the house!"

Robbie sheepishly looked at the gawking workers before perusing the entrees. "I guess I'll try the Chili Chicken," he said.

"It's spicy," Wang cautioned. "Don't get it in your eyes." He let out a thunderous laugh as he punched the order into the system.

"I'll try," Robbie said drily.

Li ordered seafood in a clay pot, and they carried their orders on orange plastic trays to a community table and sat across from one another. Robbie unwrapped his chopsticks and dipped in to the chicken, then quickly put his chopsticks down and fanned his mouth. "Fuh! Ah... ah... ah!" He sucked in a breath. "That guy wasn't kidding!" He reached for the water glass, but Li grabbed his wrist.

"Eat some rice instead," she said. "Water will only make it worse."

She looked toward the poster. "So, can you tell me what happened?"

Robbie shoveled some white rice in his mouth and chewed furiously, recalling his disaster. "As you can see, I was brutally attacked," Robbie said. "There was a crazy dentist named Dr. Littmann who had an office near here. He put his life savings into Crowe Power stock because he believed so much in my green vision. But when the stock didn't do so well, he blamed me."

"You *were* the boss, weren't you?"

"Yeah," Robbie said, "but it's not like it was my fault. I mean, people at the company were lazy as hell. I laid out all these great ideas. They couldn't fucking execute."

"So, this dentist was stalking you?" Li asked.

"Kind of," Robbie said, sheepishly. "Well, digitally anyway. He was ripping me constantly on social media, saying I was a disgrace, that I ruined the company, that I should resign. It was like, enough already! I decided I'd better just deal with it. So my security guys tracked him here and I came up to talk with him in the nicest possible way. All I wanted to do was reason with him."

"What did you say?"

"Well, first I had to get his attention," Robbie recalled. "So I sat down next to him at this table. I might have hit him with a super gentle shot to the ribs, just to let him know I was there." He jerked his elbow out to demonstrate. "That's when all hell broke loose. His hygienist was this former football player who saw what was happening. He snuck in behind me and smashed my face into my noodle bowl. It was a mess."

Li suppressed her laughter. "You poor thing," she said. "That doesn't seem fair."

Robbie glumly picked the dried hot peppers out of his dish and put them on the side of his plate. "My family blamed me for it. As if I'd done anything to merit a beatdown. Lindsey led a campaign to push me out of the job I'd worked so hard to get. The whole thing was just ridiculous."

Li fished through her seafood pot for a shrimp. "Lindsey seems to be having a lot of trouble in your old spot. Is there a chance that you could take over again?"

Robbie brightened. "There should be. Right? I mean, there's really no one else in our family who's qualified right now."

Li put down her chopsticks. "If you ever want to remake Crowe Power the way it ought to be run, let me know. I can get you the most advanced green technologies from China. Think about it. You would lead the industry. Maybe solve climate change, too."

Robbie nodded appreciatively. "Oh my God! Wouldn't I love that!"

She squeezed his thigh under the table. "She got you out of the company. Why don't you try the same thing? It might be yours again."

"Actually," he said, conspiratorially, "I've been talking to people about that possibility."

"Which people?"

Robbie dodged. "I can't say just yet. But… people with authority to do something about it."

Li shivered. "That's so exciting!"

Robbie smiled. "Keep an eye on the news. You'll see what I'm talking about."

Her eyes sparkled as she gazed at Robbie. "It's time you were recognized as a genuine hero of the planet."

He regarded her with a wry smile. "You're damn right it is!"

She dabbed her lip with a paper napkin and looked at him seductively. "Ready for dessert?"

He leered. "You bet."

"How about a little Chinese delicacy?"

"I'm all in."

She smiled and took his hand. "You will be soon enough."

16. RUB-A-DUB TUB

Marty walked carefully into Lindsey's home spa on the fourth floor, wearing a pristine white robe and carrying a bottle with two glasses. He found Lindsey comfortably settled in the jacuzzi, her head back on the tiles, her eyes closed, and her newest mobile phone laying atop a towel. The water bubbled up to her chin.

"Hope you don't mind," Marty said, holding up the bottle. "I opted for champagne." He put the bottle and the glasses on the tile around the tub, then untied the belt on his robe. "No peeking now," he said. "People would pay good money for this show."

Lindsey mockingly put a dripping hand over her eyes with her fingers splayed so that she could peek through. "I can see why."

He dropped his robe and began to climb into the tub. "Watch out. This could cause a tsunami." He sat next to her, popped the cork, and poured champagne into the two flutes. He handed one to Lindsey and they clinked glasses and sipped.

"Ahh. This is nice," Lindsey purred. "Good call."

"It's about time you caught a break. Police raids. Phone confiscations. Protesters. Lawsuits. You must be some kind of badass. All you're missing is the FBI breaking in."

Three rapid knocks loudly resounded on the door before it burst open. From the doorway, Lindsey's daughter Missy yelped, "*Ewww! Gross!*"

"*Missy!*" Lindsey shrieked as she slid away from Marty.

"*Mother!*" Then, "Marty?" Missy shook her head in disbelief. "Oh my God!" She turned on her heel, left the room, and slammed the door.

A moment later, Lindsey's phone rang. She hit the speaker button.

"You know I can't unsee what I just saw," Missy said. "I'm going to be in therapy for *life!*"

"I'm sure you'll recover, dear," Lindsey assured her.

"I assume you're both wearing suits."

"That's exactly what you should assume," Lindsey said.

"Good," Missy said, calming down.

"What's up?"

"I just had a question, is all. Is the family meeting this weekend mandatory? The girls want to go out to Montauk. First big weekend of the season. There are, like, tons of parties on the beach."

"The meeting's not mandatory, but it would be helpful to me if you were there," Lindsey said. "I don't know how the family is going to receive me. I may need your vote."

Missy hesitated. "I'll be there," she said. "You could do worse than Marty, by the way."

"Trust me," Lindsey said. "I have." *Your father, for one...*

Lindsey hung up and turned to Marty. "I think she likes you."

Marty shrugged. "Maybe. We went through a war together," he said as he poured more champagne. "I can't believe she's picking you and the family meeting over beach parties. I know what I would have picked at her age."

"The beach, right? Me, too. I think she's growing up."

"*Obvi*, as Missy would say. What's the family confab about?"

"It's our annual meeting at Grandview," Lindsey said. "All the Crowes fly in to Hyde Park to caw about the company. I'm sure all this publicity is ruffling some feathers."

"You think they're mad at you?"

"They can't be happy," she sighed. "Crowes don't like exposure, other than in the form of accolades and listings of the world's richest people. Gossip and tawdry allegations are for common folk. And they don't think of themselves as common folk. We're all special, don't you know." She sipped her champagne. "Pity you're not allowed. I'd love to have you with me for some comic relief."

Marty scoffed. "Couldn't do it anyway. I'm going to Montauk."

"Oh stop." She playfully slapped his shoulder. "You'd fit right in with the fam."

Marty scoffed. "Doubtful." He looked around at the expansive home spa, with the intricate tile work, the top-of-the-line fixtures, the plush towels and robes. When he was traveling on the corporate dime, he'd never seen better in the best luxury hotels and clubs around the world. "I know my place, and it's not in the treetops where the Crowes nest."

"You look pretty comfy."

"Don't get me wrong. I really love visiting Lindsey World," Marty said. "It's a magic kingdom, for sure."

"Rides aren't bad either," she said, sliding an arm on top of the tile.

At this, Marty sat up straighter. "Fact is, I'm a fish out of water."

Lindsey grimaced. "You're soaking wet."

"You know what I mean," Marty protested. "You come from a place of privilege I've never known, or even understood. I have a gnawing sense when I sit here that I'm pretending to be someone I'm not."

"You're no Felicity Redfeather."

"No. But I'm no scion, either."

"You're overlooking something very important, Marty."

"Which is?"

"We have a lot in common."

"Right," he said. "I've got a two-bedroom rental. You have a six-story townhouse. You're in the *Forbes* 400. I'm in the phone book. You're an heiress to two incredible fortunes, one on each side of the family. I'm the son of a cop and a lunch lady."

She sat up to meet his challenge. "We both work hard for our money."

"Fingers to the bone."

"We both worry that the world's moving in a strange and dangerous direction," she added.

"Toward some weird authoritarianism."

"We both share a resentment against people who want to tell us what to do," she said.

"Are you telling me to move over?"

"I'm telling you to maybe move a little closer. I know what you're doing. All this classism is your way of keeping me at a distance."

He peered through the surface of the water. "You look pretty close to me."

"You know what I'm saying," she said. "Maybe you need to stop worrying about whether a woman has the upper hand on you."

"You wouldn't be the first," Marty said. "I'm still sending checks to my ex."

"You're a snob, too, you know, but for the middle class." She sidled closer to him until she was inches from his face. "I like you anyway." She pushed his hair off his forehead. "Maybe more than that."

He slid down into the water. "Now you're hitting below the belt."

She put her glass on the tile and slid down with him. "I intend to."

He wriggled underwater. "You appear to be using underhanded tactics," he protested.

"Somebody needs to set you straight," she said. "It may as well be me."

17. REDFEATHER ON THE WARPATH

Felicity's advanced sense of do-goodism traced back to her years growing up in Thetford, Vermont, hometown of the Camp Fire Girls organization, a group to which she had belonged from the age of five. In her childhood, the girl then named Felicity O'Leary gladly eschewed her given name, which she found plain and uninteresting, in favor of the Native American moniker she created, ShaNeeNah, which she imagined meant "Indian Warrior Princess."

Not content to simply accumulate Camp Fire Girls' Honor Beads for her good works planting trees and building birdhouses, young ShaNeeNah created an entire persona devoted to bringing *wohelo*, or light, to the world. Girls who came from wealthy families to attend the summer camp run by her father held no edge over the fiercely competitive ShaNeeNah. She may not have their material advantages in life, but she was their moral superior, building enough birdhouses to accommodate a host of sparrows, planting enough seedlings to create a small forest, and accumulating enough Honor Beads to sew onto six or seven vests.

Her membership in the Camp Fire Girls faded as a teenager, but her unstinting passion for wohelo never did. She knew that rivals mocked her as Two Blue Eyes, but that only fueled her fire to show them how wrong they were and how right she was. Through her school years, her career as a public servant, and her ferocious campaigns for political advancement, Felicity O'Leary remained ShaNeeNah. If she had stretched the truth about her Indian heritage to climb her way up, it was for a righteous cause.

And so, as she took to the podium in the press room at her office, the woman who had become Felicity Redfeather was satisfied to know that she was bringing more wohelo to the world and shining it on the dark corners of Lindsey Harper Crowe to illuminate Lindsey's unearned privilege. Lindsey might have thought she was a big deal with all her fancy homes and cars and servants. But had she ever prevented a forest fire? Had she ever saved a family of finches? Did she have enough Honor Beads to fill a bathtub?

"For more than a hundred years, the Crowe family has unjustly enriched itself at the expense of our planet," Felicity declared to the assembled press. "I am here to announce this morning that those days are at last coming to an end. The time has come to once and for all put people and planet before profits."

As attendees behind the reporters applauded and whistled, the attorney general held up a document. "I have in my hand indisputable proof that the Crowe Power Company has known for decades that its operations could cause irrevocable harm to our beloved Earth. And yet it persisted for years, investing even more in discredited practices that choked our planet with greenhouse gases. All the while, Chairperson Lindsey Harper Crowe and her henchmen failed to alert the public, as any responsible company would do."

Lindsey, watching the press conference from her office at Crowe Power headquarters, looked at Digby and Marty. "Excuse me, henchmen. What's she got there?"

"No idea," Digby replied with a shrug.

Felicity showed the cover of the document on the screen at the back of the stage. "It's entitled, 'Climate Change: A Call to Action!' and it was written in 2001 by an extremely well-regarded executive in the strategy department of the Crowe Power Company. And we know for a fact that it was sent to the highest reaches of the company. It asserted that the danger of climate change was real, it was imminent, and the company should immediately consider ways in which to respond. Why did it not do so? Why did it not act while there was still time? And why does it continue to deny, deny, deny—*even to this day!*—that carbon dioxide emissions produced by the burning of natural gas, oil, and coal are a disaster for our world?"

Lindsey tapped Digby's arm. "Have you ever seen that report?"

Digby shook his head and turned to Marty, who shrugged. "Sounds like fun, though."

Lindsey appraised them and scoffed. "Some henchmen you are."

Felicity continued, "I should note that this document was provided to us by a whistleblower from the company. This brave soul was quite understandably tormented by the idea that he was working for a company that shirked its duty to its customers, its shareholders, our state, and our planet."

"Whistleblower?" Lindsey exclaimed. "Who is that?"

Digby was again at a loss. "No idea."

Marty mumbled, "I'm still stuck on this henchman thing."

"And so today," Felicity said, "I have filed a lawsuit in the State Supreme Court of New York charging Lindsey Harper Crowe and the Crowe Power Company with fraud. I am seeking restitution of five billion dollars, to be distributed equitably to those communities most harmed by climate change—"

"Ha! She's upped the price!" Lindsey yelped.

Felicity continued, "I am also asking the court to bar Lindsey Harper Crowe and her company from doing business in New York. A person and a company that can knowingly act so irresponsibly has no business in our state. It's time we drove a stake through the heart of this evil empire."

TV cameras panned the room, which showed activists applauding and whooping. Reporters faked objectivity by not cheering, though Felicity's suit amounted to a victory lap for their relentless advocacy. *We accomplished something! We're changing the world!*

Lindsey sighed and slumped in her chair as she watched the cameras pan to the dozens of people Felicity said would assist in her quest: lawyers, data experts, and analysts funded by her bottomless bucket of taxpayer cash, along with an advisory group comprised of universities, foundations, community organizations, publishers, and social media platforms that worked together to craft and execute a climate agenda dedicated to quashing dissent and advancing solutions.

"Would your ban on doing business in New York extend to other members of the Crowe family?" a reporter asked.

"We will follow wherever justice leads us," she replied.

"Does that include Lindsey Harper Crowe's ex-husband, Robbie?"

"That is not contemplated at this point," Felicity said flatly.

Lindsey jumped out of her chair. She pointed at the TV. "That bastard! I *knew* he had something to do with this!"

Digby grumbled, "Of course he did."

Marty looked up from his phone. "The *Daily Reaper* is reporting he wrote that memo."

Lindsey slumped against the wall. "What is wrong with that man?"

Digby stood up. "Where do you want me to start?"

Lindsey shook her head. "Get a copy of the suit, will you, Digby? I'd like to see what we're up against. And find this document that supposedly everybody in our company read."

"On it," Digby replied.

He left and closed the door behind him. Marty walked over to Lindsey, who stared at Felicity's visage on the screen.

"You okay?" Marty asked.

"I know her," Lindsey said.

"Who?"

"Felicity Redfeather," she replied. "I've seen her before."

"Of course," Marty said. "She's on TV every day."

Lindsey shook her head. "No, no. This goes back a ways," she said. "There's something about her eyes. I'm sure we've met before. I just can't remember where or when..." She sighed. "It will come to me."

On TV, Felicity shuffled her papers on the podium and looked at her audience. "Thank you all for coming to witness this historic moment," she said. "We consider this Day One of the people finally taking power into their own hands. Not just with regard to energy, but in terms of our economy, our country, and our planet."

Lindsey shook her head in wonder. "She didn't even mention the rest of the solar system."

"I'm sure there are other planets she'd like to save once she finishes with this one," Marty said.

Lindsey scoffed. "Oh, she'd like to finish us, alright."

Digby returned with a copy of the lawsuit, which he laid on Lindsey's desk. "Hate to add to your pile. I'm sure it will be a big part of the discussion at our family meeting."

Lindsey rubbed her chin. "I'm sure you're right."

"Would you like to postpone the meeting?"

Lindsey looked out the window, thinking. "No," she said. "I think we have to explain to the family what's going on. I'm sure they're wondering."

Digby pushed back. "Maybe it's just not the right time."

"No," she said. "The timing might be perfect."

"How so?"

"I need to know if they're with me. If not, I don't stand a chance."

18. FAMILY VALUES

A light rain fell over the caravan of glistening black SUVs, electric cars, and hybrids carrying members of the Crowe family up the half-mile-long driveway to the historic Grandview estate. The destination, perched on a bluff overlooking the Hudson River, was the massive stone castle built by company founder Homer Crowe in the 1920s. It had served as a summer home for Homer and, more importantly, as a monument to claim equal status with the neighboring Roosevelts, Rockefellers, and Vanderbilts. When Homer built Grandview, it was his way of announcing to the new American aristocracy that he had arrived.

Grandview had long since left the family's hands and was now managed by a non-profit foundation that handled its maintenance and provided tours to the public. The Crowe family retained limited rights to the property and used it every spring for a gathering to discuss their mutual interests in the Crowe Power Company. Top of mind today was the slow-rolling disaster that had befallen the company's stock, reducing the value of their holdings by half in little more than a month, and the reputational damage inflicted by the barrage of assaults against Lindsey and the company.

In times of turmoil, Grandview's rich history provided a comforting sense of calm and continuity for the cousins, aunts, and uncles alighting from their vehicles under the portico to the main entrance. Here is where Homer and wife Mary relaxed in the country, where they taught their children the values of hard work and honesty, and where they hosted their grandchildren on weekends. Homer, a notorious health enthusiast, stayed fit by working out his shoulders and back while rowing downstream to the cottage of his longtime secretary, Agnes Ludlow. Together, they worked out their abs in her bedroom while her husband was away on assignments for Crowe Power. Their perfectly synchronized aerobics ultimately produced twin girls, who took on the unfortunate scowling visage of the hawk-faced Homer. Family custom dictated that Annie and Fannie were never to be invited to the annual confab, nor were they to be mentioned. They simply didn't exist.

Lindsey's first order of business upon arrival was a private audience with Uncle Chuck, the aged family patriarch who had been instrumental in making her chair of the company. His wit and wisdom had sustained her many times over the years, and she needed it now more than ever. She found him in the first-floor library, a cavernous two-story room with intricately carved bookshelves stretching from floor to ceiling, a catwalk along the perimeter, and ornate wrought-iron ladders on wheels.

"So wonderful to see you," Lindsey said.

"All in all, I'm happy to be seen rather than viewed," he said, his balky knees creaking as he rose from his chair.

"Oh, please. Don't get up!" Lindsey said.

Chuck grimaced. "Too late." He stretched his back. "After all that effort, I'll be damned if I'm going to sit right back down." He embraced her lightly before pulling back to peer at her through the bottom of his black-rimmed bifocals. "You're holding up a hell of a lot better than some of our relatives."

"A little worse for wear, are they?"

"They don't much care for controversy," Uncle Chuck said.

"Understood," Lindsey acknowledged. "Wish I could make it go away."

He took her by the hand. "Come along. I want to show you something."

He shuffled slowly over to a shelf of history books. "I know you're feeling under siege these days. You're far from the first." He ran his finger along the shelf. "Crowe Power's had more ups and downs than the Otis Elevator Company. It's been a bumpy ride from the beginning."

He pointed to a book on the 1920s. "Crowe shot up like a weed around the time Homer built this creepy mausoleum. The country couldn't get enough oil. Company pipelines were humming. Refineries like ours were minting money." He pointed to a book on the Great Depression. "Then it all fell apart. Crowe Power stock crashed with the market, and it landed hard on ol' Homer. He nearly lost everything, including his girlfriend up the river."

"I thought we were never to speak of her," Lindsey said.

"He's not around to argue, is he?" Chuck pulled out a book on World War II and handed it to her. "Nothing like a world war to save an American industrial company. Gearing up to beat the Axis required all the energy we could produce. Gasoline from our refineries powered Patton's tanks across Europe." Chuck went on to explain the many gyrations that followed, from the post-war boom of the fifties to anti-trust actions against the company in the sixties, to devastating oil shocks in the seventies. Then came an exhilarating ride back up as commodity prices soared, and a harrowing decline as prices plummeted again.

"Are you saying it gets better before it gets worse? Or the other way around?"

He chuckled. "I'm just trying to give you a little context for the chatter out there." He pointed vaguely toward the mansion's ballroom, where family members were enjoying a cocktail reception. "Every time our company buckled, so did the knees of the people in our family. I love them all dearly, but they are not the most stout-hearted people in the world. It may be worse in this case. People at their clubs are looking at them all squinty-eyed. Are we really evil-doers, destroying the planet? It's enough to make them cry into their gin and tonics."

Lindsey sighed. "That sounds suspiciously like I don't have their support."

"Jury's out, my dear," Chuck said. "They don't understand what's going on and they're getting nervous. What they want to know is whether all this aggression is against you personally, or whether it's against the company."

"It seems pretty obvious it's against our entire industry," Lindsey said. "I'm just a test case to see how far they can go." Lindsey paused, thinking about the family members gathering in the ballroom next door. "Do they want my job?"

"Oh, hell no." Chuck cleared his throat. "Just to be clear: *nobody* wants your job."

Lindsey's brow furrowed. "Except Robbie."

"Nobody with a *brain*."

Lindsey sighed. "So sad that it's come to this. I think he's our whistleblower."

Chuck shook his head. "Robbie's an idiot and a blowhard, I'll grant you," he said. "But he's not your whistleblower."

"No?"

"It's Trey."

"*Trey?*" Lindsey exclaimed. "How do you know that?"

"Aunt Mimi told me."

Trey, the nickname for Homer Crowe III, was a useless forty-something ne'er-do-well. He had drifted through life by living large off his dividends from Crowe Power, which financed his lessons in guitar playing and Chinese language, playing golf and traveling the world. His social skills were pathetic, and his work skills were worse. But he had come to Lindsey two years ago and practically begged for a job. Lindsey had hired him as a favor to Aunt Mimi and buried him in the Strategy Department, where the job was to think up big ideas that nobody had to execute. It was the perfect place to stash a do-nothing patronage hire, like Robbie had been decades earlier.

"Mimi's sick about it," Chuck said. "Apparently, Trey found Robbie's memo about climate change in a file drawer somewhere. As a member in good standing with the climate cult that he helps prop up with cash, he felt duty-bound to report it. Mimi says he's always craved approval from the people who hate us."

"Just like Robbie."

"Exactly."

"I'm... I'm... I'm gobsmacked," Lindsey said. "I take it Trey's not here this weekend."

"Oh, he is very much here," Chuck replied. "And from what I gather, he's attempting to stir up a revolt."

"Against whom?"

"You," Chuck said. "Fortunately, he's incompetent, so I don't expect it to go anywhere."

"Why would he do that?"

"His mother tells me he's found a mission for his sorry life," Chuck said. "He's going to save the world, even if that means destroying you and our company. That would win applause in the living rooms of the Upper West Side, where he likes to hang out."

Lindsey shook her head in wonder. "Does he have any support in the family?"

Chuck took a deep breath. "A bit. Maybe more than that. You've got a generation in our family that grew up thinking, A) the sky opened up one day and dumped a whole lot of money on their head for no reason whatsoever and B) the world is about to end and they're responsible. They may not have acute climatosis like Missy did last year, but they've got some strain of that bug. They're embarrassed to be Crowes and they want to change the brand."

"To what?"

"Do-gooders."

Lindsey sagged. "I should have known this was coming."

"It's inevitable," Chuck said. "That's what happens when you start intermarrying between wealthy families. The kids start worrying a lot less about making money than how it was made. I think some of the chromosomes have gone haywire." He nodded toward the other room. "We better get on with the meeting."

"Any advice?"

"Keep cool. Don't get defensive. Speak with confidence because you know your job better than anybody," Chuck said. "And remember: they don't have any other good options."

19. SHOWDOWN AT THE HOMER CROWE CORRAL

By the time Lindsey and Uncle Chuck made it to the reception in the ballroom, the family shareholders of the Crowe Power Company had already departed in horse-drawn wagons to the barn down the hill. One last carriage awaited, and it provided a herky-jerky ride to what Homer Crowe had called his "shed."

The shed, such as it was, soared thirty-five feet high at its peak, where it was crowned with a giant weathervane in the shape of a lightning bolt. Its stalls still held horses, sheep, and goats, along with the visitors they and their feed attracted: mice, flies, ticks, spiders, and bats.

Lindsey helped Uncle Chuck from the carriage and steadied him as they walked slowly to the double barn doors, where they were greeted by attendants asking them to leave their phones behind.

Lindsey flatly declined. "'I'm sorry, but I must have my phone."

"Humor me," Chuck said, as he handed over his phone. "I've insisted that everyone do this. I don't want any recordings slipping out on TalkTick or whatever the hell that thing's called."

Lindsey reluctantly relinquished her phone and entered the cavernous barn, where family members were standing and chatting between the rows of folding chairs lined up between the stalls, troughs, and implements. Kerosene lamps lit the room, and the humid smell of hay, feed, and animals filled the air.

Lindsey scanned the room before taking a seat in front saved by Bits and Digby. "I see Robbie in the back sitting with Trey," she said quietly.

Bits huffed, "Two pimples on the ass of progress."

"It's worse than that," Lindsey said. "Trey's the whistleblower."

Bits' jaw dropped. "Oh, no!"

Lindsey nodded. "Oh, yes."

Uncle Chuck opened the discussion by welcoming all the cousins, aunts, and uncles from across the U.S., as well as Italy, the UK, France, Mexico, and New Zealand. It didn't escape his notice that Robbie, Trey, and a handful of cousins sat sullenly in the back row. Clearly, that was the dissenting wing of the family; he would aim his remarks at them.

"You may wonder why I chose my great-grandfather's shed for our annual meeting," he said, gesturing to the surroundings. "Don't worry. I'll return you all to civilization soon enough. But I want our meeting in this old shed to make a point about what our world was like before Crowe Power was founded."

He gestured around him. "As you've no doubt noticed, it's uncomfortable in this heat. It doesn't smell very good, unless you're a goat. You could take a sheep tick home in your ankle as a souvenir if you're not careful. And it's lacking in creature comforts, at least for humans. Which, I think, is why Homer built it. He wanted to remind himself from time to time how much he and other energy pioneers changed life in industrialized countries.

"Now, he's not around to speak for himself, so I'm interpreting here," Chuck said. "My sense is he wasn't always comfortable with what he had wrought. I've read through his private letters that he sent to a, um… let's call her a dear friend. He confessed his unease with the power he had harnessed and the profound effect it had on modern life. There were massive benefits, of course. Heating. Cooling. Electricity. Gasoline. Unimagined freedom of movement. Rapid economic growth. An incredible rise in the standard of living. Not to mention all the jobs that were created and the wealth that energy enabled, not just for our family, but for millions of people."

Chuck peered through his glasses to see how his homily was landing. So far, so good. "But there was a downside, too. Homer, like you, worried about the costs, in terms of air pollution, dislocation, and the stresses of a more modern and fast-paced life. The speed of change seemed unnatural to him, and sometimes out of control, and he longed for the simpler times that he enjoyed as a child in upstate New York. This ol' barn was a touchstone to his past."

Chuck paused as he considered his words. "I know some of you are similarly uncomfortable with our business now. That's understandable. The contempt people sometimes felt for our business in Homer's era was nothing compared to today. Everywhere you turn, there are signs of disapproval. We have protesters.

Negative press. Governments banding together to restrict or even outlaw the products we make. The Planetistas block traffic by sitting in the road. The Climate Rangers beat up anyone who doesn't buy their idiotic hockey stick theory. So-called 'experts' claim that the fossil fuels that are fundamental to our business and our way of life have caused an existential crisis for our planet. I don't believe that's the case. But whether they have or haven't, our family has its own crisis to deal with right now. The question we need to answer today is whether we stay together as a group to support Homer's magnificent creation: the Crowe Power Company."

Aunt Mimi raised his hand. "Chuck, may I ask a question?"

Chuck nodded. "Please do."

"With so much antagonism toward our company," Mimi said, "why don't we settle this lawsuit with the Attorney General and put the issue behind us?"

Digby looked at Chuck. "I'll take that question," he said. He stood and turned to the assembly. "Settling would not end the litigation; it would launch many more suits. It would be seen as an admission of guilt—and a payday—for plaintiffs' attorneys. That would open the floodgates for others to sue us. We would be in court forever."

"It seems that's exactly where we are now," Mimi replied.

Lindsey stood up and turned to Mimi. "If you don't mind, Digby, I'd like to add another point that's essential to why we shouldn't settle: we are not guilty. Felicity Redfeather offered to cut us a deal, and I turned her down," Lindsey said. "I have only been with the company a relatively short time. But from what I know, we've operated with the best intelligence we could gather regarding our impact on the planet—for better and for worse. It's important for us to defend ourselves in a public forum."

Trey, with prodding from Robbie, raised his hand. "I'd like to know what kind of company we want to be," he said. "I talk to stakeholders all the time. And they keep asking me: 'Why do you keep producing the same products that are poisoning our planet? When are you going to operate responsibly and move into the clean energy future?' If we can't do that, maybe someone else should do it for us."

Lindsey arched her back. "How are we—as you put it—poisoning the planet, Trey?"

He shrugged. "Isn't it obvious? Our carbon emissions."

"Carbon dioxide is not a poison. It's not even a pollutant," Lindsey replied. "You do realize it's the stuff we breathe into the atmosphere, right?"

Trey looked uncertain, but uttered, "Of course."

"In fact, you're emitting it right now," Lindsey continued. "And you know what? It's okay. Carbon dioxide is what plants use for photosynthesis to make food that helps them grow. It's what nurseries pump into their greenhouses to improve the vitality of their flowers and vegetables. In other words, we can't live without it."

"That may be," Trey conceded, "but it's also warming the Earth to an unacceptable level. And we don't admit that."

"We don't admit it because we don't know if it's true, or to what extent CO_2 may have an effect. Is it a lot? Is it a little? We know one thing for sure: Felicity Redfeather hasn't a clue. She and her supporters want to cut off debate, which we think is premature, so they can jam their solutions down our throat, which they're doing relentlessly," Lindsey said. "How do we know their solutions will work when they haven't accurately diagnosed the problem?"

"But they have," Trey protested. "It's human-caused climate change."

"I see," Lindsey said. "Are you saying we should get rid of humans?"

Trey paused, thinking.

"Look, Trey. If you're suggesting that the Crowe Power Company does more harm than good, I strongly disagree," Lindsey said. "As Uncle Chuck wonderfully demonstrated for us here today, life on Earth is significantly better now than it was when Homer Crowe started the company. Life expectancy is twice as high. Standards of living have soared. Deaths from extreme weather events have plummeted. It's the greatest human flourishing in history, and yet it all may be undone. We are now at a dangerous point, and it's not due to climate change. It's due to the way people think we ought to fix it. No more natural gas pipelines. No more LNG. No more fossil fuels. If they follow through on that before we have replacements, then all the progress we have made over the past century will be reversed. Deaths from extreme weather will rise. Life expectancy will fall. Standards of living will decline. And to what purpose? To make a few green entrepreneurs rich? To hand over more of our home-grown industries to China? To turn our daily decisions about how we live our lives over to politicians like

Felicity Redfeather and Frank Cardini? I'm sorry, but that's a bigger leap of faith than believing in climate change. And I'm not willing to take it."

A smattering of applause could be heard from the front rows.

In the back, Trey's cousin Mandy raised her hand. "I appreciate what you're saying, Aunt Lindsey, and you very well may be right. But you have to understand: that's not the perception of the people we talk to. They believe in climate change. And they say if we wait for all the answers before we act, it may be too late. We're near a tipping point, or a point of no return, or, I don't know… some kind of point. They look at us like we're these terrible, awful people. I can't help wondering if they're right."

Chuck rose from his stool. "It's awkward, I'm sure, Mandy, to get dirty looks from your friends," he said. "But put yourself in your Aunt Lindsey's place for a moment. She's hounded every day at the office, her home, and anywhere she goes in public. They tear into her on the news. Chase her with hockey sticks. But she takes it all for us."

Lindsey went over to Chuck and hugged him around the shoulder with one arm. "Thank you," she said, before turning to Mandy. "I'm not asking for sympathy," she said. "I'm asking for support. If we don't stand up for our business, nobody else will. This lawsuit is our chance to be heard and to make our case. It may not get through, and we very well may lose, but we have to try. Somebody needs to bring some common sense to this issue."

Lindsey sat down and Chuck turned to the group. "Everyone here should ask themselves right now: is this company worth fighting for? This is decision day. Are we in or are we out?"

Trey stood. "I'm out."

Chuck nodded. "You're selling your shares?"

He raised his chin. "I'm donating them to the Planetistas."

"Why would you do that?" Lindsey asked.

"To give stakeholders more of a voice in our company."

Chuck let out a loud phlegmy cough, a souvenir from an old smoking habit. "Read the bylaws, son," he said. "Preferred shares are traded only within the family trust. You can't give them to anyone else."

"I'll buy them," Lindsey declared.

Trey nodded. "Fine. I'm also resigning my position at the company, effective immediately."

Lindsey asked, "What is it you do?"

Trey blushed. "I'm Executive Director of Sustainable Strategies."

"I see," Lindsey said. "We're still in business, aren't we?"

Trey, puzzled, replied, "Yes."

"Then good on you," she said with a smile. "I guess we're sustainable."

"Good luck staying that way," Trey said bitterly before sliding to the aisle.

As Trey headed toward the door, Chuck said, "There's a horse and buggy that will take you back." Then he muttered, "May as well get used to it." He looked around the assembly. "Anyone else? How about you, Mandy?"

"I don't know," she said sheepishly. "I'm sorta in, I guess."

Bits stood up. "I'm in all the way." Digby rose and stood next to her. "Same."

Aunt Mimi stood. "Me, too. In until the end, which I hope is some ways off."

Missy stood up. "I think my mother is doing an amazing job," she said. "I'm all in."

Chase stood with her. "Hear, hear."

The rest of the assembly stood up and applauded to show their support.

Chuck put his hand on Lindsey's shoulder. "You have our confidence, Lindsey. Give 'em hell."

"Thank you," Lindsey said. Turning to the assembly, she added, "I deeply appreciate your support. But I have to warn you: It's going to be rough."

At the conclusion of the meeting, the family members retrieved their phones and headed outdoors for a barbecue held around a bonfire. Lindsey accepted congratulations and encouragement from most of the family members, save Trey, who had left, and Robbie, who showed that his true colors were yellow by disappearing.

***

Relaxing at last, Lindsey took a glass of Crowe Vineyards white wine and gazed into the bonfire. Bits joined her and they clinked glasses. They stood silently sipping their wine a moment, before Lindsey said, "ShaNeeNah."

"Sha—*what?*" Bits asked.

Lindsey shook her head. "I've been wracking my brain trying to think of where I knew Felicity Redfeather. It finally dawned on me while I was looking at the fire. We were in camp together one summer as kids. ShaNeeNah was Felicity Redfeather's Indian name."

"Are you sure?" Bits said.

"No, but I'd bet on it," Lindsey said. "My mother thought I was getting a little too big for my britches. She wanted me to get out of our Lake Forest bubble and associate with kids from other walks of life. So one summer, she sent me to Camp Wannabee in Vermont where there was this awkward girl with funny glasses in the next tent over. She was a Camp Fire Girl who wore this goofy vest every day to display her Honor Beads. She wore her fruit salad like a five-star general."

"Honor Beads for what?"

"All her good deeds."

"Did she ever do any?"

"She saved my life."

"Oh, c'mon. Seriously?"

"It's hard to say what happened exactly," Lindsey recalled. "The circumstances were a little murky. The story goes that an ember from our campfire ignited the wooden platform underneath our tent one night while we were sleeping. The whole thing was going up in smoke. ShaNeeNah supposedly smelled smoke and dashed over. She woke us up and got us out, just in time. Well, almost. I got a third-degree burn on my elbow."

"I've noticed that scar. Is that what it's from?"

"It is." Lindsey turned back to the fire, remembering. "ShaNeeNah was the hero of our camp. We had a ceremony where she was awarded a red feather for her outstanding leadership." She paused. "Oh my God…"

"You think that's why she calls herself Redfeather?"

Lindsey laughed. "As I recall, this girl's name was O'Leary."

"Maybe Redfeather is her married name."

"No," Lindsey said. "She never married."

"Still." Bits shrugged. "Maybe she's not so evil after all."

Lindsey shook her head. "Don't be so sure. All of the kids—me included—thought she started the fire in the first place."

"Why would she do that?"

"She hated us. And I have no idea why," Lindsey said. "I remember she was a townie. Both her parents worked at the camp. All the girls in my tent flew in from other parts of the country. LA. Detroit. Chicago. All our parents came in for Visiting Sunday at the canteen. Hers were already there, working, but ShaNeeNah didn't show up. Maybe she was embarrassed. I heard she stayed in her tent and read books."

"*Anatomy of a Murder*?"

"Maybe," Lindsey said with an anxious laugh.

"Well, well, well." Bits blinked in amazement. "It all fits, doesn't it?"

"It kinda does," Lindsey agreed.

"She lights the fire. She fans the flames. She puts it out. The world is saved."

"And she's the hero," Lindsey said. "Sounds an awful lot like Felicity Redfeather."

"Maybe she'll get another honor bead for driving you out of business."

Lindsey sighed. "Wouldn't she love that?"

PART TWO

Denial on Trial

20. DISORDER IN THE COURT

As Marty awaited Lindsey's arrival at the courthouse, he observed the growing swarm of protesters buzzing across the street in Foley Square. Full-time activists from an assortment of radical passions had found common cause in the one issue they could all agree upon: *"LOCK HER UP!"*

State Police and New York City cops attempted to keep order but were constrained in what they could do under the state's new Criminal Care and Protection Act. Police were forbidden to use force, a harsh word, or even a hurtful look to corral a disorderly crowd, lest they trigger tears, fears, or feelings of alienation.

Marty looked around for a coffee cart and noted Café Che had set up a wagon on the curb to dispense lattes to the clumpin' proletariat. Ernesto, El Supremo of the Planetistas and assistant manager at Commie Coffee on Broad Street, oversaw the operation, dressed in his finest urban guerilla gear: fatigues, shiny black boots, and a beret with a red star on the bill. Marty knew the getup would drive sales with this crowd, which would swoon over a communist in full regalia and gladly plunk down their pesos for a Bolivian Jungle Roast.

Marty ordered a plain black coffee, costing four dollars and a "suggested" tip of 22 percent, before he noticed the Climate Rangers rounding the corner and marching in formation up Centre Street. They were led by the famed climate savant Rainwater Jones, the petite activist from Seattle. She was riding a donkey, as befit her name, image and licensing brand, and her spanking new logo, which featured a silhouette of her slumped wearily atop another jackass. Rainwater had made her name as a morose fourteen-year-old revolutionary by skipping school and living in a treehouse to protest the imminent demise of the planet, which, to her disappointment eight years later, had yet to materialize. Fortunately, she and her fellow travelers were making progress in dismantling social order in the U.S.

and creating an opportunity for systemic change in the world, just in case it didn't end on schedule.

As the Rangers' climate caravan reached the courthouse, Rainwater was helped down from her mount for a video shoot and immediately laid down in the street. The police played their part by dutifully picking her up and arresting her, but Rainwater's video director was unhappy with the outcome because the cops were smiling and looking like they were enjoying themselves.

The director yelled, "Cut! C'mon guys. Look like you mean it!" She regarded their impassive faces with disgust. *Amateurs!* At least Rainwater was a seasoned pro, with more than a hundred staged arrests under her belt. "Alright," the director told the police. "Here's the scene. You're tired, you're underpaid, and you're overworked. And you really can't stand this chick. Got it? Alright. Let's run through this again." She clapped her hands. "Action!" Rainwater laid back down in the street. The police adopted more menacing looks, but not quite enough to look like fascists, so the director shouted, "All cops are bastards!" The police growled at her as they hoisted Rainwater to her feet, and the second take was deemed a success suitable for a worldwide debut on TikTok.

A roar of boos and jeers rose from the crowd as a car dropped off Lindsey in front of the courthouse, where camera crews and reporters recorded the action. Behind them, the Climate Rangers rhythmically pounded the butt ends of their hockey sticks on the pavement, as if they were rooting for a goal on a power play. Signs hoisted in the air depicted melting globes, emaciated polar bears, Lindsey in jail garb behind bars, and boldface declarations that she was a CLIMATE CRIMINAL, a LIAR, and a DENIER, and that she was somehow responsible for genocide somewhere, possibly in Darfur, a place none of these people could find on a map, could spell, or even say for certain wasn't a character on a cartoon show.

Marty maneuvered around the metal barriers and met Lindsey on the sidewalk. "Ready?" he asked.

"No," she murmured. "But here we go."

They climbed thirty steps to the entrance of the courthouse, a granite-faced edifice resembling a temple from the Roman days. Atop the pediment stood three statues symbolizing law, truth, and equity, concepts the people of New York had ostensibly believed in once upon a time. Against this backdrop of civic virtue, the good citizens of New York chanted their verdict before the trial even began. *"You SUCK! You SUCK! You SUCK!"*

"They seem nice," Lindsey said to Marty.

They stepped through metal detectors and entered the courthouse rotunda, where murals illustrated jurisprudence from ancient civilizations to the present. A security guard directed them to Room 300 on the third floor, where they found Digby and the legal team from Glickman, Edwards & Stein. Bentley escorted his clients to a quiet end of the marble hallway for a brief conference, and informed them that Felicity, facing a tight primary battle in six weeks, had decided to try the case herself. "This guarantees she'll be on TV and livestreams every day, fighting for climate justice on behalf of the people."

"That's the point, right?" said Lindsey. "Exposure for Two Blue Eyes?"

"A show trial requires a show," Bentley replied.

"Tell me something, Bentley," Lindsey said as one of Bentley's minions handed her a cup of coffee. "And I want you to be brutally honest: do we stand a chance?"

Bentley put his hand gently on her shoulder and looked her in the eye. "No."

Lindsey sagged. "Not at all?"

"You said you wanted brutal honesty."

Lindsey took a deep breath. "Not that brutal. And maybe not that honest."

"Well, I'm sorry to say, but in this court, with this judge, in this city, the odds in your favor are virtually nonexistent," Bentley said. "The verdict has likely been reached behind closed doors. The fact that Felicity Redfeather decided to try the case herself tells you everything you need to know. She expects to win. Otherwise, she wouldn't squander her political capital. The main issue before us is whether she will seize your assets."

"Tell me that's not possible."

Bentley sighed. "Roland Platt thought that was the case. He was considered, like you, a persona non grata by the late, great State of New York, which tried to drive him into bankruptcy. How far they go with you depends in large part on the verdict in the court of public opinion. Since there's no jury, the judge is allowing reporters to sit in the jury box. Their coverage will no doubt include their opinions on whether you should hang on to your business or hang from a scaffold. We know which way they're leaning but maybe there's a chance they'll at least listen to the evidence."

Lindsey sighed. Had she made the wrong call? "Is it too late for a deal?"

Bentley winced. "I'm afraid so. A settlement is off the table."

Lindsey looked down, idly studying the terrazzo tiles in the floor, before turning back to Bentley. "What would they do with our property if they took it?"

"There are a couple of options. They could manage the assets themselves, which is a truly frightening concept. Or they could turn them over to someone on her donor list. We just don't know which way that political wind is blowing," Bentley said. "Apparently, there's no shortage of interest from parties wanting to acquire the properties. We've seen lawyers from Crowe Power competitors in the courtroom this morning, as well as from big players in private equity and investment banking."

Lindsey sighed. "The vultures are circling."

"Chin up," Bentley said. "They have nothing to feed on yet."

"Would it help if I took the stand?" she asked.

"Only if things appear desperate. Otherwise, I think you simply observe and endure. It won't be pleasant."

They walked slowly down the hallway to the courtroom of Justice Hardiman. Every seat was taken. Reporters were crowded in the jury box to judge the proceedings for their audiences. Activists filled most of the rest of the room. Across the hall, an overflow room was set up to show the trial live on a large screen.

Beyond the courthouse, the overriding public interest in the case was made clear on local TV, which cut away from the usual daily fare of game shows, talk shows, reruns, and infomercials to carry Felicity's Redfeather's opening statement.

With a nod from the judge, it was showtime for the show trial. Felicity walked solemnly to the podium to launch the case of The People v. Lindsey Harper Crowe.

22. GUILTY UNTIL PROVEN INNOCENT

Standing at a podium between the press and the defendants, Felicity focused her two blue eyes on the clocks on the wall behind the judge. One broken clock featuring Roman numerals said it was three-thirty-five. The one below it, with Arabic numerals, said it was nine-fifteen. Neither was correct. Felicity held up her wrist for Justice Marvin Hardiman to see, pointed to her plain Timex watch, and offered a third version, which Lindsey thought was also questionable.

"Your Honor, it is ten o'clock on yet another hot spring day and there is simply no time left for debate," she intoned. "Our world is hurtling toward a climate catastrophe, thanks to companies like Crowe Power. With temperature records broken seemingly every other week, we no longer have the luxury of excusing denial about its cause. It comes from humans inflicting horrendous damage on our planetary home. I know it. You know it." Felicity pointed to Lindsey, seated at the table next to hers. "And, most important to this case, Lindsey Harper Crowe knows it. Not only that, she knew it long ago. And do you know what she did about it?" She paused for drama. "Nothing! Absolutely nothing! Instead of saving our planet, she saved her skin. We will prove that over the course of this trial."

Felicity glanced at the media pool camera behind her, then back to the judge. "What's even more reprehensible is that Ms. Crowe concealed this knowledge from the public, misrepresenting what her company knew about climate change to avoid taking responsible steps to address it. They acted as if it were no big deal." She shook her head in disgust. "Nothing to see here, folks!

"Call it what you will: negligence, recklessness, a lack of human decency. I call it fraud. And that fraud, perpetrated over many years, has enabled her company to double down on its investment in dirty carbon-based fuels." Felicity theatrically shook her head in disgust. "Yet Crowe Power persisted in greenwashing its image with Sunday morning commercials—fanciful stories about its supposed work on green technologies. You may recall the splashy demonstration of fusion technology two years ago atop the Statue of Liberty. What have they done with fusion since? Don't worry about that, they say. 'They're working on it.'" Felicity practically spat. "Right."

Lindsey leaned over to Digby. "I dislike everything about her. Her attitude. Her squeaky voice. Her complete BS," she said. "Most of all, I hate those clunky shoes. I thought she was an Indian princess, not a Pilgrim."

"Looks like she forgot to take the shoes out of their boxes before she put them on," Digby deadpanned.

Felicity proceeded. "It's bad enough that Crowe Power does nothing to alter climate change. More galling is that they refuse to acknowledge its cause, pretending that the issue is complex when it's simple. As the famed hockey stick graph has illustrated, the Earth's climate was steadily cooling for nearly a thousand years before Homer Crowe and his ilk came along. These unscrupulous businessmen unearthed oil and gas and coal from the bowels of our Earth to create what they claimed was a higher standard of living. The grim reality: it's our standard of *dying*. Dying species. Dying people. And, ultimately, a dying planet. Crowe Power hastens our demise, adding more greenhouse gases into our atmosphere while pretending it isn't a problem, even as they cause food insecurity, disease, and gross inequities among the peoples of our planet."

Felicity paused to turn to the gallery to gauge its reaction. Were they as appalled as she was? It sure looked like it.

"The question you might ask is this: why deny?" Felicity continued. "Why would Lindsey Harper Crowe deny what has been known for years? The answer's obvious. Greed!"

Lindsey leaned over to Digby. "She reads me like a book."

Digby rolled his eyes. "Not a book I'm familiar with."

Felicity continued, "Ms. Crowe and her company will gladly destroy our planet because she puts her own selfish needs to make a buck above the safety of our children and grandchildren. Just last summer, her daughter Missy Mayburn Crowe misled a rally in Central Park to fight the scourge of climatosis by urging the public to be skeptical, to ask questions, and demand answers before we adopt solutions. Your Honor, I submit that this was nothing more than a cynical delay tactic. We are long past the time for asking questions. The science is settled. We must act!" She pounded the podium once for emphasis.

Lindsey whispered. "Acting is one thing she knows how to do."

Digby nodded. "Like a star in a B movie."

"In the course of this trial," Felicity continued, "you will hear from this nation's pre-eminent climate wizard, Dr. George MacFarlane, whose name has become synonymous with science. Dr. MacFarlane has carefully curated a collection of hand-picked data to prove our planet is in peril. You will also hear from a close relative of Lindsey Harper Crowe who was until recently an employee of her company. This brave soul found the 'smoking gun' memo that shows her company knew about climate change long before it was acknowledged to the public. And you will also hear from Robbie Crowe, the company's visionary former chair, who authored the telltale memo during his first year at the company. Mr. Crowe is a brave environmentalist who attempted to steer the company onto a more responsible path. Naturally, that did not square with the industry's utter disregard for ethics and he was evicted from his position by his scheming and power-hungry ex-wife, Lindsey Harper Crowe."

A murmur rippled through the courtroom until the judge brought it to a halt with his gavel.

Felicity could barely contain her rising fury. "Ms. Crowe has been in her job for four years. Four long years! That's more than enough time to demonstrate that she would direct the company away from its dirty business as usual. She did not. She could have deferred to the scientific consensus about the causes and remedies of climate change. She did not. She could have shown that she cared more for her fellow humans than for her grubby profits. She did not."

Lindsey leaned over to Digby. "How can you stand sitting next to me?"

Digby shook his head in mock despair. "It's not easy."

"I submit to the Court that since Lindsey Harper Crowe has proven herself unwilling to act as a responsible steward for the people of this state, then it's up to the people of this state to take their fate into their own hands. Seize the power and give it to the people! Remove her and her company from our state! Say goodbye and good riddance! We don't need their stinkin' fossil fuels. It's time to draw the line and say, 'no more!'" Felicity paused to let that sink in. "Over the door to this courthouse is an inscription: 'The true administration of justice is the firmest pillar of good government.' It's time to administer that justice now for the sake of our state, our city, and our planet. Thank you, Your Honor."

The entire audience, save the first row behind Lindsey where Marty, Missy, Chase, Lucy, and Tom sat, rose in unison to applaud and shout its approval. *Hear! Hear!* The judge looked mightily impressed but played his part in this legal theatre by rapping his gavel and calling for order. After all, he was wearing a robe. *He had to do something.*

As Bentley walked to the podium for his opening statement in defense of Lindsey, the red light on the pool camera in the back of the room was turned off. The city's media platforms—Channel 1, the *Daily Reaper*, and all the local TV crews—had collectively agreed in advance that they would not show Lindsey's defense, lest their viewers and listeners be exposed to dangerous misinformation that they were ill-equipped to evaluate for themselves. All interpretation of the proceedings for the public would be left to the environmental journalists.

Viewers who had been watching Felicity bring charges against Lindsey on TV were returned to their regularly scheduled programming. That included a cooking show featuring quick-'n-easy macaroni and cheese, the popular talk show *Scuttlebutt Live*, a classic rerun of *Happy Days*, and an infomercial on how to get rich by investing in cobalt mining in central Africa.

22. CIVIL DEFENSE

The patrician Bentley had none of Felicity's dramatic flair. He bore instead the understated presence of a pillar of the establishment—as sturdy, upright, and quaint as the marble columns in the courthouse rotunda that stood for justice back in the olden days.

"Your Honor, there are certain aspects of this case that are beyond dispute," Bentley began. "My client agrees that we face a climate catastrophe. She does not dispute that it is caused by humans. Like the plaintiff, she fears it will cause widespread disruption, a humanitarian crisis, and possibly many, many deaths. It will also create climate refugees who will be forced to move to escape life-threatening devastation."

Bentley paused for this pronouncement to sink in. *Were people hearing this right?* It sounded for a moment as if Lindsey Harper Crowe was admitting her sins and preparing to plead for mercy.

"The catastrophe she envisions is not the one identified by the plaintiff. It is instead the very real fear of a premature push to stop our use of fossil fuels, which provide eighty percent of our world's energy. That would leave our populace vulnerable to massive blackouts as well as the collapse of the natural gas system that provides heat to our city. And if that were to occur during a winter in the not-too-distant future, the heat would stay off for a dangerously long time. Not hours. Not days. Not weeks. *Months.* And this calamity would be the direct result of The People's campaign for what it claims is 'environmental justice.' Where, I ask, is the justice in that?"

Bentley's rhetorical questions were met by a collective eyeroll from the courtroom. *You call the collapse of a planet-destroying power system a calamity? Oh, please...*

Bentley plowed ahead. "Unlike the climate catastrophe suggested by the plaintiff, where questionable computer models suggest that slowly rising temperatures could, would, or should lead to an imagined disaster in the distant future, this threat is real, and it is upon us right now." He tapped his index finger on the podium for emphasis. "Lindsey Harper Crowe and her company are not the instigator of a crisis. They are in fact our last line of defense against an avoidable crisis."

Lindsey looked around the room to see how this argument was landing. She noted that reporters seemed to be doodling in their notebooks, twirling their hair, or counting ceiling tiles. The judge had his sagging head propped up with his right fist while his eyelids drooped. And the activists in the gallery had their arms folded across their chests as they stared at Bentley with skepticism and impatience.

"To prove my client's innocence in this matter," Bentley continued, "you will hear from regulatory experts who will testify how perilously close we came to a disaster during Winter Storm Elliott in 2022, and how our risk of such a crisis is even higher today. You will also hear how our margin for error has narrowed further because of decisions by our state government that are crippling critical supplies of natural gas despite rapidly rising demand. And you will hear from experts from leading universities who will vigorously dispute that the science is settled regarding climate change. They agree climate change is occurring—as it always has—but not necessarily for the reasons asserted by the government."

Judge Hardiman roused himself into a yawn and leaned into his microphone. "You are making bold assumptions, Counselor. The Court will only hear from these so-called experts if I allow them to testify. And I am not at all convinced that they are relevant to this case."

"Duly noted, Your Honor," Bentley said. "I would merely like to add—"

Hardiman interjected. "I think we get your point, Counselor."

"May I conclude, Your Honor?"

Hardiman looked behind him at the broken clocks and somehow deduced the time, perhaps by taking the average. "If you can wrap it up quickly."

"I merely want to make this point," Bentley said. "At the end of the day, it does not matter if you 'believe in' climate change, even if it's become your religion. It doesn't matter if you think climate change is caused largely by humans. Nor does it matter whether you go along with the assertions that it comes largely from carbon dioxide, methane, or some other greenhouse gases in the atmosphere, such as water vapor. All of us in this industry can strive toward new forms of energy beyond our world's supply of fossil fuels, and we should, because as Ms. Crowe will tell you, we're going to need them.

"But an obsession with climate change that makes the end of fossil fuels the first order of business is not a luxury that Lindsey Harper Crowe can afford. Her job—the one all of us in this courtroom count on her to do whether we admit it or not—is to balance long-term concerns with pressing needs in the near term, which is to provide reliable energy every day of the year. And the only way to ensure that is to reject the extreme activist agenda championed by the plaintiff and find in Ms. Crowe's favor. Her most fervent desire is not to cause a climate catastrophe. It's to prevent one." He paused and gathered his papers. "Thank you, Your Honor."

Boos and calls of "bullshit!" rang out from the gallery, prompting the judge to rise in his seat and glare at Bentley. "The patience of the Court is already growing thin, Counselor. I will be watching closely to see if you are merely creating a diversion with this unlikely scenario. If there is truly a such a catastrophe on the horizon, why have we never heard of it?"

Bentley pointed to reporters in the jury box. "If time permits, Your Honor, perhaps we can ask them."

The reporters looked around at the others in the box. Who? *Us?* Nah...

23. WITLESS FOR THE PROSECUTION

Homer Crowe III, known as Trey, had always been considered an oddball in a family with more than its share of them. Yet until recently he had typically portrayed himself in his dress, manner, and pastimes as a member in good standing of New York's ruling elite.

Now that the good-old-boys' network had been discredited as a creaking relic of white privilege, the shiny new thing among the city's wealthiest and most celebrated individuals was radical progressivism, led by a coterie of political grifters, race hustlers, climate fanatics, and neo-Marxists bent on remaking the rules to advantage themselves.

Trey's nagging insecurity over the source of his towering good fortune had over the past two years sucked him down into the populist swales and caused him to renounce his old ways. Gone were the clean-shaven face, the conservative blazer, and the sockless loafers. The new and improved Trey 2.0 featured an unruly beard, a shirt-jacket over a T-shirt, and Red Wing Iron Ranger work boots—an intriguing fashion statement, considering he'd never performed any manual labor beyond taking out the trash. This he had last done in 2006 after a dare from his girlfriend that he didn't know how to do it. *He showed her!*

Trey nodded to the spectators offering admiring glances as he swung through the doors to the courtroom. He strolled down the center aisle to the witness stand with the swagger of a Caesar returning to Rome after victorious battles abroad. Trey loved his new friends and they in turn loved him. It was a perfect symbiotic relationship, for he was happy to unload portions of his ill-gotten blood money on them, and they were delighted to take it, regardless of its provenance. The activists appreciated the courage it took for him to buck his own family to embrace the prevailing climate wisdom. And they knew far better than he how his investment in climate advocacy was spent to advance their high-minded ideals: buying megaphones and banners to demonize Lindsey and hockey sticks to beat the hell out of her car.

Lindsey whispered to Digby. "He's trying so hard to be a hipster, but he still comes off as a doofus. I kind of feel sorry for him."

Digby squinted. *Really?* "Let's see how you feel an hour from now."

Felicity warmed up her first batter in the witness box by lobbing one softball question after another. Trey swung mightily at each pitch and dribbled them back to the pitcher. His heroic story began shortly before taking the job in the Strategy Department at Crowe Power, his first real labor since graduating from college twenty years earlier. As part of the orientation for his entry into the world of work, he met his cousin Robbie for coffee in Greenwich Village. Robbie, who at the time had been recently deposed by Lindsey as company chair and kicked out of their family home, boasted that he had written a revolutionary memo titled "Climate Change: A Call to Action!" many years earlier. It warned presciently about climate change, Crowe Power's possible role in it, and the urgent need for the company to mend its ways and change its business model. Intrigued, Trey made it his mission to find that memo and see what had happened to it. The answer, much to his dismay: nothing.

"To me, that was unconscionable," Trey declared. "Climate change is obviously an existential threat to the planet and to the company. To pretend that it was not constituted corporate malpractice. That's when I knew that if the company wouldn't change its approach, I had to change mine."

Applause from the gallery was reluctantly gaveled into silence by the sympathetic judge.

Felicity called up Robbie's memo on the courtroom's computer monitors and focused on the hockey stick chart, as central to the climate change story as Michelangelo's painting of God and Adam was to the story of creation. It was also every bit as accurate. The chart, which smoothed over both an ice age and an extended warming period, purported to show Earth's temperatures holding relatively steady over most of the past thousand years before suddenly shooting upward with alarming speed, reflecting the rapid industrialization of the West. The chart had been cited extensively in the Third Assessment Report by the UN's Intergovernmental Panel on Climate Change in 2001 to make the case that carbon dioxide emissions from human activity were largely responsible for soaring temperatures that were surely coming.

"Why was the memo ignored?" Felicity demanded to know.

"I have to believe it was because addressing climate change would have hurt the company's bottom line," Trey replied. "That's all they seemed to care about."

Aha! Felicity sneered. "Profits!" she bellowed so loud it echoed off the courtroom walls.

Bentley called out, "Objection. The witness is speculating. He has no insight into my client's motivation."

Hardiman asked, "Isn't Crowe Power a profit-making entity?"

"In good years," Bentley replied.

Hardiman shrugged. "Your objection is overruled."

Trey went on to detail how tirelessly he staged his crusade to reform the company's evil ways. He read a few reports. He watched the news. He attended a meeting or two when he wasn't working from home. He had even spent a year writing a strategy paper, "What We Should Do," outlining an array of research programs the company could undertake to transition away from fossil fuels, such as harnessing hamster wheels to generate electricity or breeding fireflies to provide carbon-free lighting. Alas, the paper never saw the light of day. The few emails he sent to people inside the company asking for their ideas about what should be done went unanswered, leaving Trey nowhere to go but out for a drink. *How was he supposed to save the world all by himself?* It was only out of frustration that he aired his grievances to Tasha, a bartender at the Capital Grille. She in turn introduced him to Ernesto, El Comandante of the Planetistas, who manned a barstool in a dark corner most afternoons to soothe his concerns over the warming planet with ice cold beers. Things snowballed from there, even in the withering heat.

***

With Trey's pure intentions established, Bentley rose to cross-examine the witness. The Court learned that Trey had studied art history at Williams College. It also heard that he had no record of achievement, other than a bevy of participation ribbons from his summer camp. He had no obvious skills, no areas of specialized knowledge, and no work history prior to joining Crowe Power. He did allow, however, that he had dabbled in investing with some success.

"Did people give you money to invest?" Bentley asked.

"No," Trey replied, tentatively. "It was mostly, you know… my own."

"I see," Bentley said. "And where did your money come from?"

"Well…" he mumbled, "I guess you'd have to say it came primarily from my dividends from Crowe Power stock."

"Which you inherited, correct?"

"Yes."

Bentley furrowed his brow. "For you, a man of immaculate conscience, wasn't that dirty money?"

"I was concerned about that, certainly," Trey admitted.

"But you got over it once you started working at Crowe Power?"

Trey blushed. "The only way I could make peace with it was to do everything I could to move the company in a more responsible direction. When I realized that was not possible, I resigned."

Bentley nodded. "I see. And when you quit, was there anyone left at the company to keep an eye on climate change?"

Trey laughed bitterly. "I don't think they gave it another thought."

"Hmm," Bentley mused, scratching his chin. "That's odd. Given your intensive interest, I wonder why so many documents escaped your notice when you were working there. Perhaps it was above your pay grade." He hit a button on his computer. "Your Honor, I would like to enter exhibits A through Q into evidence. They comprise more than ten thousand pages of Crowe Power reports analyzing climate data from reputable scientists, many of whom cast serious doubt on the so-called consensus on climate change, including the simplistic hockey stick graph. In addition, there are minutes from meetings between the company's leadership team and top experts in physics, meteorology, statistics, and other disciplines at leading universities, whose insights were used to help shape the company's strategy. I'm also presenting reports showing the company's steady decline in greenhouse gas emissions since its power plants switched from coal to natural gas. Finally, I should note that we have included sections from Crowe Power's annual 10-K filing with the Securities and Exchange Commission detailing risks to shareholders posed by climate mandates and regulations."

The judge nodded. "I'll accept these."

Bentley turned to Trey. "Do any of these materials look familiar to you?"

Trey looked blankly at his computer monitor in the witness box and shook his head. "No."

"Is it safe to say your painstaking research into the company's position on climate change was largely limited to a cup of coffee in Greenwich Village, listening to a few idle boasts from Robbie Crowe, and pulling an old file out of a cabinet, dusting it off, and handing it over to a guy you met at the bar?"

Trey raised his chin and peered at Bentley as if he were beneath him. "Obviously, it was the right thing to do if we were to save the planet."

"Since we're still here," Bentley observed, "one can only conclude you must have done a bang-up job." A loud crack of thunder could be heard outside, followed by a flash of lightning that made everyone in the court look to the windows to see rain beating on the panes.

Bentley sighed as he returned to the defense table. "Apparently, there's still work to do."

Digby leaned close to Lindsey. "Still feel sorry for Homer Crowe the third?"

She shuddered. "I can only hope is there isn't a fourth."

24. PUNCHING ABOVE HER WEIGHT

Despite Bentley's best efforts, the news media scored the first round in Lindsey's trial as a decisive win for the prosecution. The main worries for the punditry were whether the conviction could happen quickly enough and whether the possible penalties were sufficiently harsh. One commentator noted that Lindsey's lack of visible remorse at the defendant's table seemed deserving of greater punishment than the law allowed. She should wear a scarlet letter, perhaps. Or maybe a bright red "CO_2".

Marty had marveled at Lindsey's ability to maintain her composure amidst the onslaught and wondered how she managed to stay so calm. As he climbed the grand staircase to the second-floor gym in her home, Marty discovered her secret. She was beating the stuffing out of a kickboxing bag suspended from the ceiling.

He stood in the doorway and watched Lindsey pound the bag with a flurry of blows—a series of swift jabs and a straight right hand, followed by a left hook and a right uppercut.

"Glad I'm not that bag," he said.

She paused, her breaths coming in heaves. "Be glad you're not him," she said, before firing another series of shots.

"Trey?"

"Robbie." She wheeled around and launched a spinning back kick at an area just below the bag's midsection. Had Robbie been standing there, it would have directly impacted his manhood.

"Ouch," Marty said with a grimace.

Lindsey turned to Marty. "He told me many times that he wanted to be an inspiration." She smiled. "He is." She kicked the bag once more for good measure.

Marty leaned against the windowsill. "Why Robbie? Trey's the whistleblower."

Lindsey stripped off her gloves and flung them into a wicker basket. She snatched a towel off the counter and patted her forehead. "C'mon, Marty. Trey's just a proxy," she said. "You saw him on the stand. He's a dope. He's neither smart enough nor mean enough to attack me. He just wants to be seen as a cool guy by the cool people. For whatever reason, he seems to think Robbie is one of those cool people."

"But why would Robbie want to go after you? Trashing the company doesn't help his stock."

"Trust me. Any loss he's suffered is a rounding error," she said, as she grabbed a bottle of water and sat on a bench. "And it's worth it if he can see me squirm. Robbie's all about punishing anyone he thinks makes him look weak. Look at what he did to that dissident shareholder a few years back. Robbie was shown up, so had to go after him, just like he's going after me."

"You think he's still upset because you took his job," Marty said.

"No," she replied. "I think he's upset because I'm doing it better than he did."

Marty pondered that idea. "Why is that?"

"It's only because I'm smart enough to know what I don't know," she said before tossing her empty bottle into the recycling bin. "I couldn't run Crowe Power day-to-day like Lucy does. Or run finance like Armani does. Or manage the powerhouse like Dexter does. God forbid if I had to lead IT, HR, or any of those departments. Robbie always had to be the smartest guy in the room on every topic, which made Crowe Power only as good as he was."

"Which is why it nearly went broke."

"Exactly," Lindsey said. "The best thing to do in a job like this is to get the right leaders in place, review the strategy, and get out of the way. And don't burden them with some extraneous bullshit—like your 'vision.'"

"Don't say that," Marty said sharply.

"Why not?"

"Because I've made a pile of money crafting visions for chairmen and CEOs," Marty said. "It's been a good line of business, and I don't need you mucking it up."

She glowered at him. "How many of them worked?"

Marty looked up at the ceiling. "Well, let me think… "

"Yeah, right," Lindsey scoffed. "You can take your time."

Marty scrunched his face. "That's not to say they weren't great ideas."

"It's CEO theater, Marty. In the wrong hands, those vision things crash and burn, brought down to Earth by the demands of running the business," Lindsey said. "That's what happened to Robbie. He didn't understand what we do so he decided to create a new model of the business that he might understand. Crowe was going to be 'greener, cleaner, more sustainable.' Yadda, yadda, yadda. Our people didn't know what he was talking about, and neither did he. There were no specifics. It was all meaningless platitudes, a colossal waste of time. Eventually, they just tuned him out and said, 'we've got to get back to work.'"

Marty could barely keep a straight face. "But he had such good intentions."

"Yeah, right." She laughed and walked over to the refrigerator. "I've got water, Coke, and beer."

"Beer."

She popped the top on a couple of bottles of Corona and joined Marty at the windowsill. "Cheers," she said, clinking bottles.

Lindsey said, "Crowe Power's mission comes down to two words: reliable energy. We're not out to change the world; we're out to support it. If we can help people live their lives comfortably, conveniently, affordably, great. We're doing our job. If we can also do it cleaner, greener, whatever—we'll do that, too. But those are add-ons. Don't tell me Job One is to save the planet."

"I won't tell you that. But I bet Robbie will on the stand tomorrow."

She shrugged. "Poor, dumb Robbie," she said, shaking her head. "I'm sure he's still hanging on to his green dream. Maybe it gets him laid. That seems to be his priority in life." She took a big gulp of beer and softly burped. "You know, I've had one other advantage in this job that Robbie never had."

"Which is what?"

"I never felt the burden of great expectations. I didn't grow up a Crowe, which is of course a big name around the world. I grew up a Harper, which was a big deal only in Chicago." She chuckled. "I didn't grow up a boy, either."

"So I've noticed," Marty said with a raised eyebrow.

She ignored it. "It's tougher for men in a family like his," Lindsey asserted. "Every young man is expected to become the next Homer Crowe. But Homer was a singular figure, like John D. Rockefeller or Andrew Carnegie or J.P. Morgan. Nobody can follow in their footsteps, even someone with the same last name. Inevitably, you fall short." She drained her beer and put the bottle on the sill as she stood up to stretch.

"Boys are expected to grow up to become the top dogs. Girls? Not so much. Call it sexist or unfair. It's just the reality. If we join the company, great. If we don't, it's understood. In that sense, it takes the pressure off." She bent over and touched her toes. "You have to remember, Marty. I had no ambition to run this company." She stood back up and rolled her shoulders. "I jumped in only because I saw Robbie driving it off a cliff."

Marty sighed. "Do you think Robbie has any appreciation for what you've done?"

"We'll find out tomorrow, won't we?" she said with a tight smile.

Marty walked over to the bag. "Take that, Robbie." He slugged the bag with his bare fist. "Ow!" he exclaimed as he rubbed his hand. "That thing's hard. I thought it was as soft as a pillow."

Lindsey laughed. "It's not really Robbie, you know."

25. THIS DOES NOT COMPUTE

Robbie rose early for his big day. This was his opportunity to reclaim his place in the public spotlight, demonstrate his moral superiority, and show the world that he was the rightful leader of the Crowe Power Company. Whether that message would translate to shareholders was another matter, but who knows what could happen if Lindsey were out of the picture? The crown could be restored.

He padded to the kitchen of his Tribeca apartment for a cup of herbal tea, which he took to his den. Reflexively, he turned on the TV, which showed Channel One's news coverage of the crowd gathering outside the courthouse for Lindsey's trial. He opened his laptop and scrolled through his various mailboxes, deleting gobs of junk mail and solicitations. In his Crowe Power account, which he retained as a courtesy, he found an email from Li Zhang that had been sent overnight.

> Good luck today, my Sweetheart Treasure.
>
> Please see the attachment, which contains inspiration and encouragement from our Great Leader. Like you, our Comrade Mao Tse-tung was engaged in a great revolutionary struggle. It wasn't easy, but he succeeded beyond his wildest dreams. You can too!
>
> Look for me in court!
>
> *Jiayou,*
>
> Li

Robbie could live without the commie agitprop, but he knew Li meant well. He clicked on the attachment, which sent all the items on his desktop swirling like water going down a drain. Then the screen went black. He furiously punched various keys to bring his screen back up, but nothing happened. *Uh-oh...*

Panicked, he tried turning the computer on, then off again, then on again. Nothing happened. He held the power button on for ten seconds, which failed to illuminate the screen. He picked up the injured laptop, and turned it from side to side, then held it briefly over his head, as if it would magically restore his operating software, then tried hitting the power button again.

Shit! This was not a good look for a tech wizard! Did Li send him malware? Surely it was unintentional. But what to do? He couldn't call Crowe Power IT. How embarrassing would that be? *I opened an attachment from my Chinese communist girlfriend. My computer is fucked up and I'm afraid it might have been used to infect the company system.*

He slumped in his chair, thinking. If Li put him into a compromised position, maybe she could get him out. He picked up his phone and found his list of recent calls. He punched Li's name. The phone rang ten times, and Robbie decided to give up. But as he reached for the button, he heard her voice.

"Hello?" Li said in a hoarse voice.

"Li, hey. It's Robbie."

"Good morning, my darling." She paused, apparently looking at a clock. "Ooh. It's early."

"Yes, yes, I know," he said. "But I've got a problem. That attachment you sent me fucked up my computer."

"Really?"

"Yes. My screen went blank and I can't get it back on."

"That's strange," she said flatly.

"Yes, it is. I'm not sure what to do here."

"Would you like me to read you the quotations from Chairman Mao?"

"No, no. I need my computer to work. And I really don't want to call the Crowe Power IT department."

"Don't worry, my sweet, sweet baby darling," she said. "I have tech support that can help you."

"Can they help now?"

"Oh yes. They work twenty-four hours a day."

"Where are they located?"

"I don't know exactly. But that's not important, is it?" she said. "Hold on, and I will connect you."

The call went silent as Robbie tapped his foot anxiously and stared at his black screen. Maybe nothing bad had happened. Maybe it was just a hardware malfunction. If it wasn't, and the Crowe Power system was compromised somehow, maybe they wouldn't trace it back to him.

Then again, he had to consider the unthinkable: what if this was all a set-up to gain access to the Crowe network? What if Li were some sort of spy or agent and she sent him a computer bug deliberately? He had to consider that a possibility. More troubling was the question: why would she do that?

"Hello, Robbie?" Li said. "I have Deng on the line for you."

"Hello, Mr. Crowe," said a man with a thick Chinese accent. "How can I help you?"

Robbie hesitated.

"Deng?"

"Yes."

Should Robbie take a leap of faith? He might be in deep, but he had no idea how to climb out.

"Okay then, Deng," Robbie said. "I'm having trouble with my laptop."

"No worries, Mr. Crowe. You are in very good hands."

26. THE CANARY SINGS

Felicity Redfeather was hardly known for her warmth, yet she glowed at the sight of Lester Robertson "Robbie" Crowe III approaching the witness stand. What a prize for the plaintiff! The fact that this renowned prince of petroleum, a man of well-publicized conscience, had been cast aside by the ruling family was proof positive there was something rotten at the core of the Crowe Power Company. And that something was Lindsey.

Lindsey's team deliberately ignored Robbie's entrance. He returned their blatant disrespect by refusing to acknowledge them as he took his seat, partly out of fear that they had discovered his computer folly. As he cast a sidelong glance at their indifferent expressions, he sensed that perhaps his worries were unwarranted. Maybe his little laptop meltdown was a singular event, and it was over. If so, it was time to settle old scores.

He looked over the rows of activists and saw Ernesto and his comrades from the Planetistas, a row of green technology entrepreneurs ready to pounce on the outlawing of fossil fuels, and a jury box full of friendly climate reporters from the *Daily Reaper*, the wire services, and environmental websites, all on guard to prevent any misinformation from leaking out that might contradict what they had been reporting. In the front row near the podium sat a radiant Li Zhang, who blew Robbie a kiss. Should he catch it or throw it away?

The sound of a gavel ended his deliberation.

Felicity's gentle questioning established Robbie's credentials as a climate savant, making his visionary leadership sound like a dreamy combination of the best executive qualities of Steve Jobs, Bill Gates, and Warren Buffet, along with the environmental sensitivity of Rachel Carson, John Muir, and Henry David Thoreau. With little prodding, she was able to elicit from Robbie that he had tirelessly worked his way up the ranks at Crowe Power, strenuously climbing the corporate ladder, even if he happened to glide over a rung or two. He recounted the long hours he put into the job and explained that much of his work time was spent out of the office for good reason: as an environmentalist, he needed to immerse himself in nature to better understand its relationship to his company. And while his outlandish compensation had dwarfed the gross income of small American cities, Robbie noted that he kept his calendar free of appointments to afford him time to think big thoughts.

"This is more than I can take," Lindsey whispered to Digby.

"You don't have to tell me," Digby muttered bitterly.

Felicity said to Robbie, "Mr. Crowe, I'm sure you recall the memo, 'Climate Change: A Call to Climate Action!'"

"Of course," Robbie said grandly. "I wrote it."

"Tell the court, please: why did you write it?"

"Simple, really. From the time I was a child, I knew there was something very wrong with the company's environmental practices," Robbie claimed. "We were exploiting the world's natural resources without a care as to the damage it caused our planet. To have my name associated with such a massive carbon footprint was, frankly, an embarrassment. I couldn't wait to start working there so I could do something about it."

"What was it about this carbon footprint that made you so angry?"

Robbie shook his head gravely as he roused the sad memory. "Virtually every product we had was tied to fossil fuels," he said. "Oil, natural gas, and coal were used in our power plants, pipelines, and refineries. Any fool would know that wasn't sustainable. When I got out of college, I let people at Crowe Power know that I was ready to help them find a better way. Not just for the future of the company, but for the future of our planet."

Trumpets didn't sound, but a smattering of applause was heard in the courtroom, which Hardiman silenced with his gavel and a glare.

Felicity continued. "Is that why you wrote the memo?"

"It was the least I could do," Robbie said.

Digby whispered to Lindsey, "'Twas ever thus."

Lindsey didn't laugh. She was seething.

Felicity asked Robbie, "Did people at the company show any concern when you brought climate change to their attention?"

"Not a bit," Robbie said sadly. "Nobody wanted to even think about it, much less talk about it."

"Why not?" Felicity asked.

Robbie shifted in his seat. "You'd have to be there to fully comprehend the mindset at work. To me, they were in denial, living in a bubble," he recalled. "Most of them were engineers and accountants and logistics people. All they wanted to do was think about the same old, same old, you know? Heat. Light. Power. I mean, c'mon. There's got to be more to the company than that. I wanted to run through the halls screaming, 'Look at the big picture, people! Think about the planet!'"

Felicity shook her head in despair. "Were you the only one in the company thinking about the long term?"

"It sure seemed that way," Robbie recounted bitterly. "I kept saying, 'Let's go, guys. We can change the world if you just stop what you're doing for a second and give it some thought.' People looked at me like I was crazy. Maybe because it was too hard for them. They'd say, 'Oh, there's no time for that today. I've got an operations meeting' or 'We'll save the planet tomorrow. I've got to make sure our refinery doesn't blow up.' Okay, that's important, of course, but it was mundane, you know? Honestly, they had one excuse after another."

"Why didn't you think like they did?"

"I'm just not cut out that way," he said. *I didn't take math, for one thing...*

"You needed more out of your job?"

"Absolutely," he said. "I guess it's just my nature, but I needed a bigger challenge. Something to get my engine running in the morning."

"Like what?"

"I desperately wanted to pull our people out of their rut. One day I said, 'C'mon. Let's do an offsite meeting. Go off to a lodge in the mountains. Get everyone away from the grind for a few days and think about the future. We'll bring in some facilitators to help us think outside the box.' The constant focus on the day-to-day operations of the company was driving me nuts."

Lindsey leaned over to Digby. "And he wonders why he lost his job."

Felicity continued. "Did you continue to push your case as you assumed more senior positions in the company?"

"Of course! I made my views known every step of the way. At least to anyone who would listen."

"And did they?"

"Oh, they'd nod their heads, but they would never do anything," Robbie lamented. "I hate to say it, but a lot of them were just dead on their asses."

A disapproving murmur was heard in the court. Felicity pointed in the general direction of the Crowe Power Company headquarters to the south. "Your father was CEO. Your name was on the building. How could they ignore you?"

"That's a mystery to this day," Robbie claimed as he shook his head in wonder. "All I could do was make my views known to anyone who'd listen."

"That was brave."

Robbie shrugged. *Yeah, well. I'm just that kind of guy...*

Felicity continued. "Tell the court what happened when you finally became chairman. At last, you were in position to do what needed to be done for our planet, regardless of the resistance. Is that right?"

Robbie nodded. "To a point, yes."

"It was reported in the *Daily Reaper* that you were moving the company out of the, quote, 'deep darkness of climate denial into the sublime sunshine of solutions.' Is that why you bought Greeneron, which brought the company a treasure trove of green technologies?"

Robbie nodded vigorously. "That's exactly right. I believed the time had come to make a bold stand and put our money where my mouth was."

"And how were you rewarded for your courageous leadership?"

Robbie glared at his ex-wife. "I was fired. Lindsey staged a coup within the family and pushed me out of my job."

"By 'Lindsey,' you mean 'Lindsey Harper Crowe,' the defendant?"

"Yes," Robbie said.

"Is she in the courtroom today?"

Robbie nodded. "She is."

"Point her out, please," Felicity said.

Robbie raised an accusatory finger toward Lindsey. As he glimpsed her impervious expression, his finger started to wobble, before it went limp. Then he dropped his hand to his lap and felt around for some reassurance from his manhood. *You're okay, bruh...*

Felicity took a step toward the witness stand. "After your career at Crowe Power met its unwarranted demise, it was said by some in the media that Robbie Crowe was the canary in the climate coal mine. Did you see it that way?"

"Absolutely. When people saw that investing in solutions for climate change cost me my job, they thought, 'Hey. If it could happen to Robbie Crowe, it could happen to anybody. I'm not going there. It's too dangerous.' Lindsey is the mother of my children, so I obviously do not want to say anything bad about her—"

"Here it comes," Lindsey said quietly to Digby.

"—but I must admit she not only killed the progress I would have made at Crowe Power, she set the entire industry back years, maybe decades. And with it, she harmed one of our best shots at saving our one and only planet."

Felicity nodded knowingly. "Imagine for a moment that you had survived her coup against you, and you had kept your job," Felicity said. "What would be different about Crowe Power today?"

"I know one thing for sure," he said with a bitter laugh. "The chair of the company would not be on trial."

Bing. Bang. Boom. Felicity turned to the judge in triumph. "No further questions, Your Honor."

27. DIGBY GETS CROSS

As Lindsey conferred with Bentley and Digby about Robbie's cross-examination, she noticed something strange about her general counsel and former brother-in-law. The normally unflappable Digby was flushed red, perspiring, and his hands were trembling. *Good Lord! Was he having a heart attack?*

Lindsey patted his arm. "Digby. Are you okay?"

"No," he replied.

Alarmed, she asked, "Should I call for help?"

"It's not that," Digby said. "I just can't stand… Robbie. He's so full of *shit*."

Lindsey's head snapped back. "You didn't expect anything different, did you?"

Digby wrung his hands under the table and stared at the floor. "He shouldn't get away with it. We could lose a chunk of our company and he doesn't even care. As long as he comes out looking like a hero to the idiots in the gallery, he's okay."

Lindsey leaned close. "Don't worry. Seriously," she assured him. "Bentley won't let this go unchecked. He'll contest everything Robbie said."

Digby raised his head. "I want to do it."

Bentley said, "Do what?"

Digby leaned over. "If you don't mind, Bentley, I'd like to do the cross-examination," he said. "Don't get me wrong; you're doing a great job. But I've been hearing this BS for years. I've sucked it up long enough."

Bentley rubbed his chin, thinking. "You know all the exhibits, right?"

"We've been over them many times," Digby assured him.

"And you've seen our questions?"

"Of course. I wrote most of them."

Bentley shrugged. "I'm okay with it, if you are, Lindsey."

She nodded. Bentley added, "I would urge you to gather yourself first, Digby. You don't want to go in too hot. This isn't exactly a home game."

Digby nodded and took a deep breath. "I'll keep it together," he said, rapping the table. "We'll see if he does."

At the sight of his brother-in-law Digby rising from the defense table and buttoning his suit coat, Robbie breathed a sigh of relief. Bentley had been a ruthless negotiator for Lindsey in the divorce settlement, extracting more concessions through his relentless pressure than Robbie expected. Digs, as Robbie called him, had been easily steamrolled when Robbie was his boss. His presence now behind the podium suggested a more feeble opponent. *This should be a breeze!*

"Mr. Crowe. May I call you Robbie?" Digby asked pleasantly.

"You always have," Robbie said with an easy smile.

"Thank you, Robbie," Digby said. "I'd like to clarify portions of your testimony that don't quite jibe with the record as I understand it."

"Fire away," Robbie said.

"You stated that you wrote the memo, 'Climate Change: A Call to Action.' Did you write this memo yourself?"

Robbie shifted in his chair. "Of course. I wrote most of it," Robbie said cagily. Then, "Well, some of it." He tried to read Digby's inscrutable expression. *Where's he going with this?* "I remember quite clearly that I edited the headline on the cover."

"I see."

Robbie sensed from Digby's expression that his answer was inadequate. He hastened to add, "But that's not all."

"No?"

"I added the exclamation point."

Digby stared at Robbie and said nothing—a surefire way of making Robbie squirm.

Robbie gulped. "I realize that may sound trivial, but that punctuation was actually very important. You know, "'Climate Change: A Call to *Action!'* You get that? I wanted to emphasize the action part. It was—"

Digby cut him off. "Understandable," he said. "You are, after all, a man of action, as you indicated in your testimony."

"That's right," Robbie assured him.

"So please tell the court what sorts of action you took to implement your climate vision as you worked your way up the corporate ladder."

Robbie scoffed. "That was never my job."

"No? What were you doing?"

"They had me rotate through various roles in the company to give me an understanding of our operations around the world. I spent a year in marketing. Another year in refining. A year in finance and one in HR. They also sent me to our office in Paris for a couple years, Buenos Aires for six months, and to Singapore for a year-and-a-half."

"Sounds like you were getting groomed to run the company. Is that accurate?"

"I believe that was the board's plan, yes," Robbie said.

"Did you ever work in a Save-the-Planet Department?"

Robbie scoffed. "We didn't have one, obviously."

"Is that because that's not the company's mission?"

"In my view, that was everyone's mission."

Applause erupted in the courtroom, which Robbie acknowledged with a smile and a nod to the gallery. Justice Hardiman rapped his gavel and called for order.

"Let me see if I understand this correctly," Digby said. "While you were busy on your world tour, you intimated that the listless shmoes in operations at Crowe Power were focused on such dull tasks as providing light, heat, and power around the world. Wasn't that their job?"

"Well, yeah, of course," Robbie said. "And don't get me wrong. I mean, heat, light, and all that jazz is fine. But I thought, what good will that do if you kill the planet in the process? You can't turn on the lights if you're dead, right?" Robbie paused for applause before continuing. "I wanted them to stretch their thinking, to consider providing energy the right way."

"Ah," Digby said "The *right* way. And in your view, Crowe Power was providing energy the *wrong* way."

"Exactly," Robbie said. "We had an awesome responsibility to Mother Earth."

Digby dug deeper. "What's a more awesome responsibility than keeping Earthlings safe and comfortable in their homes, schools, hospitals, businesses, and places of worship? What am I missing?"

Robbie paused, thinking. What *was* he missing? There was a stock line he used in speeches that he was forgetting. Ah... "I wanted us to be 'The *And* Company,'" he claimed.

"What does that mean?"

"I wanted us to provide power *and* do it responsibly," Robbie said. "To generate energy *and* leave no carbon footprint. To serve our planet *and* leave it better than we found it."

"To go woke *and* go broke?" Digby asked.

"That wasn't the plan," Robbie retorted.

"What was the plan?" Digby pressed. "Did you ever develop a strategy to make all these wonderful things happen simultaneously?"

"Not explicitly," Robbie claimed. "I told them what I wanted. How they did it was up to them."

"Was that because you were out enjoying nature? Or was it because you didn't know?"

Robbie seethed. "That wasn't my job to know."

"Ah. There again is that sticking point," Digby said, shaking his head. "What was your job exactly?"

Robbie gathered himself. "My job was to inspire people to a higher calling."

"I see. And how did you inspire them?"

"Well," Robbie said, "we put together a campaign for our employees around developing 'The And Company'. Our marketing team created videos, town halls, that sort of thing. And we followed that up with TV commercials and social media to reinforce the message."

Digby pulled up a sheet of paper off the podium. "Do you recall the budget for that?"

"I believe it was fifty million dollars."

"So it was. Do you recall that budget was pulled from employee bonuses?"

"We had to make a difficult choice," Robbie claimed. "And I felt strongly that the best employees were motivated by more than money. They wanted to make a difference. This was a way to show who was really committed to our vision."

"Did your campaign inspire people as planned?"

Robbie nodded. "I believe it did."

Digby put a document on the computer screen. "According to the Crowe Power HR department, it inspired them to quit," Digby said. "This chart shows that from the time you cancelled bonuses and launched 'The And Company' campaign, management turnover jumped fifty percent."

"And you know what? I was totally fine with that," Robbie declared indignantly. "People who couldn't get with the program should have left. We needed a cultural shift if we were going to move the company in a more sustainable direction. There was no time to mess around. My vision required a little housecleaning."

Digby pulled up the company proxy and put it on the screen. "According to company filings, the cultural shift did not extend to the chairman's office. Your bonus wasn't scrapped. Rather, it went up twenty-two percent. Why was that?"

Robbie bristled. "That was up to the Compensation Committee. I was told they were extremely happy with the progress I was making, even if the rest of the company was not yet keeping pace."

"Everyone else was still 'dead on their asses'?"

"They were making some progress," Robbie sighed, "but not fast enough for my liking."

"That's why you bought Greeneron?"

"Exactly," Robbie said proudly.

Digby could imagine Lindsey's expression, but he didn't look back. "Do you think your departure had anything to do with your overspending on Greeneron's grab bag of science experiments? You took five billion dollars from the operating budgets of the employees who maintain all that 'jazz,' as you call it, and blew it on a green spending binge, ninety-five percent of which was deemed useless by the company and written off after you left."

"I was showing them a better way."

"Are you an expert on climate change?"

"I was chairman of the company."

"I was not aware that such an exalted position made you an expert on climate change."

"I don't need to be the expert," Robbie contended. "My responsibility was to come up with solutions, which is exactly what I did. If people want to criticize me for spending too much money, have at it." His tone ratcheted up from defiant to indignant. "I make no apologies. I'm proud of what I did. When it comes to saving our planet, I say cost be damned."

"Spend like there's no tomorrow?"

"Exactly," Robbie said. "Because there is no tomorrow if we don't figure this out."

The courtroom erupted in cheers. What a brave and fearless leader!

Robbie acknowledged the applause with a smile and a wave as he scanned the room of glistening, rapturous eyes. He was among friends. Activists who tirelessly demanded action. Journalists taking advocacy to another level. Investors ready to offer expensive and futile green solutions once the old power system collapsed. But Li Zhang, his sweet little communist tootsie, was nowhere to be found. Where had she gone? Back to Chengdu?

Robbie bit his lip as he headed for the door. No way she's a spy. *No way…*

28. INDIGESTION ON THE MENU

Lindsey and her team repaired to the Italian restaurant Locanda Verde in Tribeca for lunch, where they glumly looked over their phones as a steady stream of news reports poured out of the courthouse. Team Lindsey was losing as badly in the court of public opinion as it was in the court of law. Coverage celebrated the trial as a necessary step for the governments of the world to get control of the global thermostat and crank it down by whatever means necessary.

The *Daily Reaper* reported:

Redfeather Gains Upper Hand Against Climate Scofflaws
AG shows the way to force compliance
She means business in public beatdown of Crowe Power

Digby listlessly scanned the menu as he played back in his head his cross-examination of Robbie. Bentley sensed Digby's frustration and patted him on the shoulder. "You did as well as anyone could expect," Bentley said. "You can't embarrass a man who has no shame."

Digby sighed. "I thought I had him. He just slithered out of my hands."

"Forget it," Bentley said. "We're all doing the best we can."

As the people around the table considered what to order, Lindsey looked across at Bentley.

"What's next on the menu?" she asked.

"I'm thinking of a sandwich," he said, rubbing his chin.

"I'm thinking of the courtroom."

"Ah," Bentley said, putting down his menu. "We're scheduled to hear from the Science—with a capital 'S.'"

"Spanky?"

"Yes," Bentley said with a sigh.

"Is he going to tell me anything I don't know?"

"Actually, you might be surprised," Bentley said. "Try Googling his name and 'impact on climate change' with whatever topic you like. Hitting a baseball. Grilling a hamburger. Feeding your goldfish. You'll be amazed to find Spanky and his gang have done a study on it. They apparently learned a long time ago: there's no activity in the world that can't be linked to climate change. And the implication is *always* that humans did it."

"I thought farting cows were responsible for some of it," Marty said.

"Only because humans raise them," Bentley replied.

Lindsey asked, "How much damage are we causing by going out to lunch?"

Bentley consulted his phone. "Easy enough to find out." He typed in his browser. "Lunch... restaurant... Ah. Here's your answer. It says we're producing thirteen percent more emissions by going to a restaurant than if we ate lunch at home." He put the phone down and looked around. "I don't know how you people live with yourselves."

Lindsey felt a tap on her shoulder and turned to see her CEO Lucy Rutherford with Faraz Rahman, Crowe Power's head of IT, and Tom Michaels, her security chief. "May we have a word?" Lucy asked.

"Of course," Lindsey said. She followed Lucy into a private dining room at the rear of the restaurant and noted their worried faces. "What's going on?"

"We've had a data breach," Lucy said.

Lindsey responded with a helpless shrug. "Of course we have." *What next?*

"Faraz and his team were able to stop the hack," Lucy said. "But the hackers kept finding access. We're trying to figure out how."

Faraz explained that hackers used a botnet of more than one million computers to penetrate the system, performing more than a half-billion probes of Crowe Power's computer network in a single day. That escalated to more than three billion probes before Faraz's team stopped them.

"They could have shut down our operations, but they didn't," Faraz said.

"What was the point?" Lindsey asked.

"We think it was a reconnaissance mission."

"You're saying they'll be back?"

"That's our guess."

Lindsey sighed. "For what? Customer data?"

Faraz shook his head. "They didn't go near that. It appears they were trying to map out our system. Hackers affiliated with the Chinese Communist Party have been aggressively targeting American infrastructure—pipelines, the electric grid, and water supplies. We've alerted the FBI and Homeland Security."

Lucy added, "The feds tell us the hackers may try to take control of our pipelines. Not sure when, where, or why, and the CCP certainly isn't saying. But, as you know, they have a vested interest in disrupting our economy."

Lindsey looked puzzled. "For what purpose?"

Lucy replied, "It could be to distract us from what's going on with Taiwan. It could be to force a reduction in this country's fossil fuel use and gain a further advantage in manufacturing. If the U.S. and the West continue to deindustrialize because we don't have sufficient energy, that opens the door for China to grow its position as the world's dominant manufacturing hub—and take the lead in AI."

Faraz added, "The FBI says China's Ministry of State Security oversees their cyber spying operations. They contract criminal hackers offshore so that the government can maintain plausible deniability. Most of the cyber invasions can be traced to the island of Hainan in the South China Sea."

Lindsey shook her head. "It seems we're under attack from all sides."

Tom said, "Yes, and we think the attacks are related."

Lindsey stepped closer. "How so?"

"We have reason to believe the CCP is funneling money to climate activists in this country as well as the foundations that finance them. The feds tell us they do that through a foundation they've established in the States, the Center for Unity and Cooperation," Tom said. "The CCP is not the sole source of money, of course; there's a good deal more coming in from Silicon Valley and from fellow travelers on the East Coast. But between them all, they provide money to candidates who advance their agenda and to activists who cause disruption."

"There's one other issue you should be aware of," Lucy said, before turning to Faraz.

Faraz inched closer and spoke in a near whisper. "The feds tell us that a Chinese intelligence agent who works for the Center for Unity and Cooperation is a woman named Li Zhang," he said. "She was in the gallery at your trial yesterday."

"Why would she show up?" Lindsey asked.

"Perhaps to support a man she's dating," Lucy said.

Lindsey knew instantly where this was going. "Oh, please. Don't tell me..."

"Robbie," Lucy said.

Lindsey threw up her hands. "Of course!"

"An email between the two of them may have provided the hackers with access into our system," Faraz said. "It appears Robbie opened an attachment that he shouldn't have."

Lindsey flushed with anger. "Of course he did. They couldn't have found a more useful idiot."

"We suspended his account pending further investigation," Faraz said. "Unfortunately, we think the damage is done. The feds told us we can expect another hack—probably at a time when we're most vulnerable."

"Can you defend against it?"

"I've got my best people on it," Faraz replied.

Lindsey thanked them for their work and returned to the table. She offered a taut smile to her companions and placed her linen napkin back on her lap. As Bentley and Digby discussed Spanky's upcoming testimony, Marty leaned over to Lindsey and whispered, "Everything alright?"

She sighed. "The hits just keep on coming."

Marty leaned back in his chair as Bentley addressed him. "Marty, maybe you can explain something. There are so many accomplished scientists with better credentials than Spanky. Why don't the media ever talk to them?"

Marty shrugged. "I guess because most of the media have been riffing on the same theme for years about climate change. I can't imagine a reporter walking into the newsroom at the *Daily Reaper* and telling the editor: 'We decided to interview scientists outside the usual doom loop. And guess what? We got this all wrong! We fell for a bunch of unproven theories based on faulty models, manipulated data, and faculty lounge bullshit.'"

"I don't understand," Bentley said. "Isn't the definition of news to say something new?"

Marty shook his head. "How quaint, Bentley. No, the modern definition of news is advancing favored causes in the newsroom. When the facts don't support the narrative, they just attribute their stories to 'experts predict,' or 'scientists say.'

And as we've seen, some of them will say anything. There's no shaking their belief."

Lindsey shut her menu. "I know what I believe."

Bentley looked over. "Which is what, my dear?"

"I believe I'll have a glass of wine," she said, signaling a waiter. She looked at Bentley and shook her head. "It's just that kind of day."

29. FOLLOW THE SCIENCE

Lunchtime at the protesters' encampment across from the courthouse was a catered affair, with commie cuisine offered by a row of food trucks lining the perimeter of Foley Square. Che's Chuckwagon, Pol's Potstickers, and Ho Chi Munchies were crowd favorites, serving up revolutionary fare to demonstrators hungry for dumplings, tacos, and systemic change.

Some of the protesters set down their plates long enough to shout the obligatory obscenities at Lindsey as she left her car and climbed the stairs to the courthouse. She shut out the noise by telling Marty about her disturbing conversation with Lucy and Faraz.

"We've had a cyberattack aimed at our pipelines," she said quietly. "Faraz brought in the FBI."

"Do they know who did it?"

"The Chinese Communist Party, with the help of Robbie and his girlfriend."

"No," Marty said. "I can't believe he'd do that."

"I'm sure it was a mistake," Lindsey said. "If he'd tried to do it, it never would have worked."

They continued up to the courtroom, where a hush had fallen over the assembly as it awaited the arrival of the eminent Dr. George "Spanky" MacFarlane. Widely acknowledged as the greatest climatologist the media had ever paid attention to, Spanky was accustomed to a certain degree of reverence in public forums. Accordingly, all spectators except for Lindsey's small team rose as he entered. Spanky smiled and nodded to both sides of the aisle as he walked to the witness box, clasping his hands as if in prayer. *So humbling to be so great!*

Over the course of his long career, Spanky had assumed a mantle of authority over all matters related to climate change. His ability to oversimplify a massively complex issue by focusing on a single variable made his version of science understandable for even the dimmest bulbs. Justice Hardiman's cranial filament practically lit up from the spark of such a presence.

Felicity welcomed Spanky to the witness stand with the blush of a teen crush. She then ran through his list of credentials, including his studies of physics and chemistry, his dozens of papers, thousands of appearances on TV, podcasts and news platforms, and his best-selling *Dr. MacFarlane's ABCs of Climate Change* coloring book. He served as chair of the Climate Conference, an association of news media, universities, foundations, search engines, and popular entertainment companies dedicated to squelching debate on the scientific merits of climate change while promoting all manner of expensive, unworkable, and counterproductive solutions. Depending on who you listened to, Spanky was the organization's Pope of Prognostication, the Climate Caliph, or the Guru of Global Warming.

"The *Daily Reaper* refers to you as 'the last word in climate science,'" Felicity noted. "Would you agree with that assessment?"

Spanky sighed, as if acknowledging the massive burden piled on his slight shoulders. "Far be it for me to judge," he said. "But I would hope that I'm not the last word."

"How so?"

"It would mean we reached the end of the world."

A horrified murmur went through the crowd.

Under gentle nudging from Felicity, Spanky outlined the parameters of his beliefs. The Earth was warming. It could not be explained by natural variability, apparently because it was too complicated. Rather, climate change was caused by the wasteful activities of humans, who were not sufficiently bridled by the guiding hand of enlightened leadership from people like him. All media-sanctioned experts agreed. Deniers, skeptics, climate realists and other deplorables were either right-wing nutjobs, oil company shills, or garden variety nincompoops. Smart people in the in-crowd of the coastal cocktail circuits realized we were fast approaching some kind of tipping point. "We are seeing the beginning of our cataclysm already," Spanky claimed. "Climate change is causing the collapse of ice shelves, a massive rise in sea levels, and a cascading series of catastrophic events: droughts, floods, storms, wildfires, sinkholes, potholes..."

"Assholes," Lindsey added in a whisper to Digby. "He's got everything on that list but bunions and bad breath."

"Give him time," Digby replied.

Felicity summarized. "In other words, Dr. MacFarlane, virtually anything thought to be a problem can be largely tied to climate change. Is that what you're saying?"

Spanky nodded. "That sounds like an exaggeration, but it's true. You see it every day in the news. Even if climate change is not the primary cause of a particular issue, it will surely make the problem worse," he assured her. "It could be as mundane as crabgrass or clogged sinks, or as serious as boiling oceans and raging rivers. It doesn't matter. Climate news is bad news, and we have thousands of government-funded studies to prove it."

Felicity sighed. "What happens if we fail to take the proper measures to stabilize our climate?"

Spanky shook his head gravely. "I fear the future is very bleak indeed."

Felicity let that sink in before proceeding. "Tell us, then. What can we do to avoid a climate catastrophe?"

Spanky raised his chin and peered down his nose through his glasses. "To really crank down our global thermostat, you need to put the control dials in the hands of experts," he said. "That requires a transfer of power from people who hold narrow interests, such as profit-making companies, to people of broad interests who consider the greater good. And I'm not talking about the greater good of only this country, but the entire world. If we are as serious as I believe we need to be, controlling our climate requires nothing less than the entire reordering of society. And I mean everything—top to bottom, here and around the world."

Felicity nodded with appreciation. "Given your reputation as 'the Science,' I think we can all feel better knowing that you're there to guide us," she declared, turning to the audience for affirmation before resuming her questioning. "And you believe we must act immediately?"

Spanky flashed anger. "I hate to be the bearer of bad tidings, but immediately is not fast enough. We should have acted long ago. I hope we're not too late."

Felicity leaned over the podium and fixed Spanky with a stare. "Are we?"

Spanky put his index finger under his chin. "I can't say for sure. But I do know this: the time for debate is over. The planet is in peril. It desperately needs our help *right now*. If you think we can wait for the liars and deniers to come around, it will be game over. And I mean, *done!* The planet will have lost, and we will have lost, too. And our children and grandchildren will have no chance at all. None!"

Felicity turned again to the audience for a moment and extended a hand toward the witness stand. She returned to her star witness. "The state is alleging that Lindsey Harper Crowe and her record profit-making company engaged in fraud. Crowe knew about climate change, but the company covered it up to avoid alarming the public so it could continue to sell their poisonous products unimpeded. Dr. MacFarlane, you have seen the documents in question. Would you agree with that assessment?"

"I don't see how an objective person could come to any other conclusion," Spanky asserted. "All they had to do was look at the memo written by Mr. Crowe back in 2001. That's your smoking gun right there."

"Can you think of any reason why they would cover that up?"

Spanky chuckled at the question. "Isn't the answer obvious?" Spanky said, slapping the arm of his chair. "They did it to make money."

"That leads to my final question, Dr. MacFarlane," Felicity said. "Given your vast understanding of climate change, and your evaluation of Lindsey Harper Crowe's base motives, could you in good conscience approve of Crowe Power's continued operation in our state?"

Spanky cast a droopy-eyed glance toward Lindsey, then turned to Felicity. "Sadly, no," he said, shaking his head. "To my mind, they have forfeited their chance. The Crowes appear to be greedy capitalists who have exploited our planet to feather their own nest. They've had more than a century to prove they could act responsibly. And they've failed to do so. I don't see how another hundred years, or even another thousand years, would help."

A rumble of concurrence was heard from the observers, as Felicity recognized she had scored a pile of points. She studied the microphone on the podium: was there some way to pick it up so she could drop it on her way out? Alas, it was attached. "No further questions, Your Honor."

Justice Hardiman looked at Bentley with a triumphant smirk, as if there was nothing more to be said. "Your witness."

30. CRANKY SPANKY

The patrician Bentley approached the witness box with a gentleman's grace. "Good afternoon, Dr. MacFarlane. What an honor it is to meet you," he said. "May I call you Spanky?"

"I would rather you called me Doctor," he replied tartly.

Bentley put his right hand over his heart. "My deepest apologies if I overstepped."

"Apology noted."

"So, then tell me, *Doctor* Spanky..."

Spanky bristled. "Dr. *MacFarlane*."

"Heavens," Bentley said, as if he were momentarily confused. "What was I thinking?"

"Hard to say," Spanky sniffed.

"Dr. MacFarlane, *sir*. Under your direction, Bartleby College was a veritable funding machine for climate studies, was it not?"

"We had great success, yes," Spanky allowed. "If you did your homework, Mr. Edwards, you would know we led the country in attracting research grants."

"Due in no small measure to your reputation, I'm sure," Bentley said. "From what I understand, a nod from Dr. MacFarlane is like a *Good Housekeeping* Seal of Approval for the planet."

"I've heard that said," Spanky said.

"Is it fair to say that your grant funders expected a particular conclusion in advance of your research?"

Spanky fluttered his eyes impatiently. "I can't speak for their motivations. All I can tell you is that anyone with a background in science would expect the sort of results we have found. It's not like we don't know what in the world's going on. We do. We're past the point of understanding whether climate change is occurring and why. Our studies were designed to point out its far-reaching impacts in order to instigate action."

Bentley nodded. "I've read some of the reports you directed in your role at Bartleby," he said. "And I must say you've had remarkable fields of inquiry. I've got a couple of them on screen. There's 'Oyster Flatulence: A Cause for Climate Concern.' Then there's 'Climate Change and the Sex Habits of Green Sea Turtles.' Now, if I'm not mistaken, these are real reports, aren't they? They're not publications from a satirical website like the Babylon Bee?"

"No, sir," Spanky said, bristling. "We conducted those studies. And I'm proud to say we did. Climate change is no laughing matter. My responsibility is to help ordinary people know exactly what's going on, why it's happening, and who's doing it."

"If I read this correctly, sea turtles are doing it, but not as often?"

"Our observations confirm that."

"What a fun group you must be," Bentley said. "Let's explore your studies as they pertain to humans. Here's one: 'Inhalers used by people with lung diseases contribute to global warming with every puff they take. Every push of the button is the equivalent of driving a mile in a gasoline-powered car.' Should people with breathing problems stop using inhalers?"

"We make no judgment on that," Spanky declared. "We're simply trying to make people aware of the impact of their activities on the climate. Everyone should know these things and modify their behavior accordingly."

Bentley picked up a paper and read from it. "Here's another: 'MRIs and other medical imaging programs contribute one percent of global greenhouse gas emissions.'" He put down the paper and eyed Spanky. "Should we stop looking for tumors and simply wait until they announce themselves? Maybe when they poke their way through the skin?"

"What the study shows," Spanky said, "is that people don't need as many exams as they think. Perhaps that MRI could wait a year or two."

"I suppose if they wait long enough, they won't need an MRI at all?"

Spanky nodded thoughtfully. "The situation could resolve itself."

Bentley paced in front of the witness stand. "If I listened to you, Dr. MacFarlane, rather than my gastroenterologist, I would skip my scheduled colonoscopy this summer. According to your studies, colonoscopies are terrible for the climate." Bentley picked up a paper and read from it. "Energy use and plastic waste from such procedures produce nearly 86,000 metric tons of carbon dioxide a year, the equivalent of nine million gallons of gasoline. I'm feeling guilty just thinking about it."

"Objection, Your Honor," Felicity complained. "I fail to see the relevance of these studies to the accusations against Crowe Power."

Hardiman sighed. "I am losing patience as well, counselor. Where are you going with this?"

"I'm merely pointing out that burning fossil fuels is not the only offense the witness has found against our climate," Bentley said. "Virtually every human endeavor is a cause for concern."

"You may proceed," Hardiman ruled, "but not for much longer."

"Thank you, Your Honor." He turned to Spanky. "Dr. MacFarlane?"

"We didn't say you shouldn't get an exam," Spanky said. "That's up to you and your doctor. All we're saying is, you must balance your personal health against the health of the planet. What do you value more? Are you one for all, Mr. Edwards? Or all for one?"

"Let's say I'm a 'one for all' kind of guy," Bentley claimed. "And let's say that you—the Science—have convinced me that I'm causing great harm to the planet by trying to stay healthy. Consequently, I don't use my inhaler. I avoid MRIs. I skip colonoscopies. And I die prematurely in service of the climate. How many carbon emissions would I prevent?"

Spanky looked up at the ceiling, calculating.

Lindsey leaned over to Digby. "Is he adding this up?"

Digby shook his head in amazement. "I can't believe he took the bait."

Spanky punched numbers into the calculator on his phone. "Considering what the average person emits…" He looked up and assessed Bentley's physique. "I'll factor in that you look relatively vigorous for your advancing age…"

"Looks deceive," Bentley said.

Spanky continued punching numbers in his phone. "Should you die seven years earlier than your life expectancy, that would mean you have prevented more than four tons of carbon dioxide emissions from breathing alone."

"That's quite an achievement," Bentley said. "I should feel good about that, I suppose."

Spanky looked up and smiled. "That doesn't begin to count the emissions you wouldn't generate for transportation, heating, lighting, and so on. Thanks to your early demise, you would prevent roughly one hundred tons of carbon dioxide emissions."

Bentley clapped his hands together. "Perhaps they can etch that on my tombstone," he said, excitedly. "If I'm hearing you correctly, Dr. MacFarlane, my premature death is a good thing."

"For the sake of the climate: yes," Spanky said.

"That makes me wonder: What are we saving the planet for if not for people?"

Spanky shook his head at the naivete of Bentley's question. "Earth is for *all* species—not just one. To use up our planet's resources for the comfort and enjoyment of one genus over all others is speciesism."

Muffled applause was heard throughout the courtroom. *Tell him!*

"Oh dear. Specie—what? I don't know what that is," Bentley said. "Is it a bad thing?"

"It's immoral and extremely short-sighted," Spanky sniffed. "The degradation of our atmosphere will ultimately destroy humans as well as other species."

"When will that occur?" Bentley asked.

"Sooner than you think," Spanky replied tartly.

"Ten years? A hundred years? A thousand?"

"At the rate we're going, I believe we are five years from reaching a point of no return."

"I would find that frightening if you hadn't made that prediction so many times before," Bentley said. He picked up a notebook. "You said we were five years away from doomsday in 1992. You said it again in 2001, in 2008, and most recently in 2018."

"It will give me no pleasure when I'm eventually proven right," Spanky claimed. "I would rather we take measures now to stabilize our climate while we still can. That begins with holding energy companies such as Crowe Power to account for the damage they are causing."

Bentley walked over to the defense table and sat on the edge. "How much?"

Spanky flinched. "How much what?"

"How much damage is Crowe Power causing?"

"That's difficult to quantify," Spanky said.

"You don't know?"

Spanky guffawed. "I can't give you a precise number."

"Is that because you would have to know all the factors that figure into climate change, including natural variability—solar activity, cloud formation, ocean currents, volcanic eruptions, the Earth's orbit around the sun, and the tilt of its axis? Has your research ever looked into these things?"

"Our focus is aimed at the variable we can control, which is human activity."

"But what if that amounts to almost nothing compared to the other factors? Why are we going through all this fear and bother and expense if human activity doesn't really make much difference at all?"

"We don't know that. It very well could make a huge difference."

Bentley stood up and approached the witness stand. "Let's suppose Crowe Power stops using fossil fuels today. Crowe would rely exclusively on wind, solar, and hydro-electric power, which is about twenty percent of its current mix. They slash power to the people of New York, but they align climate emissions with the state's goal to reduce emissions 85 percent by 2050. Would that have an impact on global temperatures?"

"Immediately," Sparky claimed.

"How much?" Bentley pressed.

Spanky scratched his chin. "Hard to say exactly."

"Wouldn't it be negligible?"

"Perhaps. But it would be something."

"Wouldn't any reduction in carbon dioxide emissions by Crowe Power be easily wiped out by the rapid growth in emissions from China and India?"

Spanky shifted in his seat. "Yes, but that does not relieve us of our obligation to do our part."

"Does that mean we should deindustrialize, lower our standard of living, stop eating beef, give up our gas stoves, and on and on and on, while our chief competitor in the world builds two new coal-fired power plants every week? What possible benefit do we derive from this?"

"You have to understand, Mr. Edwards, China builds well over half of the green technology in the world today. We need them to ramp up their manufacturing to make our wind turbines, solar panels, and batteries for electric cars so that we can be green, regardless of what they do."

"I'm confused," Bentley said. "Don't their emissions and our emissions go into the same atmosphere?"

"Yes."

"Then why shouldn't we generate enough energy from every possible source to make things in this country?"

Spanky sighed. "The West has had its run, Mr. Edwards. It's time we passed the baton."

Bentley looked at Lindsey and shrugged. *This is what we're up against.* He then turned back to Spanky and fixed him with a stare. "How did you do it, Dr. MacFarlane?"

"Do what?"

"How did you convince the Western world that carbon dioxide is a pollutant?"

Spanky blushed. "I can't take all the credit for that," he said. "I've had lots of help."

"Impressively so," Bentley said. "I thought carbon dioxide was essential to life on this planet. A higher concentration of CO_2 in the atmosphere makes green plants grow faster. It makes crops more drought-resistant and improves yields. Recent studies show it is greening land around the world that was once considered desert. Yet you've made millions of people feel guilty about their carbon emissions because they drive a car, heat their home, or take a breath."

"It's not a problem to inhale," Spanky said, raising his index finger. "Just to exhale."

"Don't those things go together?"

Spanky flinched. "Generally speaking, yes."

"That brings me to my last area of questioning for you, Dr. MacFarlane," he said. "There are eight billion people in the world today. You have written that each of them is impacting the climate from their first breath to their last. What's an optimal number of people for the world?"

Spanky took a deep breath and drummed his fingers on the armrest. "No more than one billion."

Bentley gasped. "I'm sorry," he said. "Did you say *one* billion?"

Felicity, alarmed, shot up from her chair. "Objection, Your Honor! Counsel has baited the witness."

"I merely asked a logical question based on the witness's testimony," Bentley said.

"This is highly speculative," Felicity insisted.

Hardiman looked conflicted. As deeply in the bag as he was for the prosecution, his curiosity over his own survival was suddenly getting the better of him. "Overruled. The witness may answer the question."

Spanky looked at the judge and nodded. Then he turned back to Bentley. "You asked for an optimal number," Spanky said. "There are global organizations that look at such issues with a mindset of benefiting the greater good. Not just for people, but for all living things and for the planet that supports them. A global population of one billion would allow for the proper balance of things."

Bentley looked to the judge. He was allowing this? Apparently so. Bentley decided to press further. "Do you think, Dr. MacFarlane, that we need to actively cull the human herd?"

"No," Spanky said, nonchalantly. "I believe the problem will take care of itself."

"How so?"

"Wars. Pandemics. Euthanasia. Low birth rates. Not to mention droughts and famines caused by climate change. I'm optimistic the world population will decline rather dramatically in the years ahead."

Bentley felt a chill run up his back. That's *optimism?* "And if this problem, as you put it, doesn't take care of itself?"

Spanky cocked his head and smiled. "Then it will simply have to be taken care of."

Bentley wanted to flee and take cover. "No further questions, Your Honor." He turned away from the podium and looked at Spanky's fan club in the gallery. *Some of you will not make the cut.*

31. OUTLIERS AND DENIERS

Based on the bands of red, purple, and charcoal gray that covered the local TV weather map, it appeared to Marty that the forecast for New York City called for its imminent incineration. Temperatures were expected to soar to ninety-six degrees, a "near record" that the meteorologist insisted was another sign of the climate apocalypse.

Marty wondered: how close to the record was it exactly? He plugged the question into the browser on his phone and found New York's highest temperature recorded for this day was 106 degrees set in 1936, a time when air-conditioning was rare and carbon dioxide levels were 25 percent lower. *Hmm*, Marty mused. *That might have been worth mentioning.*

The stack of newspapers that had been piled against his door the night before prominently featured coverage of *The People vs. Lindsey Harper Crowe*. The *Daily Reaper* didn't bother masking its opinion; it applauded Felicity's pursuit of the energy evildoer and suggested on its front page that Lindsey's prosecution was only the first of many steps that needed to be taken across the nation. There could be no justice and no peace "until every one of the nation's climate criminals is punished for the destruction they have wrought upon our lands and seas."

Marty pondered that as he adjusted his thermostat, turned on his coffee machine, and popped a bagel in the toaster—all courtesy of the horrible, terrible, incredibly rotten Crowe Power Company. Where, he wondered, would the city be without them? His gut told him they would find out soon enough.

In the interest of saving money to pay for his kids' college tuition, room and board, books, and, possibly, protest signs, Marty decided to take the subway downtown. His journey served as a reminder of the many routine offenses that New York's ever-vigilant prosecutors declined to address.

He stepped over a passed-out addict splayed out on the curb, dodged a motorcycle roaring down the sidewalk, and made a wide circle around a man defecating on the stoop of a jewelry store. Descending the steps to the station at

Columbus Circle, he declined an offer to buy knockoff Gucci bags, swiped his card to get through the turnstile while fare beaters pushed through an open door, and ignored illegal vendors selling candy stolen from retailers. He stayed far away from the tracks with his back against the wall as he awaited the train, lest a lunatic push him into its path, then stepped into a train car where a man was smoking weed, a woman was sprawled out on a bench sleeping with her bare bum exposed, and a shirtless man with astonishing abs was swinging from the handlebars to thumping music while his menacing partner demanded tips.

Still, according to the news feed on Marty's phone, the only person who deserved public scorn from New York's ruling establishment that day was the elegantly attired and perfectly mannered Lindsey Harper Crowe. She took her seat at the defense table for day three of her show trial as Marty arrived. He gently patted her shoulder and took his own seat in the row behind her. Lindsey turned and offered a weary smile.

Bentley rose to summon his first witness. "I would like to call Dr. James Freidkin," he announced.

Hardiman demanded to know, "As what?"

"Dr. Freidkin is an expert witness on climate change, Your Honor."

"Not in this trial," Hardiman said.

Bentley's expression was incredulous. "Your Honor, Dr. Freidkin is a highly credentialed scientist, a professor emeritus of meteorology at MIT and Harvard and the author of more than two hundred papers and books related to the climate."

Hardiman scowled. "Dr. Freidkin is an infamous climate change denier operating outside the realm of scientific consensus. Unless he has direct knowledge of Crowe Power's activities related to climate change, then Dr. Freidkin has no standing in this case."

Bentley showed his irritation as he proceeded to his next witness. "I wish to call Dr. Harold Olmstead, former professor of physics at Princeton, who is an expert on carbon dioxide and its effects on our planet."

Again, Hardiman shook his head. "Carbon dioxide is not on trial here," he declared. "Lindsey Harper Crowe is. You may *not* call Dr. Olmstead."

Bentley was on to the judge. He looked down his list and realized that none of his expert witnesses would be allowed. All would be silenced in the court, just as they were in the news media. Still, he wanted to get his requests on record with the hope they might help an appeal. "Would it please the Court if I called upon a recent Nobel laureate in physics who can speak to serious public misunderstandings about climate change?"

Hardiman looked at his watch, then at Bentley. "The Court would not be pleased at all."

Bentley glanced further down his list. "What about the former chair of Earth and Atmospheric Sciences at Georgia Tech to discuss why she changed her mind about climate change?" He looked up to see Hardiman shaking his head. "The developer of the system of satellites that measure temperatures around the world? An astrophysicist? A founder of Greenpeace? The author of the best-selling book on climate change, who makes a compelling case the science is unsettled?"

"No. No. No. No. And no again." Hardiman muttered to himself as he counted on his fingers. "Was that enough for you, Counselor? Do you get the point?"

"More than you know," Bentley said hotly.

Hardiman pointed at him. "Did you just roll your eyes at me? My patience is wearing thin, Mr. Edwards!" He pointed to Bentley with his gavel. "One more sign of your disrespect and I will hold you in contempt."

Exasperated, Bentley said, "Your Honor, all my witnesses are world-class experts with credentials that are at least the equal of Dr. MacFarlane's and in most cases far more impressive. Just because the news media refuse to report on their findings or even acknowledge they exist does not mean that their points of view aren't credible. Indeed, I would argue they're essential to this case. They would show you that the effects of fossil fuels on the climate are debatable. These charges against Lindsey Harper Crowe and the Crowe Power Company rest on assumptions that are unfounded and unproven."

Hardiman, irritated, cleared his throat. "For the record, Counselor, this Court regards the science as settled and Dr. MacFarlane's testimony beyond reproach. I've reviewed the curricula vitae of all your expert witnesses, none of whom witnessed the internal workings of Crowe Power first-hand. All I see is a collection of outliers and deniers. These so-called experts are far out of the mainstream of contemporary beliefs about climate change."

"That is precisely why they should be heard," Bentley said. "The science around climate change is far from conclusive, Your Honor. To suggest it requires no further study beggars belief."

"We're moving on," the judge declared.

Bentley shook his head in frustration and slowly returned to the defense table. He leaned over to confer with Lindsey and Digby. "As you just heard from the ringleader of this circus, they want to fold their tent. Word in the corridor is that Felicity has a fundraiser at the Met this afternoon." He paused. "I still think we need to offer a rebuttal for the record."

Digby said, "How? The judge won't allow it."

Bentely looked at Lindsey. "I'm afraid it's all on you, my dear."

Lindsey was alarmed. "What?"

"I think you should take the stand."

Lindsey looked at Digby, then back at Bentley. "I thought we agreed that was not a good idea. Given their obvious bias, I don't see what's to be gained."

Bentley replied, "If we're to have even the slightest chance at an appeal, we'll need to get a defense on record. He can't deny you the right to testify."

Lindsey reluctantly agreed. "Can I at least get some time to prepare?"

Bentley looked over his shoulder at the judge, who was staring lasers at him and rapidly slapping the top of the bench. He turned back to Lindsey. "I think it's game on." Noting her concern, he said, "Don't worry. I go first. I'll tee up the questions. You just hit them out of the park."

"What about Felicity? She won't be so gentle."

"I'll make sure she doesn't get her shot until tomorrow."

32. LINDSEY TAKES A STAND

Lindsey was determined not to let her haters see her sweat, nor to return their ire. She appeared unruffled as she approached the witness stand, recited her oath, and took a seat, carefully folding her skirt under her legs. Behind her calm exterior, she was a jumble of nerves as she looked over the courtroom. She counted eight friendly faces among the hundred or so people in the room.

What if I say something stupid? What if they all laugh? What if... whatever? As her thoughts clashed, she tried to calm herself by remembering Bentley's advice: "Keep your answers brief. Stick to what you know." He had told her his questioning would be relatively easy—a round of friendly fire before Felicity's anticipated assault the following day. "What do they tell you at the dentist? This won't hurt a bit," he'd said.

Bentley stood behind the podium and smiled. "Good afternoon, Ms. Crowe." Sensing her discomfort, he tried putting her at ease with a question that required no thought on her part. The idea was to get her mouth moving and to get her used to hearing her own voice in this venue. "How are you today?"

"I'm fine, thank you," she said with a tight smile.

"Excellent. Take us back, if you will, to your becoming chairperson of the Crowe Power Company," Bentley said. "It was asserted yesterday by your predecessor Robbie Crowe that you 'staged a coup' within the family to oust him from his job. Is that an accurate description?"

The thought of Robbie made Lindsey forget her nervousness and she began to focus on the topic at hand. "It's true I was alarmed by his leadership, such as it was. Robbie seemed very focused on missions that were well beyond our company's reach, such as saving the world. He showed little interest in the core mission of Crowe Power."

"And what is that?"

"To provide safe and reliable energy to people in a clean and safe way. It's not complicated, but it does require a great deal of attention."

"Did your actions lead to his departure?"

"No," she said, shaking her head. "*His* actions led to his departure. We were married at the time, and I saw our net worth dwindling because of his poor stewardship of the family enterprise. He lost money. He wasted time. Essentially, he forgot the plot. I felt I had no choice but to act if we were to leave something for our children and for future generations of our family. To my mind, he had his chance. He blew it." She shrugged.

Bentley nodded. "There was criticism at the time that you lacked the experience necessary to become the top executive of a company the size of Crowe Power. Were you aware of that criticism?"

"I heard it, yes."

"Did that bother you?"

"It might have if I were an executive. I'm not. I'm a non-executive chairman. I was elected by our shareholders to look after their interests. That means ensuring the company is well-run and sticks to its knitting."

"How has that worked out?"

"Very well, until recently. Our share price hit record highs this spring. Clearly investors were pleased."

Bentley moved away from the podium and paced in front of the witness stand. "The plaintiff charges that you defrauded shareholders by failing to inform them of climate change and your company's role in it. Do you deny that accusation?"

"Of course I do. You must understand, Mr. Edwards," she said, lightly punching the air with an index finger. "My extended family and I are investors, too. We hold a greater stake in this company than anyone else. There's no percentage gained from deluding ourselves or our other shareholders about the risks we face."

"And yet the plaintiff alleges the company took enormous risk by ignoring the so-called 'smoking gun' memo authored by Robbie Crowe. Do you believe there's any merit to that claim?"

"I wasn't at the company at that time," Lindsey said. "My understanding is that the leadership of Crowe Power was very much aware of the concerns that Robbie and his ghostwriters expressed. After all, climate change—or global warming, as it was called then—was hardly a secret. It was widely publicized, just as it is today."

"If that's the case, why didn't the company act on the memo?" Bentley asked.

"There was nothing to act on, Mr. Edwards. The memo suggested we repurpose the company. But to what? It didn't say. If we were to change our business model, we would have to rely on more than a vague suggestion that we do something different. We do things a little differently every day. But we stay constant in our purpose."

Bentley nodded. "Is it inaccurate to suggest that the company ignored the issue of climate change in the hope that it would simply go away?"

"It is inaccurate. We want to understand what's going on with our environment. We have to. That's why I have an advisory group of leading scientists to help us observe how the climate is changing and determine whether there's anything we can do about it."

"Is there?"

"Based on what we know?" She shook her head. "There's very little."

"How little?" Bentley asked.

Lindsey moved her head from side to side. "I'd say... somewhere between a little and nothing."

A murmur of disapproval rumbled through the courtroom. A voice from the back of the room called, *"Liar!"* Another shouted, *"Denier!"*

Hardiman waited a moment to see if anyone else wanted to yell at Lindsey before rapping his gavel to show he sort of disapproved. Felicity, meanwhile, furiously scribbled notes as she prepared for her next round of Honor Beads.

"Ms. Crowe, you heard Dr. MacFarlane's testimony," Bentley continued. "He said that if Crowe Power somehow ceased all use of fossil fuels, that would immediately reduce the threat of climate change. How do you account for the vast difference in your points of view?"

She looked directly at Spanky, who was sitting in the front row. "Well, for one thing, I can't afford to be wrong."

Spanky flinched as Bentley pressed on. "Are you suggesting Dr. MacFarlane can?"

Lindsey asserted, "Dr. MacFarlane has been wrong in every one of his predictions for forty years. Florida was supposed to be under water by now. The polar ice caps were supposed to melt. The sea level was supposed to rise six feet. We were supposed to see record numbers of hurricanes. None of those things have occurred, yet he's still celebrated as a great prognosticator. When I'm wrong in my judgments, my company pays for it. We could lose a great deal of money, and I could lose my job."

"Is that what happened to your predecessor?"

"He was held accountable."

"I see," Bentley said. "During your tenure, have you made any adjustments in your business strategy to accommodate climate change?"

"We've made many," she replied. "Not for the science, which is inconclusive, but for the politics, which are never in doubt. There's a powerful coalition of forces pushing for all kinds of mandates and regulations over what we do and how we do it. After we meet their demands, they ask for more, even if they provide no tangible benefit for our consumers, investors, or employees."

"Can you give me an example of a change you have made?"

"I'll give you several," she said. "We shuttered two nuclear power plants, which are carbon-free but politically toxic. We converted six power plants from coal to natural gas, which reduced carbon emissions by nearly fifty percent, but made them less reliable because of our limited pipeline capacity. We shut refineries in California because of climate regulations, which sent the price of gasoline soaring on the West Coast. We're seeking permits for more liquefied natural gas at our East River Powerhouse in New York because our pipeline applications have been denied and we need more backup."

"What happens if you don't get it?"

"I'm afraid rolling blackouts are likely in our city," Lindsey said. "Even more concerning is the potential for long-lasting disruptions of supplies of natural gas to homes and businesses for heat and cooking. Activists claim they're defending poor neighborhoods. In our view, quite the opposite is true. It is the people in marginal neighborhoods who are likely to be hit the hardest by unreliable energy."

"Objection!" Felicity yelled. "The witness is speculating."

Bentley pushed back. "Your Honor, the state has cited the interests of disadvantaged people to support its case. It's fair to ask whether their claims have merit."

Hardiman looked out over the gallery's sea of white faces used to claiming the high moral ground on climate change because of its supposed impact on the poor.

Did their claim have merit? "The objection is overruled," Hardiman said over a murmur of disapproval from the crowd. "You may proceed, Counselor."

Bentley nodded and returned to Lindsey. "Ms. Crowe, why do you say people in marginal neighborhoods are most likely to be harmed by power outages?"

"Wealthy people who fund climate activism can go to their second or third homes or take a vacation when the trouble starts," Lindsey said. "That's far less likely in the predominantly black and brown working-class communities in Queens, Brooklyn, and the Bronx. Where do they go when the lights are turned off? There may not even be enough heat for community shelters. What do they do then? We're putting disadvantaged residents on a path to needless privation. To my mind, that's indefensible."

Bentley nodded. "Isn't that an inevitable outcome if we're going to manage climate change? We all need to sacrifice, don't we, if we're to reduce carbon emissions?"

"The state would have us believe that carbon dioxide is our control button. I agree—but not for climate. It's the button they push to control people, restrict freedom, and corral people into behaviors they find more acceptable, like buying into their green programs. When carbon dioxide is your hammer, everything you see is just a nail."

The gallery grew more restive with this shot. "If the odds are so stacked against you, Ms. Crowe, why don't you simply join the crowd?" Bentley asked. "Why not create your own lines of business around climate change and make some money like so many of your critics are doing?"

"We see some opportunities in the future, especially for cleaning up the mess from today's climate solutions," Lindsey said. "Somebody's going to have to dispose of the toxic waste from solar panels, and the dead birds, bats, and whale carcasses from wind turbines. There will be a need to build community warming centers for people to gather when their heat goes out, and cooling centers for days when blackouts prevent air conditioning. We also see a need to restart our old nuclear power plants once the politicians realize that closing them was a colossally stupid and reckless idea."

"Thank you, Ms. Crowe," Bentley said, before turning to the judge. "I have no further questions."

Justice Hardiman rapped his gavel. "We'll pick up with the cross-examination tomorrow morning."

33. BAR EXAM

Team Lindsey left the courthouse to jeers from the dozens of demonstrators who had set up an encampment across the street. Lindsey, Marty, Bentley, and Digby jumped into a pair of cars waiting to take them to Crowe Power headquarters on Broad Street in the Financial District. They squeezed into the small executive elevator, headed to Lindsey's suite, and settled in her conference room, where Winnie had arranged beverages and snacks on the credenza.

Bentley grabbed a bottle of water and sat next to Lindsey to prepare her for the next day's cross-examination. "Felicity will press you on the basics," he said. "What did you know and when did you know it?"

Digby, taking a seat across the table, added, "And what did you do about it?"

"Obviously, whatever I did was not enough to satisfy them," Lindsey said.

"Let's work on that answer," Bentley said. He turned to Marty, "Marty, help us with some wordsmithing here."

For the next three hours, the legal team ran Lindsey through a "murder board"—a grueling practice session of aggressive questioning to ready her for Felicity. As the hour approached six o'clock, Lindsey fell back in her chair, exhausted. "I think I'm about as ready as I'll ever be."

"Agreed," Bentley said. He put his files away in his leather satchel and the team dispersed, leaving Lindsey and Marty alone, sitting across from one another at the conference table.

Marty clapped his hands together. "Let's get out and grab a beer."

Lindsey laughed bitterly. "Are you kidding me? I can't go anywhere," she said. "I'm a pariah."

"No, you're not," Marty insisted. "You just need to get outside the echo chamber where the elites hang out."

"I don't know where that is."

"How about a place where they serve burgers and beer instead of snails and sherry?" Marty said. "Maybe they play rock instead of Rachmaninov. The furniture's a little nicked up and so are the people because they're working for a living, instead of gluing themselves to the pavement."

"You know a place like that?"

"I do."

"They're not going to hate me?"

"They might, but it won't be because of climate. It will be because of their electric bill."

Lindsey sighed and shook her head. "I don't think so…"

Marty stood up and took her hand. "C'mon. You need a change of scene."

Lindsey stayed seated. "Tom says I can't go anywhere without security."

"Don't worry," Marty said with a laugh. "You'll have plenty where we're going."

She stood. "This is on you."

Marty stripped off his tie and rolled up his sleeves. He looked at her designer suit. "Can you dress down a little?"

"I'm not as good at that as you are."

"Is that a shot?"

"Might have been," she said. "I've got jeans in the back."

"That will help."

Andrei brought the car around to the rear entrance of Crowe Power headquarters on New Street. After picking up Lindsey and Marty, he was directed through a maze of one-way streets to Cedar and Greenwich on the perimeter of the World Trade Center campus. Andrei pulled up to the curb, and Marty helped Lindsey out of the car in front of O'Hara's Pub. A group of young people wearing shorts, sneakers, and t-shirts were clustered around the door, chatting, smoking cigarettes, and laughing.

Lindsey looked at their attire and said, "Good call on the jeans."

Marty nodded. "Next time, I have to get you a baseball cap."

He held the door for her and they entered the bar, which was packed with firefighters from Engine Company No. 10 around the corner, cops from across the city, and tourists visiting the 9/11 Memorial across the street.

The crowd was standing room only, but Marty spotted a man leaving a cash tip on the counter. He grabbed the back of the chair as the man stood up to leave and offered the seat to Lindsey. He helped carefully push it up to the brass rail as the bartender brought over a couple of typewritten menus in plastic sleeves. She looked up at the TVs over the bar. They were mercifully showing sports channels rather than her trial. She breathed a sigh of relief.

"What will you have?" Marty asked, as he looked over the drinks list.

"Hmm... I'm thinking this is not the place to order Chateau Margaux," Lindsey said.

"Only if you want to get thrown out."

Lindsey was mesmerized by the décor. All around her—on the oak-paneled walls, the pillars, the coolers, the ceiling—were thousands of colorful uniform patches from police and fire departments from around the world. The Joliet, Illinois Police Department. The Rockville, Maryland Volunteer Fire Department. The Mashantucket Tribal Police. First responders in France, England, and Germany. It dawned on her that this was a worldwide clubhouse for people united in a mission to keep people safe.

"What a privilege to be here," she marveled. "When I think of idiots like the Climate Rangers endangering people's lives... then I look around here at people who save them, putting their lives on the line every day—" After another emotionally draining day, the thought of it made her struggle to keep her composure.

"Kinda puts things in perspective, doesn't it?" Marty said. "Maybe it's because my pop was a cop. But the people behind these badges are my idea of heroes."

"Good call to come here," Lindsey said with a nod and a smile. Suddenly, her challenges seemed small. Nobody was asking her to run into a burning building, stop a robbery, or rush a critically injured person to the hospital.

"This one's on the house," said a voice.

Lindsey looked up to see the bartender putting a tall glass of beer in front of her. "Really?"

"Absolutely," he said, before putting down a glass for Marty, too.

"Thank you," she said. She turned to Marty. "Is this your doing?"

Marty shook his head as the bartender grabbed a battered scrapbook from the counter and laid it in front of her. "Check this out if you get a moment," he said before moving off to serve other customers.

On the scrapbook cover was a large circular emblem bearing the crests of the New York City police and fire departments and the police department for the Port

Authority of New York and New Jersey. At the top around the rim, it said, "September 11, 2001. World Trade Center." A ribbon at the bottom said, "Fallen Heroes."

She opened the book to see photos of the pub in the aftermath of the 9/11 attacks, when it was shrouded in dust and gray debris from the collapsed towers. Another photo showed a firefighter on the first anniversary of 9/11 removing the patch from his shirt to tape it to the wall. Thus began a tradition that had been emulated thousands of times.

The bartender returned holding a beer of his own. "Our power was out for four months after the towers fell," he said. "We don't take our electricity for granted here." He raised a glass and clinked it against hers. "Thank you for your service, Ms. Crowe."

"What?" she asked, flabbergasted. "*My* service? I wasn't even at the company back then."

"You are now." He nodded toward the TV. "I've seen what's going on over there at the courthouse. It's a rigged deal, and I'm sorry you're going through it. They're making a mockery of our justice system."

Lindsey was genuinely speechless. "I... I... don't know what to say."

"Just tell me how you like your burger cooked," the bartender said. "That's all I need to know."

Lindsey fought back a tear and ordered a Brooklyn burger medium rare. "How nice was that?" she said to Marty.

He could barely speak himself. "Cool. Very, very, very cool."

"Imagine: 'my service.'" She shook her head in wonder. "How does that equate with what these people do every day? It's not even close."

"Welcome to the world outside the bubble. They don't hate you here."

"Most of them don't think about me."

"Even better," Marty said. "Hear that?"

Lindsey cocked an ear. "Pretty sure it's not Mozart."

"Lynyrd Skynyrd."

"Oh yeah. 'Free Bird.'"

"Don't tell me you know the song," Marty said, with surprise.

"Are you kidding me? I even know the lyrics."

"Nah," Marty guffawed.

"Oh Lord," she said with a laugh. "My girlfriends and I used to belt this out at the bar in college." She sang along softly so that only he could hear. "'*And this bird you cannot cha-a-a-ange.*'"

He tapped his glass to hers. "I hope you never do."

34. TWO BLUE EYES ON THE PRIZE

Fortified by her journey outside her discomfort zone, Lindsey walked into the courtroom for her cross-examination, ready for battle. If she was going down, she would go down swinging.

As she stepped up to the witness stand, she noticed Justice Hardiman glowering at her. Clearly, nothing about her testimony yesterday had altered his views, and there was little chance she would move him today. His verdict was likely in his pocket. Felicity, meanwhile, was greeting her supporters in the gallery with double handshakes, hugs, air kisses, and quick poses for selfies. The People v. Lindsey Harper Crowe was going as expected: as a highly successful campaign event.

After Hardiman brought the court to order, Felicity came face to face with Lindsey for the first time since Camp Wannabe. Lindsey studied her, trying to square the puckered puss of her adversary with the strange campmate from what seemed like a thousand summers ago.

Still, Felicity's inscrutable expression showed no flicker of recognition. She raised her chin and peered through her granny glasses at her prey with a cold, clear eye. "Let's pretend for a moment that I'm a customer of Crowe Power and I know nothing about energy or climate change."

Lindsey smiled. "That should be easy enough."

"What have you done to educate me about how your products are driving climate change?"

Lindsey stared back at Felicity. "Nothing."

Felicity blinked several times. "Why not?"

"For what purpose?" Lindsey asked. "To scare you with unfounded speculation? I'm not sure what the point would be. Our customers still need to heat their homes and charge their phones. Are you suggesting they wouldn't if we slapped a label on their electric bill?"

Felicity smiled imperiously. "I'm suggesting you pushed energy on an unsuspecting public in the same way tobacco companies promoted cigarettes, as if there was no possibility of danger. Let me take you back to 1959," she said. "The famed nuclear physicist Edward Teller warned then that the burning of fossil fuels could lead to global warming." She punched a button on her laptop that brought up a magazine advertisement from the early 1960s, entitled "Life without Crowe Power."

"Yet the only warning your company issued was what life would be like without Crowe Power and its fossil fuels. No ice cubes. No electric shaver. No vacuum cleaner. No hair dryer. Would that be such a tragedy?"

"You're asking the wrong person," Lindsey replied.

"Who should I ask, if not you?"

"How about our customers?"

"Don't your customers have a right to know what they're consuming?"

"I'm pretty sure they do, Ms. Redfeather," Lindsey said. "Thanks to the endless efforts of our media friends in the jury box, to schools immersing students in climate doctrine, and to our activist government, there's not a living soul in our market who hasn't heard at least one report suggesting the climate is in peril and that it is due to their use of fossil fuels. Yet they still turn on the lights, do they not?"

Felicity moved away from the podium and began to pace. "Ms. Crowe, are you familiar with the precautionary principle?"

"Yes, if you mean the notion that we should take action to prevent the possibility of something occurring in the future, even before we have all the evidence."

Felicity nodded. "That's exactly right. Given the scale of the disaster that could be caused by climate change, wouldn't it be prudent for your company to do everything in its power to head it off?"

Lindsey paused, thinking. "I believe, Ms. Redfeather, that you and I have very different ideas of what constitutes disaster. The state regards it as a minor uptick in average temperatures that may or may not be caused by human activity. It sees the accumulation of carbon dioxide in the atmosphere, which is near a historic low, as a problem from which we'll never recover. My bigger worry about a coming disaster is a dangerously low supply of energy at times when we'll need it most, such as summer heatwaves and winter storms. That possibility is real and it's here now."

Felicity dismissed Lindsey's claim with a shake of her head. "Do you deny, Ms. Crowe, that wind and solar are better sources of energy than fossil fuels?"

"Better for what?"

"For our planet, obviously."

Lindsey scoffed. "Is that a serious question?"

Felicity shot back. "The fate of your business may hinge on your answer."

Lindsey laughed. "Let's not kid ourselves, Ms. Redfeather. The fate of our business in this state was likely sealed before I walked into this courtroom on Monday. That said, I would suggest wind and solar are niche sources of energy. They're only about three percent of our energy mix, and I don't see that going much higher."

"Why not?"

"They simply can't reach the scale necessary. We use them because the state insists and rewards us with subsidies to make them appear to the public as economical. But they are unpredictable, unreliable, and nobody wants them in their backyard."

"Do you not even consider them part of the answer to our climate crisis?"

"First of all, I don't consider our climate in crisis. Secondly, I think that's a question best put to you should you become governor, Ms. Redfeather. How many acres of farmland and forests do we need to destroy in our state to create enough solar farms to power New York City? How many wind turbines must dot the horizon of our shorelines and crown our mountaintops? How much harm would that cause to plants and animals? And how much fossil fuel capacity would you still have to build to back up renewables when the sun doesn't shine and the wind doesn't blow?"

"You tell me the answer," Felicity shot back.

"More than is currently possible," Lindsey asserted.

"How do you know that?"

"Do you have any idea how rapidly electricity demand is soaring?" Lindsey said, heatedly. "In fifteen years, we'll need forty percent more electricity than we produce today. That's because they're creating new capacity for artificial intelligence, chip manufacturing, and battery plants. That requires huge amounts of electricity, and I don't know where I'm going to get it. Add to that the demand from consumers to power up all their ever-multiplying electronic devices. Consider, too, the push by government authorities to make all transportation, cooking, and home heating electric—and doing so at the very same time they're curtailing our supply of fuel we need to generate that electricity. There is simply no way to meet the demand in the way you imagine. It's a fantasy—and a dangerous one."

"So you say," Felicity scoffed. "And yet the lights stay on."

Lindsey blushed. Felicity was getting on her nerves. "For how long, Ms. Redfeather?" she asked. "Are you okay with increasing blackouts and brownouts? Can you live without air conditioning in the summer? Without heat in the winter? Is all that a worthy price to pay for what I would regard as a futile attempt to influence our climate?"

"All the more reason to bring renewable energy projects online. Why haven't you done so?"

"We've tried, repeatedly," Lindsey said, exasperated. "We can't get permits." She pointed toward the front of the courthouse. "All your friends out there protesting in Foley Square won't let us do it. They file lawsuits to keep the wind turbines out of their line of sight or to block the transmission lines from going through their backyard. They pressure our legislators. They tie us up in legal knots to delay, delay, delay. Nobody wants these things in their backyard."

"You seem to have all the answers, Ms. Crowe. So tell me: how do we save the planet?"

"We don't."

Felicity practically spat. "That's it? We just let it go?"

"Rumors of our planet's demise have been greatly exaggerated," Lindsey said. "There are many stupid things humans can do to destroy life on our planet, such as nuclear warfare. But it's probably the ultimate conceit of humankind to think we can manage the world's temperature. I would suggest to you that the controls are beyond our reach. We can't manage solar activity. We can't tilt the earth's axis or adjust its orbit. We can't control the temperatures of the ocean or put a cork into undersea volcanoes. Honestly, when I hear some of the solutions people are proposing, I'm scared half to death of the unintended consequences."

Felicity crossed her arms and glared at Lindsey. "So you'll continue merrily along, business as usual. Is that what you're saying?"

"I'm not sure how merry it is, but yes." Lindsey replied. "I make no apologies for providing people with the energy they need to live their lives. Can we do things better? Of course. That's one reason we're working on fusion as a possible replacement for fossil fuels someday."

Felicity scoffed. "The joke is that fusion is twenty years away and always will be."

Lindsey said, "So's the end of the world."

35. DE-PRESSED

With his poll numbers sinking faster than Crowe Power stock, Governor Frank Cardini tried desperately to remind pearl-clutching voters that he was every bit as worried about climate change as Two Blue Eyes. He summoned a busload of union pals, a dozen of his top non-white political appointees, and a few protesters-for-hire to a forlorn patch of broken asphalt outside a Brooklyn housing project and called a press conference.

At ten minutes past the appointed time, there were still no reporters in the audience, and Frank's press secretary, Mona DeLisi, sensed the governor was about to blow his top. She approached him to delicately suggest he make his announcement soon. The union people, she reminded him, were off the job at three o'clock whether he was finished or not.

Frank shook his head. "I thought this was a photo opp."

"That's the idea."

He turned to her, seething. "Then why don't we have some fucking photographers here?" He scanned the meager crowd. "I don't see anybody from the press. What the hell do you do all day long?"

Mona thought back to her day, which started at 4 a.m., when she got up to monitor news reports coming in overnight. That was followed by a screaming call from the governor at 6 a.m. when he saw Felicity booked on three morning news shows while he had none. Then came the last-minute logistics to arrange this presser, frantic calls begging reporters to come to the event, choking back a bagel for breakfast on the subway, and monitoring the governor's interview with a cute young reporter from an obscure website. Frank apparently liked that interview because he smiled at Mona afterward and patted her butt. Mona then hammered out two press releases, ten tweets on the governor's account, and munched on rice crackers for lunch. That's right, guv. *I do nothing all day.*

"Governor," she said quietly, "I advised you the timing was risky. All the climate reporters who would normally cover an announcement like this are downtown at the Crowe trial."

Frank seethed. "What am I supposed to do, Mona? Huh? Just wait until the trial's over before I tell 'em my ideas? The election will be over. And you'll be out of a fuckin' job. You get that?"

"Governor, please. We'll put your announcement on the wire ourselves if we have to. And we'll run our own photo with you in front of the apartment building. It will all work out fine." She tapped her watch. "But we need to get going."

Frank sighed and stepped to the podium, as three TV news trucks and a van full of reporters pulled up, followed by three black cars. "Alright, alright, alright," he said out of the side of his mouth. "Now we're talkin'."

"Almost," Mona muttered, as she motioned with the back of her hand to get going.

Then, as the TV crews set up their cameras, Frank noticed the emergence of attorney Melinda Truscott, a close personal friend of Felicity Redfeather, who was famous for suing high-profile celebrities for sexual harassment. Beside her were three former members of his staff. It quickly dawned on the governor that he was about to be ambushed. "Oh shit."

Mona saw what was happening, too. "Start talking!" she commanded him. "*Now!*"

Frank leaned into the microphone and spoke rapidly. "Thank you all for coming today. I'm here to announce that I've signed legislation mandating that our state will be completely fossil-fuel-free by 2035. This bold initiative will—"

A local resident who meandered into the press conference out of curiosity blurted out. "Who you kiddin', boss? Our building is fossil-free now. Ain't no gas in there since March."

Frank backpedaled. "I... I don't know... uh, what?"

"Governor!" Truscott called as she approached the podium with her clients in tow. "You have to answer for your behavior!"

With his announcement falling into chaos, Frank looked to Mona, who motioned vigorously for him to continue. He spoke as loudly as he could. "We take this action in the name of environmental justice, to stop climate change from ravaging our communities..."

"We're after justice, too, Governor!" Truscott hollered. She practically shoved the governor out of the way as she commandeered the microphone while cameras flashed. "I'm here to announce a lawsuit on behalf of fourteen women who accuse Governor Francis Xavier Cardini of using his position of authority to harass the women who served him. This includes his chief of staff, his head of human resources, three staffers in his campaign office, a security guard, a cleaning lady, a FedEx delivery person, three cocktail waitresses, and a chanteuse."

Frank, staggered, asked, "What's a chanteuse?"

"A singer, Governor," Mona said quietly.

"Oh," he said. He tried to think back. *Which one…?*

Truscott continued, "Basically, any woman the governor encountered was treated as his personal property that he felt entitled to grope. This conduct would not be tolerated from anyone, but especially a person in a such an exalted leadership position."

Frank tried to move Truscott out of the way with a nudge of his shoulder. He grabbed the microphone and declared, "Please disregard this obvious political stunt. Anyone who works closely with me will tell you this is simply not true."

He glanced at Mona, who angrily approached Truscott. "I want to see that lawsuit right now."

Truscott motioned to an aide, who handed Mona a copy. She glanced through it quickly. "Is it too late for me to sign?"

Truscott smiled. "Happy to squeeze you in."

"So was the governor," Mona said.

Mona took off her employee badge, slammed it on the podium, and glared at Frank. "I'm done here." She looked at him in disgust. "So are you."

36. CLOSING TIME

As the downtown courtroom filled up for closing arguments, Felicity conferred with the other members of her legal team for a pulse check. Despite Lindsey's strong pushback in her testimony that morning, Felicity was advised her case was going very well, indeed, with a surge in donations to her campaign for governor, and a 5 percent bump in poll numbers. Best of all, a sneak peek from her ballot harvesting indicated a slight edge in early voting over Frank Cardini. Now with the announcement of a sexual harassment case against the governor knocking him further back on his heels, a strong close to *The People vs. Lindsey Harper Crowe* could assure Felicity's victory in the primary.

She took the podium with a fortified confidence in her moral authority. "At its core, this case is about lies, disinformation, and deception," she said. "You heard Lindsey Harper Crowe claim she doesn't know the exact cause of climate change. Why is that? Everyone else in this room knows. We heard it straight from the pre-eminent climate scientist of our age, Dr. George MacFarlane.

"I ask the court: what more do we need to know to take action against these climate scofflaws, who ply their products on an unsuspecting public? Do they think we'll never notice the carnage all around us? Horrendous droughts. Raging wildfires. Violent storms. Rising seas. Scorching heat. It was little more than a decade ago that Superstorm Sandy wreaked havoc on our city, killing more than forty people and causing nineteen billion dollars in damage. What comes next?

"Like cigarette companies failing to warn their products cause cancer, Crowe Power failed to tell us that their products were destroying our climate, creating ever more powerful storms. Yet the evidence is undeniable. And it was present in their very own secret files more than twenty years ago. That was all the proof we needed. Crowe Power has known for decades that its products lead to climate change, yet they said nothing. If only they'd had the integrity to tell us. What could we have done differently to save our planet?"

Lindsey leaned over to Bentley. "Nothing."

"Your Honor," Felicity continued, "this case presents an opportunity to send a message to all the deniers and skeptics out there. You can't ignore the science and get away with it. Not in this town! We are coming after you. We are naming names. We will root you out and we will hold you accountable. It is time for one and all to get behind the solutions. There is simply no time to lose."

Felicity was filled with the righteous fervor of an itinerant preacher from the Great Awakening. "Crowe Power says it's doing everything it's supposed to do simply by providing reliable power. Well, I'm sorry, Your Honor, but that's not enough. We have a right not just to energy but to *clean* energy. It's time we get it through a publicly owned and democratically operated energy system that keeps our disadvantaged communities free from deadly pollution. That, Your Honor, is the very definition of environmental justice. And that is exactly what we are seeking here today."

Bentley extended his arm across the table and briefly grasped Lindsey's hand before rising to take the podium. He looked around the room at the hostile expressions. There was no moving this crowd, but he plunged ahead anyway.

"Your Honor, if Crowe Power is a polluter because of carbon dioxide, then so are you." He gestured toward Felicity. "So is the plaintiff." He swept his arm behind him toward the gallery. "So is everyone in this courtroom. As we heard in testimony this week, the inconvenient truth about blaming carbon dioxide for climate change is that it makes everyone in this world complicit simply by breathing. Everything we do after our first breath compounds the problem. According to Dr. MacFarlane, the damage done to our climate is made worse by exercising, using an inhaler, and getting an MRI. Nothing will please our climate masters—not even dying, which we apparently can't do soon enough. Where does this madness stop?

"The plaintiff contends that so-called 'clean energy' is a right. I would like to know where that is enshrined in the Constitution. Even if it were, there was nothing offered by the prosecution that definitively ties carbon dioxide to climate change. Nor did they quantify the impact of other greenhouse gases, such as methane, or water vapor. That's because they simply don't know. And all their computer models won't help them. What they say about our climate is nothing more than projections, estimates, and wild guesses that have been consistently disproven over time. And that is why Lindsey Harper Crowe and her company do not invest their money in educating the public about these causes, which are poorly understood.

"The debate about the extent to which humans may impact climate change has been undermined by the dishonesty of this theory's proponents. By scientists whose incomes depend on the foregone conclusions favored by the entities that finance them. By journalists funded by foundations that use climate change as a tool to advance their agendas to control our lives. By search engines that bury or disclaim their results to align themselves with the United Nations' mission to transfer wealth from one part of the world to another."

A murmur of disapproval from the gallery was gaveled by the judge, as Bentley pressed ahead. "You can't run a power plant with politics, Your Honor. High-voltage power lines and high-pressure gas lines do not respond to ideology. The professionals who run these assets have to deal with hard facts and rapidly changing scenarios. What is the demand for energy right now? What will it be in ten minutes? How much power do they have? Do they need to produce more? Do they have too much, which will upset the balance? Should they shut down generators? Export energy? Import?" He snapped his fingers three times rapidly. "These decisions need to be made in seconds, on the spot, in real time by real people who know what they're doing. They can't be decided by an ideologically driven committee pondering whether it's the 'right' power from wind, or sun, or moonbeams.

"The plaintiff would have you believe she's delivering environmental justice. Yet, if she gets her way, this city won't let anyone even deliver a pizza. You can't use coal or wood in your oven. You can't use gas heat in your store. You can't offer plastic forks and knives. You can't use a gasoline powered motorcycle or automobile to deliver the pizza. And, if you take the plaintiff's arguments to their logical conclusion, you shouldn't even pedal a bike, which increases a person's carbon emissions through heavy breathing.

"Your Honor, the fraud in this courtroom is the one perpetrated by the state. It is misleading the public to suggest that a climate catastrophe is near. No doubt, extreme weather events will certainly occur, just as they have throughout history. But don't be fooled that it's certain that these are caused by anthropogenic climate change. There is no evidence supporting that conclusion."

Bentley glanced at the jury box to see if he was getting the journalists' attention, but none of them met his eyes. He found that unfortunate, since he was about to make a few historical points that they didn't appear to know about.

"Long before the industrial revolution dramatically drove up the use of fossil fuels, the world saw many weather-related disasters that were far more deadly than anything we're seeing today," Bentley continued. "I'm sure you've heard of the Great Chicago Fire. It occurred in the autumn of 1871. The devastating fire followed a long period of unseasonably hot, dry, and windy conditions. It killed three hundred people, destroyed seventeen thousand buildings, and left nearly a third of the city's population homeless.

"No doubt, you're also aware of the Great Flood of 1889 in Johnstown, Pennsylvania. A dam burst after several days of extremely heavy rain, and the rushing water killed more than two thousand people.

"History is replete with such examples of extreme weather, yet the plaintiff would have you believe that weather-related disasters are a recent invention of the Crowe Power Company. That's nonsense. She would like you to imagine that Hurricane Sandy in 2012 was the fault of energy companies, yet the Galveston Hurricane of 1900 remains the deadliest Atlantic hurricane on record, with more than eight thousand people killed. At that time, carbon dioxide in the atmosphere was a third less than it is today."

Bentley turned to Felicity, who could become the next governor, but she was looking down at something in her lap, perhaps her phone. "The state needs to consider four questions when it comes to climate change. One, what is tolerable risk? Two, what is simply intolerance for the way people freely live their lives and how Crowe Power serves their wishes? Three, is a slight warming in temperature, regardless of the cause, worth stealing Lindsey Harper Crowe's business? And four, is climate change merely an excuse to reorder our society more to the plaintiff's liking?"

Bentley turned back to the judge to conclude his remarks. "Since the industrial revolution began, energy has been to modern economies what carbon dioxide is to plants. It's the source of life. The greater the quantity, the more abundance you get. It should not be casually discarded or placed in the hands of amateurs."

Bentley took his seat, and Lindsey leaned close. "That was eminently sensible."

He sighed. "Only to a sensible audience. Let's see what we have here."

37. SUMMERY JUDGMENT

On the morning of the expected verdict, carpenters hammered nails into a terraced media platform outside the New York County Courthouse, banging out a somber beat. A huge crowd of media was expected to record the final humiliation of Lindsey Harper Crowe and present her demise to their audiences as an abject lesson to climate deniers: *Get with the program!*

Lindsey eschewed a black shroud for her execution and chose instead a summery cream-colored outfit with splashes of green in her silk scarf and emerald earrings. Marty laughed to himself as he greeted her curbside amid the boisterous crowd clamoring for an execution.

"Green's a bit in-their-face," he said quietly.

"My quiet riot," she said as they climbed the steps to the courthouse. "I'm sure they'd rather see me in orange."

Every seat in the courtroom was filled, including the jury box, from which a steady stream of guilty verdicts had emanated from the media all week. The red light on the camera at the back of the room was back on to record the final drama, and two overflow rooms were at capacity. It was time to burn the witch who magically conjured wildfires, hurricanes, droughts, and other perversions of the climate.

As the room quieted, Justice Hardiman announced: "I find the defendant guilty of fraudulent business practices, as evidenced by her reckless disregard for the impact her company has made on our climate. Through her neglect of the scientific consensus on climate change, she has failed to warn the public about the continued use of her products. Had her customers been sufficiently educated, it is possible they would use less energy today. As a result, her company would produce fewer deadly emissions, and our planet would suffer less grievous injury. Moreover, her company would not need the extra capacity for energy generation she claims it needs to operate."

Bentley reached under the table and squeezed Lindsey's hand. She showed no emotion as she awaited the judicial guillotine that would sever her business ties in the Crowe Power Company's historic home.

"I am hereby cancelling Crowe Power's business certificates and placing all the company's assets in the State of New York in the hands of a receiver. This action will serve as recompense to the people of our state for Crowe Power's damage to our climate. It also serves to prevent further destruction of our planet by placing these assets in more responsible hands. Any entity providing power to the people holds a sacred public trust. Clearly, that trust was broken for reasons that can only be described as the defendant's reckless disregard for the citizens of our fair state and her utter lack of personal accountability."

Even though Lindsey had known this was coming, it still felt like a punch in the gut.

"Tomorrow," Hardiman continued, "we will begin the process of transferring control of the following properties to the people: Crowe Power Company headquarters at 62 Broad Street in Manhattan, the East River Powerhouse in Queens, all of Crowe Power's natural gas pipelines within the boundaries of the State of New York, and all entities related to electrical transmission within our borders. This court is adjourned."

The judge rapped his gavel, which led to an explosion of cheers from the gallery, and from the jury box, where reporters put their pens down to applaud. The bailiff called for all to rise as Hardiman left the courtroom for the safety of his chambers, a slug off a pint, and a friendly snuggle with his matron, Felicity Redfeather.

Lindsey turned to Bentley. "What's the penalty for grand larceny in this state?"

"Four years in Albany," Bentley replied, nodding toward Felicity.

"She deserves a sentence like that," Lindsey declared as Digby, Marty, Bits, Missy, and Tom gathered around her. "Let's wait here a moment before we go."

The jubilant crowd shuffled out of the courtroom, casting triumphant glances at the disgraced executives as they left. When the room cleared, Bentley faced Lindsey. "I know what you're going to say, and I can assure you: we're already on it. We're filing our appeal first thing in the morning."

Lindsey shook her head. "Don't," she said.

Bentley blanched. "I'm sorry?" He looked around at the others in the circle, all of whom registered surprise, if not shock.

"Obviously, I anticipated this verdict, Bentley. I've had a chance to think about whether it would make any sense to contest this. I concluded it wouldn't." She shrugged. "We're done here. Two Blue Eyes can have it."

"I know you're disappointed," he said. "But… seriously? You can't just give up."

"Oh yes, I can, at least as far as this state is concerned. Their hostility to me and to our business is more than I can take. The juice, as they say, isn't worth the squeeze. We have many other parts of our business we can build upon in more friendly environments."

Bentley saw an endless annuity of legal fees disappearing before his eyes. "Even if we were to lose on appeal, I could see this case going to the Supreme Court. There are important constitutional issues involved here. You could strike a blow for all corporations that are under pressure from antagonistic governments."

Lindsey squared up to Bentley. "And how many of those companies rose to my defense?" She made a circle with her thumb and index finger to indicate zero. "They'd rather mouth platitudes about how they're part of 'the solution,' whatever that is, and run for cover. No, Bentley, I'm not fighting their battles, and I'm finished with mine. Life is too short to spend years litigating one chunk of our legacy business that's only marginally profitable. You know, there are still places in this world where we're welcome. This state consumes way too much of my money, my time, my thoughts. I've already spoken to our board, and they agree. Let's cut our losses and get on with building our business elsewhere."

"I'm not sure how you do that," Bentley said.

"Well, we're doing it," Lindsey said, picking up her handbag. "Armani has run the financials. She's figured out how to write this off in a way that won't cause too much pain. My guess is that our stock will see a bump when people realize we're out of this hostile climate for good."

Lindsey and Tom were the last to leave the courtroom. Lindsey paused at the door, taking one last look at a place she vowed to never see again. She locked the image in her memory and stepped out into the corridor, where she was shocked to find Robbie leaning against a pillar looking at his phone.

"Wait here a moment," Lindsey told Tom.

"Are you sure?" Tom asked. "I don't want to see someone get hurt."

"Don't worry," Lindsey said, patting his arm. "I won't hurt him."

She approached Robbie and cleared her throat so that he would look up. "I thought of calling you as a character witness," Lindsey said, "but that would require you to have some."

Robbie batted his eyes innocently. "I'm sure you want to blame this verdict on me, like you blame everything else. But I take no pleasure in what happened in there."

"Right."

"Look," Robbie said, "this trial didn't have to go down the way it did. All they needed to hear from you was a little contrition, and a promise to do better. I don't know why you couldn't do that."

"That would require me to believe it. I don't."

"I'm not saying you have to mean it," Robbie insisted. "I'm saying you just have to say it."

Lindsey studied her ex, who reminded her with each encounter why dumping him was the best decision she'd ever made. "I know that's your standard MO, Robbie. But, unlike you, I'm a terrible liar. I also don't suffer fools, which means you've got another thirty seconds."

Robbie flinched but kept his cool. "Give me the keys."

"What?"

"You should step aside after this debacle and let me run the company," he said. "Take a break. Go back to hanging out with my sister. Go drinking. Go shopping. Do the stuff you're really cut out for. You're in over your head in this job, whether you know it or not."

"And make way for you?"

"I know how to work with these people," Robbie claimed. "I can get our assets back and get the company back on track."

"The track you were on? That was headed for bankruptcy." Lindsey struggled to contain her anger. "Let me tell you something, Robbie. That's the *last* thing I'm going to do. You were a lazy do-nothing inside the company, and you're even worse outside. Do you know that your little fortune cookie Li Zhang is an agent of the Chinese Communist Party?"

Robbie took a step back. Lindsey pressed her advantage and stepped forward. "And did you know her job was to infiltrate our company and that you helped her do it? We had a massive cyberattack thanks to your stupidity. And we know they're coming back. We just don't know when."

Robbie stuttered. "How was I supposed to know that?"

"You weren't," she said, "because you think with this." She reached out and grabbed his balls and squeezed as hard as she could.

He grabbed her arm to push it away and Lindsey released her grip. "What's the matter with you?" he asked.

"You're a menace to our company, Robbie. Not only are you not getting your job back, you're not welcome at Crowe Power anymore," Lindsey said. "I've cancelled your badge, shut down your email, and taken you off the family advisory committee."

"You can't do that."

"I can and I did."

Robbie ran a hand through his thinning hair. "You're just mad because of my testimony."

"You're damn right I am," she said. "I'm even more pissed that you put our company at risk yet again." She wagged a finger in his face. "Don't come around anymore." She pointed to Tom down the hall. "Or I guarantee you: one of us will kick your ass."

38. POWER TO THE PEOPLE

Felicity made her victory march down the courthouse steps, where she was applauded by cheering townspeople for slaying the fire-breathing climate dragon. With mere days to go before the primary, Felicity had struck electoral gold, and it showed. She beamed as she stepped up to the podium on the sidewalk and took the microphone. She gazed out at the dozens of staff and campaign workers beside her and the hundreds more supporters in the audience jostling for space behind the bank of TV cameras. ShaNeeNah had triumphed again! She had brought more wohelo to the world! *A few Honor Beads, please!*

"Today we took the first essential step toward healing our broken climate," Felicity said. "We have done so by achieving what we, the people, have long desired: a publicly owned, democratically run energy system. This is an essential step toward delivering an affordable and equitable transition to clean green bountiful energy. I think I can say without equivocation: *environmental justice is served!*"

The crowd roared its approval. "As we proved this week, Lindsey Harper Crowe and her company acted irresponsibly, shirking their duty to protect our community and our planet. But now, I believe it's safe to say: the days of corporate greed are over when it comes to energy in our state. Power is back where it belongs: in the hands of the people. The long-delayed transition away from fossil fuels begins right here and right now. No more pipelines for New York City. No more LNG. Today, we begin to heal."

The activists were ecstatic. They had brought down the plundering, polluting power structure built by the greedy Crowe family and placed their faith in the pandering populism of a Pretendian. What could go wrong?

Felicity called for quiet to introduce the receiver of Crowe Power's assets: Boyd Meriwether, a community organizer and doctoral candidate in Translocational Positionality at Bartleby College.

"Thank you, Attorney General Redfeather! And thank you, New York!" Boyd bellowed. "It's a great honor to be part of this long overdue celebration. I know that a lot of you in community groups and in the non-profit sector worked tirelessly to achieve this outcome. I, for one, am deeply gratified that it is finally here. As Attorney General Redfeather stated in court, clean energy is a right. And starting today, we are going to ensure that all New Yorkers lead the world in ending our society's sick addiction to fossil fuels. And we can do that because all these assets will be publicly owned and operated by you—" he pointed to the crowd, "the *people!*"

The crowd roared its approval as Boyd continued. "Remember this historic moment: day one for New York's first collectively owned non-profit energy company, People's Power!"

With that, a banner unfurled behind him, featuring the logo of the new company: a red raised fist in a power salute holding a yellow lightning bolt against a black background, with the words PEOPLE'S POWER stenciled underneath.

As the crowd cheered, Felicity leaned in. "Let's go see our new HQ."

The People's Power banner was brought to the front of a procession, as was Lindsey's papier-mâché head on a spike. Felicity took Boyd's hand and led the way down Centre Street as the environmentally minded crowd noisily fell in line behind them, blasting vuvuzelas, rattling cans with peas inside, pounding hockey sticks, blowing horns, smoking joints, and leaving the grounds behind them littered with coffee cups, paper, plastic bottles, discarded blankets, and signs.

Police on motorcycles cleared a path as the crowd marched past the Tweed Courthouse, a historic monument to New York's long history of political corruption, followed by City Hall, the more contemporary vessel for contractor payoffs. Then it was onto Nassau Street through the Financial District, passing Federal Hall, the site where George Washington took his presidential oath of office, and the New York Stock Exchange, where a symbol showed CRO up four percent in heavy trading. By the time the procession reached Crowe Power Company Headquarters, half the marchers had dropped off to seek relief from the heat in air-conditioned coffee shops, bars, and restaurants, where they could charge their phones and upload their videos showing how they stood up to The Man.

Or in this case, The Woman.

39. MOVERS AND SHAKERS

Two eras ended on an unseasonably cool day at the end of June. Governor Frank Cardini was beaten soundly in his primary bid for re-election by Felicity Redfeather, virtually assuring that she would be the next governor in the one-party state. And Lindsey Harper Crowe's last day in her New York office was spent supervising the packing of her files, mementos, and company artifacts. The new owners of what had been the Crowe Power Headquarters for nearly one hundred years were scheduled to take possession the following day.

"They're here now," Winnie announced in the doorway.

"Who's here?" Lindsey asked.

"The movers for People's Power."

"No, no, no," Lindsey snapped. "That's not right." She stepped quickly into the reception area, where she encountered Boyd Meriwether and his team of movers lifting the bronze bust of Homer Crowe off its stand.

"Do *NOT* touch that!" she commanded.

The workers looked at her.

"What do you think you're doing?" she demanded to know.

The workers put the bust down and stood up. Boyd turned to her. "We're moving in," he declared triumphantly. "And you're moving out."

"Not until tomorrow," she insisted.

They didn't move.

"Get *out!*" she said heatedly.

Boyd huffed and puffed but retreated. She followed him into the hallway to make sure he and his crew found the exit. There, she saw her own movers taking down the portraits of Homer Crowe and his descendants from the walls of the Hall of Fam. The visages of Lester Crowe, Charles Crowe, Robbie Crowe, and Lindsey had all been removed from the gallery and set on the floor. On the opposite side, People's Power artwork celebrated the uprising of climate activists around the world and their seizure of Crowe Power properties.

There was a print of the Mona Lisa spattered with orange paint. A color photo of a climate march with a banner proclaiming: *We're on Fire!* A charred planet dripping blood. A portrait of climate savant Rainwater Jones wearing a keffiyeh as she was carried from a protest by police. A black-and-white photo of Felicity addressing her fans outside the courthouse following Lindsey's conviction. The largest piece of all was the sculptural red-fisted logo of People's Power, which was destined to replace the bust of Homer Crowe.

Lindsey looked at the collection and turned to Marty, who had just come up the elevator.

"Barbarians are not at the gates," Lindsey said. "They're inside."

Marty looked at the bust of Homer Crowe on the floor. "They love toppling icons in this town, don't they?"

"It's what they put up instead that scares me," Lindsey said.

She returned to her inner sanctum to continue her own packing as Marty followed her in. Winnie appeared at the door.

"Lindsey, it's Governor Cardini on the line," she said.

Lindsey was puzzled. "Why in the world would he call now?"

"Shall I tell him you're not here?"

"No," she said, glancing at her watch. "I can speak to him." She pushed the button on her telephone console and Frank came on.

"Looks like we both took it on the chin," Frank said.

"I had an assist from you," Lindsey said.

"I did what I had to do," Frank replied dully.

"I don't know who was advising you, Frank, or if you were just following your own worst instincts. But you can't beat Felicity at her own game. You could have stood up to her. You still might have lost, but at least you would have shown some guts."

"Like you did?" he said. "What did that get you? A one-way ticket to Jersey?"

"It's only temporary. I'm moving the company to Florida," she said. "And frankly, Frank, I can't wait. What are you going to do?"

"I dunno yet," he said. "Did you hear they're dropping the sexual harassment suit against me?"

"Not surprised," Lindsey said. "It served its purpose."

Frank sighed. "Yeah, well… I didn't harass all those women, you know."

"That's a relief," she said. "It made me wonder why I was the only woman in the state of New York you didn't grope. I mean, what am I? Chopped liver?"

"You may find this hard to believe, but I have too much respect for you to consider such a thing," he said.

Lindsey chuckled. "C'mon, Frank. You're pulling my leg—figuratively, anyway. Are you grooming me for another donation? Is that why you're calling?"

"Not at all," he said. "I just have this sense it's not the end for either one of us in this state. I know we're both a little bruised right now. But I'm not giving up. I hope you don't either."

Lindsey considered his pitch. "Never say never, but... never," she said flatly. "That said, I think Felicity and her team are in for a rough time with our assets. They have no idea what they're getting into."

"Well, that's still my responsibility through the end of the year, which is why I'd like you to stay close."

"Alright. I get it now, Frank," she said. "How about this? I'm happy to provide a little friendly advice if you need it. But that's as far as I'm willing to go."

"I can live with that," he said. "Keep in touch, will ya?"

Lindsey hung up the phone. "I think he's worried about the power plant."

"He should be," Marty said.

"How long do you think Dexter's going to last with the new regime?"

"My over/under is Halloween."

"I'll take that bet," Lindsey said. "I'd be surprised if he makes it past Labor Day."

40. A NEW YORK STATE OF MIND

As Dexter watched over the control room at the East River Powerhouse, he wondered how long he could last without blowing somebody's brains out—his or theirs. All the protocols he had established over the past ten years to ensure energy dependability had been set aside by Boyd Meriwether and the People's Power Revolutionary Work Council. Every decision was to be made through a lens of racial, social, and ecological justice, rather than heat, light, and power.

"Dexter?"

He turned to see a young person of undetectable gender.

"You're wanted in the conference room."

Dexter could only guess what this latest incursion was about. He followed his courier into a conference room where the walls were festooned with manifestos and directives about the Council's mission to create an equitable, diverse, and inclusive workplace.

"Dexter," said Boyd, who was sitting at the end of the table. "Come on in. Have a seat." He glanced at his watch. "A few other peoples will be joining us in a moment or so."

Peoples? On cue, six members of the new management team entered the room and took chairs around the table. At the sight of them, Dexter confirmed in his own mind that he had not been called in to receive a promotion. None of the new managers had any appreciation for the responsibilities of running a power plant. Ten minutes into a tour of the control room during her first day on the job, Betty Biddle, the new head of HR, decided it looked no more difficult than playing a video game, and declared it time for a break.

Boyd said, "Betty, why don't you get things started?"

Betty sat up and folded her hands on the tabletop.

"Dexter, did you read the DEI materials that we sent around?" she asked.

"Can't say I have," Dexter replied, scratching his chin. "We've been kinda busy working in some new equipment."

"For what?"

"To keep our energy flows balanced."

"They're not balanced?"

"No, they are," Dexter said. "But that's because we work very hard to keep it that way."

Betty looked at Boyd and rolled her eyes. She turned back to Dexter. "You think that's what we're about here?"

"It's an important part of our job," Dexter replied.

Boyd leaned forward and stabbed the table with his index finger. "Well, this is *very* important."

"I'm listening."

"That's good," Boyd said. "Because, as you know, we're building a culture of diversity and inclusivity at People's Power. We want to make sure you're bought in."

Dexter shrugged. "I'm cool."

"That's good," Boyd said. "See, under People's Power's new regime, we're all about tolerance—with one exception. We do not tolerate a difference of opinion on the matter of diversity, equity, and inclusion. In fact, we have zero tolerance for intolerance directed against people who have historically not been tolerated." Boyd studied Dexter for a reaction, but he looked puzzled. "You, um… *dig?*"

Dexter pursed his lips. "No."

Boyd picked up a notebook. "Let me put the question to you more bluntly: are you on board with our DEI initiative, or aren't you?"

Dexter looked around at the seven pale faces around the table. "No offense, but I don't need DEI to get ahead. Maybe you do, I don't know. As far as I'm concerned, it attaches a stigma to people that I don't appreciate. People look at you and wonder, 'did they get the job because they know their stuff? Or are they checking a box on some scorecard a boss is using to get ahead?' I need people next to me who can do their job. And I don't care what color they are, who they sleep with, how they worship, or what they eat or don't eat."

Betty studied Dexter. "I'm curious, Dexter. Do you identify as a black man?"

Dexter looked at her incredulously. "Are you visually impaired in some way?"

"No..." Betty said uncertainly.

Boyd interjected. "Dexter, please understand. She asks you that question out of respect."

"You call that respect?"

"Absolutely," Boyd said.

Dexter held up his arm. "You think this is a tan?"

"Well, no," Betty said. "It's just that..."

Dexter glared at her. "It's just what?"

"You don't think like a black man," she said.

"Is that right?" Dexter said. "How is a black man supposed to think?"

"Well... like you think, of course. Only different."

"Different how?"

Boyd squirmed. "Well, for one thing, you seem really hung up on data," he said. "We all know the use of data is a construct of white privilege to prevent inclusivity."

"You can't run a power plant without data," Dexter replied. "How do you not understand that?"

They looked at him blankly.

Dexter sighed. "I've got to get back to work," he said. He stood to leave.

Boyd picked up a piece of paper. "Hold on, Dexter. There's a personnel issue we need to discuss."

Dexter pointed with his thumb to the control room. "I've got an operation to run," he said.

"We need to talk about this *now*," Boyd insisted.

Dexter sighed heavily and sat back down.

Betty said, "We have a report that you mis-gendered a colleague."

"When?"

"Yesterday," she said.

"Who?"

"You referred to KJ as 'he,' when KJ prefers 'zhe.'"

Dexter blinked hard. "I didn't know he was a zhe."

Betty looked at Boyd and sadly shook her head. "There he goes, Boyd. He did it again."

"I did what again?" Dexter asked.

"You said 'he.'" Boyd said. "KJ is a *zhe!*"

"You know what? Fine. I'll call her—"

"Not her!" Betty exclaimed. "*Zher!*"

"—Zher." Dexter slapped his forehead. "Whatever zhe wants, zhe gets. I really don't give a flying fuck."

Boyd sadly shook his head. "That doesn't sound tolerant at all."

Dexter clenched his jaw. "It's not."

"See? That's the problem, Dexter," Betty said. "This is one of our core principles at People's Power. We're all about *people*. It's your duty to know the preferred pronouns of your colleagues."

Dexter took a deep breath. "I don't understand this. We seem to get along fine. Did zhe complain?" he asked.

"No," said Betty. "He did." She pointed to the back of the room at Elliott, a short balding person, presumably a man, with a gnarly sweater and horn-rimmed glasses.

Dexter turned to him. "You did?"

Elliott sniffed. "Yes," he said.

"Who are you?"

"I'm Elliott Grindleburg, director of environmental justice."

"Elliott? That's your name? Seriously?"

"Yes," he said, icily.

"The last shitstorm that blew through here was named Elliott, too."

"I take exception to that."

Dexter nodded. "Well, here's what I'm taking, Elliott—the next bus out of town." He flung his ID badge on the table. "I'm hopping a Greyhound on the Hudson River line. Good luck with your revolution, comrades. Try not to blow up the plant."

PART THREE

Ivan the Terrible

41. A GATHERING STORM

For the first time in five years, an extreme weather event in New York wasn't Lindsey's problem. It was just another good reason to get out of town.

Safely removed from the city at her temporary headquarters in a New Jersey high-rise overlooking the Hudson River, she stood at her desk packing a phone, keys, and a week's worth of reading materials into her handbag to spend the holidays in the Caribbean with Marty, Missy, and Chase.

"Lindsey," Winnie said at the door to Lindsey's office. "Governor Cardini is on the line for you."

Lindsey laughed. "I thought his term was up."

"Not until January 1," Winnie replied. "He says it's urgent."

Lindsey sighed. "Alright. Guess I can take a minute."

"Line one," Winnie said, before closing the door behind her.

Lindsey pushed a button on her speaker phone and heard Frank Cardini's voice.

"Lindsey, this is your governor."

She played dumb. "Governor Wertheimer. What a pleasure," she said, warmly.

"Your governor in *New York*, smart ass—at least until the end of the month," Frank said. "You still live in my state, don't you?"

"Not for the next two weeks," she conceded. "I'm outta here."

"Where are you going?" Frank demanded to know.

"I don't believe I owe you an explanation," she said, looking at her watch. "But if you must know, I'm heading to St. Bart's for the holidays."

"Have you heard the weather reports?"

"Eighty degrees and sunshine."

"For *New York*."

"The forecast calls for an extended period of high taxes, hostility to business, and poor governance," Lindsey replied. "Did I leave anything out?"

"Our weather. In case you haven't heard, Winter Storm Ivan is on its way," Frank said. "It's the freaking storm of the century."

"Yeah. Well, there's one every year it seems," Lindsey said.

"This one sounds like the real deal."

"Did you call to give me the weather, Frank? I could have gotten it off my phone."

"I called to say you can't leave now, not with Ivan barreling toward us."

"Pretty sure I can," she insisted. "I don't think it's within your jurisdiction to stop me. I'm in Jersey, in case you've forgotten." She glanced out the window toward Lower Manhattan, which suddenly seemed light years away. To the south of the World Trade Center, she could make out the peak of her company's old headquarters on Broad Street, now topped by a logo for People's Power. There was no sign of a storm yet, but dark political clouds were surely gathering to the north in Albany. Otherwise, Frank wouldn't be so worried. "I've got to be at the Teterboro airport by one if I'm going to beat this storm."

Marty entered her office pulling his rollaboard. He was dressed in khakis, a red Tommy Bahama shirt with palm trees, and a windbreaker. Lindsey looked at him aghast and muted the phone. "We're going to St. Bart's, not Orlando."

Marty looked down and shrugged. *What's the difference?*

Lindsey returned her attention to the governor as Marty flopped on her sofa, glumly tapping the handle of his suitcase.

"Please, Lindsey." Frank's tone was desperate, almost as if he needed just five dollars more to meet that week's fundraising goal. "The people running your old powerhouse don't know a control switch from a doorknob. They don't even answer the phone. I have zero confidence they can keep our power on in this shitstorm."

"Who's running the show over there?"

"*The People!*" Frank said. "And they're doing whatever the hell they like!"

"That's a shame, Frank. But you know, the People, or the Peoples, or whatever they call themselves, got exactly what they asked for," she said tersely. "It's not my problem."

"It's your plant," he insisted.

"You broke it. You bought it."

"I didn't break it," Frank pleaded. "That was Felicity."

She laughed bitterly. "You did your part," she said.

"Lindsey, look. I'm sorry, alright? I know you're probably still pissed at me..."

Lindsey seethed. "Pissed? No, no." She sat down on the edge of her desk and took a deep breath before plunging ahead. "I'm past that, Frank. I'm done with you, Two Blue Eyes, and your entire state. I warned you a long time ago what could happen in a storm, but you wouldn't listen. Now you have idealogues running a power plant. How stupid is that? You may as well hand toddlers a box of matches. Congratulations to you, Governor, and to your successor. You've got the climate catastrophe you always predicted. Merry Christmas."

There was a long pause as the governor considered another tack. "Linz—" *baby, sweetheart, darling*—"you and I can sort out later what happened and why. Right now, I need you to help me prevent a humanitarian crisis."

"Which is... what? You could lose the next election, too?"

Frank paused to collect himself. "If this storm goes down like I'm thinking, I'll be hurt, sure, but so will a lot of other people. We've already had a run on supermarkets and gas stations. The store shelves and gas pumps are empty. Now people can't even leave if they want to. They've cancelled all flights out of LGA and JFK after 6 o'clock tonight. And the roads out of town are impossible."

Lindsey winced. "All good reasons to leave."

"Put aside how you feel about me for a moment," he implored her. "How are you gonna relax on a beach while this city faces a disaster you could have helped us prevent?" Frank asked. "If this goes down the way it looks, and the power goes out, people are going to die. It may be hundreds. It may be thousands. It may be a lot more than that. And if that happens, yeah, the blame will be on me, and maybe on Felicity Redfeather. But you're still going to have to live with yourself, and I don't know how you're going to do that. You're a better person than this."

"You're testing that concept, Frank."

"I'm testing your character," he said.

Lindsey sighed. "Hold on a sec." She muted the phone and looked at Marty, who was laying back on her sofa with his hands clasped behind his head while he idly stared at the ceiling. "What do you think, Marty?"

"I'd prefer to dip my toes in sand rather than snow." He sat up. "Wouldn't you?"

She gnawed a fingernail. "I don't know how I refuse him."

"That's your problem, Linz. You've got a conscience."

"And you don't?"

"Not that I'm aware of."

Lindsey unmuted the phone and resumed her conversation with the governor. "What is it exactly you think I can do?"

"We've got—what?—twenty-four hours before we feel the full brunt of this storm. I need your people to go back to the East River Powerhouse and make an assessment," he said. "Can the crew we have over there get us through this storm or not? And if they can't, how can your people help?"

"The court revoked my permit to work in New York."

"I'll override that," he said. "It's a State of Emergency. I'll issue an Executive Order."

"Felicity would file an injunction and—"

"*Fuck* Felicity! She's not in charge here. I am! We're wasting time, Lindsey!" Frank said. "I'll worry about the politics and the law. I need you to worry about the powerhouse."

Lindsey walked to the other side of her office and craned her head to look west. She could see a long line of unusually dark clouds on the horizon. "I don't know who on our team is even around," she said, walking back to her phone. "People have plans for the holidays, including me, and my plane leaves in an hour."

Frank exploded. "Don't give me that shit! You're on a private jet! I've got the tail numbers right here on my computer. Your plane is sitting out on the tarmac right now, ready to leave whenever you say, 'wheels up.' All I'm asking is that you hold off for a while to help me sort this out. Assure me the plant is operating the right way, and I'll get you a police escort to Teterboro."

"Can you get me a snowplow, too?"

"Whatever it takes."

She looked toward the door, where her suitcase stood. "Let me talk to my people and see what—if anything—we can do. I can't guarantee results."

"I guarantee one result, Lindsey," he said. "You'll sleep better knowing you did the right thing."

HOSTILE CLIMATE

Lindsey said, "I doubt I'll sleep at all."

42. DAMNED IF THEY DON'T

A deeply disappointed Marty shook his head as Lindsey hung up. "Nobody pulls off a snow job like Frank Cardini."

Lindsey shrugged. "I'm sorry. What else could I do?"

Marty shrugged helplessly.

"How does Christmas in Queens sound?" she asked.

"Like a bad episode of *All in the Family*."

"I hope you packed warm clothes," she said.

"That wasn't exactly the plan when I got up this morning."

"Well, neither was this." She flicked on the local news on television, where coverage of the approaching Winter Storm Ivan was breathless. While she had learned long ago to discount forecasts of the latest Snowmageddon, Ivan had already made a convincing case that it was the real deal. Temperatures in the Upper Midwest had plummeted forty-six degrees in five hours. Blizzard conditions blanketed the Dakotas and there were whiteouts in the Great Plains. Freezing rain and heavy snowfalls were reported all the way down to Texas and as far east as Ohio. It was all headed New York's way, with snow beginning in the afternoon, gusty winds picking up in the evening, and temperatures plunging around noon the following day.

"If you want to go, go ahead," Lindsey said. "You can take the plane. I'll meet you down there when I can."

"You're going to stay?"

"I don't know," she said. "I need to talk to the team first." She looked at Marty, who was clearly feeling sorry for himself. "You don't have to stick around."

Marty took a deep breath. "No, no. I'm not leaving unless you are. I don't know if I could drink enough pina coladas to forget about what you're going through up here."

Lindsey nodded. "Thank you." She hit the button on her intercom. "Winnie, I'd like you to organize a conference call for one o'clock. I need everyone on the leadership team to attend, so follow up with phone calls to make sure they get the message."

Lindsey walked to her bank of windows on the east side of her office. She could only imagine what was going on over at the powerhouse. It had come perilously close to disaster several times under Crowe Power's competent professional management. What was the risk profile now that it was operated by Felicity's climate crusaders?

Lindsey brewed a cup of coffee in her pantry and settled into the chair at the head of the table in her conference room to face the screen. Marty looked on from his laptop on the sofa back in her office to make it appear they were in two different places. She scanned the assembling checkerboard of faces, few of whom were at company facilities. Most of her team members were already visiting their families in other states, sitting poolside in Florida, shopping for last-minute presents, or preparing holiday meals.

"Thank you all for calling in. I know many of you are out of town for the holidays," Lindsey said. "As you may have heard, we have a winter storm approaching the city that appears very dangerous. Governor Cardini has asked for our help." Her comment elicited a collective groan from the assembled leadership team before she read through the particulars. Weather emergencies had been declared in eight states so far, with a dozen people killed in car crashes on icy roads. Another twenty-two people had died from exposure, electrocution from downed power lines, falling through ice into frigid water, or getting crushed by falling tree limbs. In Detroit, a power failure prompted a desperate family to start a fire inside their wooden frame home to get warm, leading to a fast-spreading inferno and six more deaths.

"My first question is this: do we help, or don't we?" Lindsey asked.

Lucy bristled. "Are you kidding? After what the state did to us?"

"Especially after what they did to you personally," Armani added. "As far as I'm concerned, they're on their own."

Digby shook his head and blinked hard. "I'm shocked you'd even consider this, Lindsey. It sounds to me like the governor is setting you up as a scapegoat."

Lindsey acknowledged the risk. "I have no illusions about how this could play out," she said. "If we jump in and the powerhouse fails, he's going to stick it to us."

"And if we help avert a tragedy, Frank Cardini takes credit for bold leadership," Digby said. "It's lose-lose. You'll get credit for nothing."

Lindsey sighed. "Honestly, I could care less about credit. I'm worried about what's going to happen to innocent people whose lives are endangered through no fault of their own." She looked at the people in the squares and saw Marty running his hand through his hair as he studied his laptop. "Marty, what's your take?"

Marty put his hand down and sighed. "Much as it might ruin your holidays: this is what your company is all about."

"What do you mean?" Lindsey asked.

"Energy is your product. But your service is that you help people. You take care of their most fundamental needs even when they don't realize it, acknowledge it, or appreciate it. You're an essential part of their support system. You've always been there for them when they turn on a light switch, charge their phones, turn on the oven, or turn on the heat. You are dependable, reliable, and always willing to help, especially in times of greatest need."

"That's lovely, Marty," Lindsey said.

"It should be. I'm reading it on your website."

"Oh."

"Jesus," Lucy said, with a laugh. "You can't hold that against us."

"Is it true?" Marty said. "Are you who you say you are? Or was this just some corporate BS to throw the public?" He paused and studied the skeptical faces on the screen. "I know the people of New York turned their back on you. That doesn't mean you turn your back on them. It's still your hometown."

"They stole our assets," Lucy said emphatically.

"I'm not justifying what they did," Marty said. "But you can't let yourselves be defined by your critics. You need to define yourselves. You do that most convincingly when your actions match your words." He tapped his screen. "This is who you say you are. If it's true, it's something to be proud of, maybe even to fight for."

Lindsey sucked in her breath and looked at the others. "I think we have to try," she said.

Lucy made a 'T' with her hands. "Timeout, Lindsey," Lucy said. "You do know what we're signing up for, right? We're already struggling with our power plants in the Midwest. They call this storm 'Ivan the Terrible' for a reason."

"How terrible is it?"

"We've reduced output at our plants in Missouri and Nebraska, and we're bringing in extra crews in Illinois and Kentucky to make repairs in the field. My biggest worry is the grid. Given the size of this storm, all the regional power authorities are getting peak demand for electricity at the same time. If that holds, we won't have the opportunity to import power from elsewhere. We'll be on our own, and we won't have enough gas. That plant's at the end of the pipelines."

Lindsey sighed. "Does anyone have intel on the People's Power team running the plant?"

"I know Dexter quit months ago," Lucy said. "Last I heard, the people who worked for him were training a new crew to take their jobs so People's Power could hit their diversity quotas."

Lindsey had heard enough. "Tom, call the governor's office. Make sure they issue security passes for everyone on our team—including Dexter. Marty, you know him. "

"I know he doesn't answer his phone."

"Can we get him to come in?"

Marty sighed. "I don't know. I hear he's deep in the Gunks."

Lindsey shook her head. "Aren't we all…"

"I mean he lives in the Shawangunk Mountains," Marty said.

"How far away is that?"

"Couple hours by car."

Lindsey nodded. "Pull him out of his Gunks, will you? And get him to the powerhouse."

43. MOUNTAIN MAN

Marty barely remembered how to drive as he steered his ten-year old Audi Q5 up a winding road in the Shawangunk Mountains. With so many transportation options in Manhattan, Marty rarely drove. His car had gathered dust in the cheapest garage he could find, a half-mile from his apartment.

"Turn right in two hundred feet," came the directions from his phone.

Marty slowed as a pickup truck came racing around on his left, nearly running him off the road. Marty waited for the truck to pass, caught his breath, then turned onto a gravel driveway and followed it up a hill to a clearing. He came upon a rustic cabin with solar panels on the roof and a wind turbine peeking out over a shed in the back. Was this Dexter's place?

Boom! A gunshot answered the question.

"What the *fuck!*" Marty yelped. He turned to see Dexter grinning at his driver's side window, tapping the glass with the barrel of his handgun.

"You lost, city boy?" Dexter laughed.

Marty rolled down the window and felt a blast of cold air. "In more ways than you know." He shut the window, opened the door, and felt Ivan's first flurries land on his ears. "That's some welcome," Marty said as he stretched.

Dexter slapped him on the back. "I don't care much for visitors."

"Could have fooled me."

"Come on up."

They climbed the steps to the cabin, which featured a large pine-paneled room with a bed, a kitchen, a sofa, and a couple of chairs. Dexter invited Marty to join him in front of a crackling fieldstone fireplace and offered him coffee.

Marty waved him off. "We don't have a lot of time."

"We?"

"I hope it's 'we.'"

"We what?"

"We are preventing a possible catastrophe, I hope. Frank Cardini, who's Governor of New York for—" he looked at his watch, "the next eight days, is worried that the lunatics running your old asylum don't know what they're doing."

"This is an historic day, Marty."

"How's that?"

"For once, I agree with that asshole," Dexter said. He nodded toward the snow, now falling a bit harder outside. "This is no time for amateurs."

"Is that who's running the show?"

"They were training a bunch of hippies to take over the control room when I left," Dexter said. "We had a PhD candidate in philosophy. A 'street theatre professional,' whatever that is. There was a beekeeper, a poet, and a goat herder. None of them had any experience in running a power plant. Their bosses were public defenders and community organizers. But I'm tellin' you, brother: they couldn't organize a bag lunch." He shook his head in wonder. "And they took Lindsey Harper Crowe to court to put those dumbasses in charge? What kind of bullshit was that?"

"Do any of your people still work there?"

"All of them. But they're leaving the first of the year—forced out because they don't check the right boxes. And with the holidays, who knows if they're still around. I doubt the People's Revolutionary Work Council cancelled vacations. They gave one dude a month off because his dog had puppies."

Marty looked at his watch. "Can you help?"

Dexter sighed. The powerhouse was his baby, even if it had been kidnapped, tortured, and possibly mortally wounded. What choice did he have? "I'll get my go-bag." He stood, picked up his pistol from the table, and tucked it in his waistband.

"You think you're going to need that?" Marty asked.

Dexter shrugged. "I'm taking it so I don't."

In the car ride back to the city, Marty listened to weather reports on the radio while Dexter sat in the passenger seat, calling and texting his former team members, checking availability, and gathering intel about the current operations. Overhearing one of Dexter's pleas to a former colleague, Marty said, "Tell her we'll pay double."

That piqued Dexter's interest. He covered the phone. "I can do that?"

Marty nodded as he watched the road. "There's no time to negotiate. Do whatever it takes."

Dexter barked into the phone, "I'll pay you triple overtime."

"I didn't say that!" Marty protested.

Dexter covered the phone. "This is Jeanette, my old admin. I'll need her."

"Alright," Marty said with a wave. "Fine."

By the time they reached Queens, Dexter told Marty he'd gathered enough information from his former teammates to understand the depth of the challenge.

"Is it as bad as I think it is?" Marty asked as he turned onto the RFK Bridge toward Queens.

"You see the movie, *Titanic*?" Dexter asked.

"Too many times."

"We're heading for the iceberg. And we've got stoners in the wheelhouse." Dexter leaned over to see how fast Marty was going. "Can you move this crate a little faster?"

"Not if I want to stay on the road," Marty said.

"Pull over," Dexter said. "I'll drive."

"Oh, hell no," Marty said. "You can drive the powerhouse once we get there. That will be enough excitement for me."

44. TAKING THE WHEEL

Marty and Dexter arrived at the East River Powerhouse as darkness descended on Queens. The lights in the parking lot illuminated the light snow that had begun to fall more steadily. Marty parked his car near the employee entrance as the afternoon shift's trainees and supervisors exited carrying gifts from their holiday luncheon.

Evan Beckwith, who had replaced Dexter as plant superintendent, wore a cockeyed Santa hat on his way to the car. He had the bleary-eyed look of a man who had been partying all afternoon and needed a nap.

"Yo, Evan. Hold up," Dexter called.

Evan stopped in his tracks.

Dexter asked, "Where's everybody goin'?"

"Show's over, Dex," Evan said. "Best office party ever. Karaoke was hilarious. You should have seen—"

Dexter cut him off. "Wait a second. You had a party? *Today?*"

Evan rolled his eyes. "It's the holidays, man. *Helloooo.*" He resumed walking.

"Evan!" Dexter called.

Evan stopped in his tracks and glared at Dexter. *What?*

"Who's running the show in there?" Dexter asked.

"It's, um... I dunno. What's-her-face. Maggie, Melanie, Margaret. Somethin'." He paused, thinking. "What do you care? Didn't you quit?"

Dexter held up his hands. "You know there's a shitstorm heading this way?"

"Of course I do," Evan scoffed. "Why do you think I'm getting the hell out of here? Gotta get to my in-laws in Pittsburgh before the roads turn to crap."

Evan continued to his car. Dexter called after him. "What about the powerhouse?"

"I'm clocked out," Evan called. He dismissed Dexter with a wave of his hand.

"I can't believe that," Marty said to Dexter.

"Good thing he's leaving. If Margaret's in there, we're better off without him," Dexter replied. "Let's go." As they headed toward the employee entrance, they were caught in the headlights of an approaching Subaru with its horn tooting. Dexter waved and waited for Jeanette, whom Marty sensed immediately was an all-business administrator. The three of them headed for the employee entrance, where a member of Tom's security team handed them badges that would allow them access to all buildings on the property.

They hustled down the corridor and entered the control room, where a warning flashed on one of the big screens: an Energy Emergency Watch had just been issued by the New York grid operator. It asked the state's energy customers to reduce their energy usage immediately by turning down thermostats to sixty-two degrees, turning off holiday lights, and avoiding unnecessary cooking.

"Good luck with that," Dexter said. "My aunt in Brownsville is burning up the kitchen right now." At the center of the room, Dexter was relieved to find his former colleague, Margaret Quinlan, on the bridge. After greeting her with a quick hug, he said, "Thank God you're here. You're the floor manager?"

"I'm not sure. Evan's supposed to be on duty," she said, looking around. "But we haven't seen him."

"He's on his way to Pittsburgh," Dexter said.

Margaret's jaw dropped. "No."

"I just saw him in the parking lot. He was loading up his trunk."

"That jerk." She groaned. "He left me a mess, and no time to clean it up."

"You just got yourself a battlefield commission," Dexter said. "I need you to run point in here."

"You can order that?" she asked.

"I just did." He looked around the room. "Who's up?"

"You've got your A-team. Consuela. Steve. Luis. Their shift just started."

"Why are they working a holiday shift?"

"The new hires were all granted seniority over your people. Something about equity."

"For tonight, anyway, that might turn out to be a blessing." He turned toward the wall that displayed constantly updated reports and recognized instantly why Margaret was so distressed.

On one screen was the Weather Channel, showing rapidly falling temperatures in Ohio and Pennsylvania. Winds were gusting up to sixty miles per hour. The precipitation pattern was a hellish mix of freezing rain, sleet, and blowing snow, falling at the rate of two inches an hour around the Great Lakes.

Trend lines for energy supply and demand were moving in opposite directions. The forecast for electric consumption indicated a steady rise over the next six hours as homes began to chill under the plummeting temperatures outside, but demand was projected to rise even more rapidly the following day when the mercury would drop to zero. Meanwhile, the monitor tracking supply showed a sharp decline.

"What's the problem with supply?" Dexter asked.

"Everything," Margaret replied.

Dexter said, "I'll make the rounds."

Dexter summoned Jeanette to follow him as he walked over to the desk that managed a small network of peaking power plants that were called upon in emergencies. Consuela Corazon, the woman handling auxiliary power, shrugged helplessly. "Wellheads are frozen again in the Marcellus. We can't get gas."

"Nothing for the peakers?"

"Sorry," she said. "I'm looking for a work-around."

The walls shuddered as a wind gust smacked into the building, making the overhead lights flicker. Dexter locked eyes with Consuela. "Preview of coming attractions," she said.

Dexter patted the back of her chair. "Let's hope it's not a horror movie."

He walked to the next desk where veteran dispatcher Steve Mitchell managed imports and exports of electricity with other systems in the eastern US.

"Hey, brother," Dexter said, offering a handshake.

"Hey, Dex," Steve said. "Great to see you. You back in the saddle?"

"Until the horse throws me again," he replied. "Finding any power?"

Steve sighed. "Santa better drop coal in my stocking so I have something to burn," he said. "Everyone's tapped out."

"Nothing?"

"I've begged. I've borrowed. I'd steal if I could. Got a few commitments early in the day, only to get cancelled at the last minute. Everyone's struggling. They're dipping into their reserves to cover their own requirements." He nodded toward a map of the grid covered with purple, black and blue circles indicating outages. "See for yourself. Twenty percent of the generating units in the Eastern Interconnection are knocked out already."

Dexter took a deep breath. "Nothing from TVA? Carolinas? Kentucky?"

"They're all having blackouts. Our only hope may be a break in the weather." Steve called over to the next desk where Luis Menendez, the in-house weather forecaster, nervously pecked at his computer keyboard as he studied an array of maps and monitors. "Throw me some sunshine, Luis."

Luis didn't turn around. "Sorry, Steve," he shouted. "National Weather Service says we're stuck with this system until Tuesday."

Dexter absorbed that news and moved back to the center of the room, where he scanned all the meters, looking for answers. Finally, he turned and spoke to Margaret and Marty. "I have some thoughts. Might even be a plan," he said. "We'll have to move fast. Marty, can you get HQ on the line?"

Marty nodded toward the door. "HQ is here."

Lindsey had just stepped inside the door, knocking the light dusting of snow off her boots.

"Good," Dexter said. "I'll also need the governor."

"Lindsey's got his number," Marty said.

"Get the mayor, too," Dexter said.

"On it," Jeanette replied

"We'll meet upstairs," Dexter commanded. "I'll be there in a sec." He walked to the front of the room and clapped his hands loudly. All the heads looked up from their computers.

"Listen up, people," he said. "Just want to say I'm glad to see you all. Not the best circumstances, but you're the best people this plant's ever had. I don't know who's scheduled to relieve you, but I want to ask that you stick around through tomorrow. I know it will be Christmas Eve and many of you have plans, but this is no time for on-the-job training. I need pros. Which means I need you. Can you stay with me?"

It was less a request than a command, but Dexter saw nodding of heads as he scanned the room. Steve called out, "We got your six, Dex," which prompted further shouts of agreement.

"Thank you," he said before he turned for the stairs. "Glad I can count on you."

45. A MAN AND A PLAN

Dexter entered the conference room to see Marty taking off his coat and revealing his colorful poolside shirt with palm trees.

"Wassup, Marty?" Dexter asked. "You a contestant on *Wheel of Fortune*?"

Marty shrugged. "I just... um... I don't know." He scowled. "Why?"

Dexter pulled a Dayglo orange vest off a hook and tossed it to Marty. "Cover that shit up, will you? You're burning my eyes."

Marty held up the vest and studied it for a moment. "It clashes with the little trees."

Dexter put both fists on his hips and glared. "You can't be in a serious meeting wearing a clown outfit. Alright?"

Marty sheepishly slid on the vest and took a seat at the conference table, where he was joined by Lindsey and Margaret. Jeanette dialed up a video call to bring in Lucy, Armani, and Digby, as well as Frank Cardini and his chief of staff. Jeanette advised Dexter that Mayor DeAngelo Brice could not make the call.

"Does he realize we've got a problem that could take down his city?" Dexter asked.

"I told his answering service," Jeanette said.

"Did they say when he'd be available?"

"They said he's off duty."

Dexter shook his head in disbelief. "When's a mayor off duty?"

"About half the time," Frank interjected. "You can probably find him at Club Spiff in Manhattan."

"I tried that," Jeanette said. "They wouldn't tell me if he was there or not."

Dexter turned to Margaret. "You know Club Spiff?"

"I know they're a customer."

"Turn off their lights."

"Will do," she replied, grabbing her phone.

Dexter turned to the screen. "The mayor will be joining us shortly," he said. "Alright. I don't know how to put it delicately. But we're going to need everything to go exactly right or this town's in a world of hurt."

Frank sighed. "What does that mean?"

"It means voluntary measures aren't working," Dexter said. "Any power that doesn't absolutely have to be turned on should be turned off—now. The Christmas tree in Rockefeller Center. The colored lights at the top of the Empire State Building and the World Trade Center. The signs in Times Square. The lights on the Radio City Music Hall. Everything you can think of. We're going dark."

"We're hours away from Christmas Eve," the governor whined. "Is that absolutely necessary?"

"If the system crashes, y'all can cancel Christmas," Dexter said. "And a happy New Year is out of the question." Dexter paused to let that sink in before continuing. "The New York grid operator has called for rolling blackouts to begin in twenty minutes. This will exclude hospitals, nursing homes, police and fire stations, but blackouts will roll through every neighborhood in the city, two hours at a time. If that's not enough, they'll extend the blackouts to four hours. Governor, we need you to shut down all the subways and train stations across the city to avoid stranding people when the blackouts hit."

Cardini leaned back in his chair, wincing. "Done."

Dexter studied the other faces on the screen and saw that tuxedoed Mayor DeAngelo Brice had joined the call, along with his chief of staff, Joyful McGee, who was wearing a slinky red dress.

"Thank you for joining us, Mister Mayor," Dexter said. "We're discussing blackouts."

"You're discussing… what?" the mayor said. "Did I hear you right?"

"We've got to turn off some lights, mayor. You've been through this drill before. When lights go down, crime goes up," Dexter said. "You'll need all the police you can get to prevent looting. Criminal gangs will want to do their Christmas shopping with sledgehammers and pillowcases. If we can keep the blackouts to two hours, we'll minimize the damage. If not, well… I guess we'll find out."

"Couldn't you at least give me a warning?" the mayor whined.

"I just did," Dexter replied. "In the meantime, people with electric heat are going to get cold, especially in public housing with poor windows and insulation. We need to warn people: don't heat your home with gas ovens. They could start fires. Or they could die from carbon monoxide poisoning."

"We'll take that on," the mayor said, nodding to Joyful.

"*We'll?*" she asked, her tone full of irritation.

"Yeah, *we*. I need you to handle that."

"On December twenty-third? I ain't—" Joyful placed a hand over the lens and their camera went dark.

Dexter pressed ahead. "We also need to advise people to fill buckets, tubs, and pots with water," Dexter said. "Their water and sewage systems won't work without electricity. I recommend you go building-to-building and talk to people."

The governor said, "I'll get the National Guard to help with that and coordinate with the mayor, if he ever comes back on."

"I'm here," said the mayor, who reappeared on the screen. He was clearly less Joyful.

"Which neighborhood goes first?" Frank asked.

"I don't know. It's done through a computer program," Dexter said. "But I promise you: Nobody gets a pass. Everyone from the Upper East Side to Bed-Stuy will get their turn in the barrel."

Frank looked irritated. "You all know how this works. We'll get criticized for who gets hit the hardest and who gets hit the least."

"We'll spread the pain as evenly as the system allows," Dexter promised. "That brings me to my last point. I know this will cause agita for Felicity Redfeather and her fan club, but I have no choice: we need to vaporize our entire reserve of liquefied natural gas. I know she promised we'd never use it again, but there's nowhere else to turn. LNG's the only way to go."

Margaret leaned over to Dexter and said under her breath, "We don't have any."

Dexter turned to her. "Don't have any what?"

"Liquefied natural gas."

Dexter cocked his head, disbelieving. "Wait. *What?*" He had trouble comprehending. "No LNG? You didn't use it already, did you?"

"It never arrived," she said.

"That can't be," Dexter said, his voice rising. "I ordered the shipment last summer."

"Boyd cancelled it," Margaret said.

"Boyd—" Dexter felt as if his head was about to explode. "Why would he do that?"

"You know—carbon emissions. Boyd said they were drawing the line. New era and all that."

Dexter was dumbfounded. "You're telling me our tanks are empty."

"Yeah."

"Is the building open?"

"Yes," she said.

"Do we still have tanks?"

"Yes. They're mothballing them, but not until next month. In the meantime, they've got a skeleton crew over there."

Dexter looked at the camera. "Hold on. I'll be with you in a minute." He turned off his camera and microphone, stood up and stepped over to the window overlooking the control room. Margaret joined him as he studied the monitor showing pressure in the gas lines continuing to fall.

"Do you see where this is going?" Dexter asked her.

"I do."

"How long before the pipeline system collapses?"

"At this rate?" She anxiously looked at the clock. "I'd say we have until noon tomorrow."

Lindsey and Marty exchanged alarmed glances. *Holy shit.*

Dexter calmed himself with a deep breath and spoke in measured tones. "Alright," he said to Margaret. "Put out an APB. Find me an LNG shipment that can get here tomorrow morning. Don't bother with the Gulf of Mexico; they'd never make it. Focus on the Mid-Atlantic and New England. We have to find a ship and get it here as soon as possible."

"On it," Margaret said, before running out of the room.

Dexter turned to Jeanette, the admin. "Get me a crew that can prepare our LNG tanks for a delivery. I'll need another crew to offload the ship, assuming we find one. Pay 'em whatever it takes." He turned to Lindsey. "Don't worry. You can bill the state."

She nodded. "Damn right I will."

Dexter turned back to Jeanette. "And alert all our first responders that we may have ourselves a situation here," he said. "We need their help."

Dexter turned back to the screen and switched on his camera and microphone. "Sorry to report this. But thanks to People's Power's inept management, we have no backup fuel for electricity generation or home heating. We're trying to find a ship with LNG that can get here by midday tomorrow, but there's no guarantee. Not with the holidays, and not with this weather. I recommend you order an immediate evacuation."

Frank looked shaken. "Of what?"

"New York City."

The mayor asked, "What part?"

"The Big Apple."

"That's eight million people!" the mayor said. "I can't do that."

"If we don't get LNG here on time, the gas system will collapse, and you won't get it all back until spring."

"C'mon, man," the mayor said with a chuckle. "You puttin' a brother on. It doesn't take three months."

Dexter started ticking the process off on his fingers. "You go to every home and building in the city that uses gas. You have to close every valve. You purge all the lines. You make repairs before you turn on the pilot lights. That takes months, an army of utility workers, and a whole lot of money. In the meantime, people will freeze to death."

The mayor sat back in his seat, dumbfounded. "I had no idea."

"You got one now. This system goes down the tubes, so does New York City." He stared at the governor, and then at the mayor. "It might never recover."

Frank ran that calculation through his mind. He would no longer be governor, but the catastrophe that Dexter described would still be his legacy, even if it was Felicity's stupidity that had put the city in this dangerous situation. The number of deaths could dwarf 9/11. The economy would be in shambles. Businesses and residents would be forced to move elsewhere. The earthquake caused by America's largest city falling to its knees would consume the markets, require cash from the country's deeply indebted treasury, and send shock waves to allies and enemies around the world who might find opportunity in the chaos.

"I know you want a better answer than evacuation," Dexter said. "I don't have one. Anyone who doesn't have a place to go in the city—an emergency shelter or apartment building that uses fuel oil—should get out of town."

Frank considered the logistics of an evacuation as the windows at his home north of the city were rattled by the high winds and driving snow. Reports all evening had said that roads were increasingly treacherous. Trains would soon be shutting down because of the blackouts. Bridge and tunnel entrances were already clogged with holiday traffic. And ferries had limited utility since people couldn't reach the terminals to board the boats. Whether people tried to leave, or they sheltered in place, it all added up to significant casualties unless Dexter could acquire LNG in time.

The mayor had his own pressing issues. Fresh from a holiday ball, he had counted on going to bed, preferably with Joyful, who had left him in a snit. "This doesn't sound like a decision that needs to be made right now. Let's see how things go overnight."

Lindsey grew impatient with the dithering. "If you're going to evacuate, Mayor, you should do it now," she said sharply. "If you wait, it will be worse. Imagine everyone trying to leave at once when the lights are off and the elevators aren't working. It will be dark inside these buildings. It will be freezing cold. And somehow, they will all have to find their way to their cars, if they have them, or buses if they're running, and travel over bridges or squeeze through tunnels. Isn't it better to get out while most of the lights are still on?"

"What if your ship arrives on time?" Frank asked.

"That's right," the mayor said emphatically. "We'll evacuate the city for nothing. Everyone's gonna blame me."

"And me," the governor said.

"You can say you did it out of an abundance of caution because you both care so much about people," Lindsey said. "Sorry if that came off sarcastically."

"As a matter of fact, I *do* care," Frank said indignantly. "That's why I don't want to put millions of people out on the road at the same time in a driving storm. That's dangerous, too, you know." Frank pointed offscreen. "Look out your windows. It's too late to evacuate. We'll have people freezing in their cars and on the streets. That's even worse than dying in their homes. There's got to be another way."

HOSTILE CLIMATE

Lindsey sighed. "Your call."

"Find the LNG," Frank said.

"That's the only way," the mayor added.

Dexter leaned toward the camera. "Better hope your ship comes in."

46. GAS PAINS

The first desperate calls for LNG were frustrated for lack of availability. One source had only foreign-flagged ships on its docks, which were prevented by an antiquated federal law from moving from one American port to another. Other cities had empty vessels, crews off on holiday, or advisories from the Coast Guard not to sail in such treacherous conditions.

An extremely tense Margaret hung up her phone and signaled for Dexter, Lindsey, and Marty to gather around.

"We have two possibilities," she said. "One is a ship at an offshore terminal in Gloucester, Massachusetts. It's got a crew available and a full container of LNG. The other is at Cove Point, Maryland on Chesapeake Bay. It was scheduled to go to Georgia, but Georgia agreed we were more desperate. The challenge is whether either boat can get here on time in this weather."

"Which one's closer?" Dexter asked.

Margaret called up nautical maps on a computer screen. "They're both a little over two hundred miles away. Allowing for prep time, navigating out of the harbor, and hitting a top speed of maybe twenty knots"—she punched the calculator on her phone—"there's a chance they could get here in ten hours if all goes perfectly."

Lindsey asked, "Can we count on that?"

"No," Dexter said. "You better build in a two-hour cushion on top of that. The water is very rough. And the wind is getting worse by the minute."

Margaret looked anxiously at the clock. "We're cutting it close, either way."

Lindsey said, "Order both ships. Maybe one of them will get here in time."

Dexter nodded. "Do that." He turned to Margaret. "Let the guys in the annex know we're expecting a ship. Maybe two."

Out of the corner of his eye, Dexter noticed his former colleague, KJ, standing at zher desk, talking on the phone and glowering at him. Had zhe been listening?

He had no time to find out, or tend to zher sensitivities. He grabbed his coat, hardhat, and gloves.

"Don't tell me you're leaving," Lindsey said.

"I'm heading to the LNG Annex," he said. "Need to make sure we can unload a tanker."

Lindsey sucked in her breath. "I'm coming with you."

"Me too," Marty said.

Dexter tossed them each a hardhat. "Fasten your chin strap."

It took a hard push from Dexter to open the door against the blistering gusts blowing off the river. A small plow circling the parking lot was fighting a losing battle against the swirling snow, with five inches on the ground already and drifts piling up against cars. Marty noted that his car had been socked in by the plows. Regardless of what happened with the ship, he was stuck for the foreseeable future.

The three of them bowed their heads and leaned forward as they trudged along the dock toward the LNG facility on the far side of the property. "First thing I gotta do is make sure our tanks are cooled before the LNG arrives," Dexter shouted as they walked.

"Wouldn't they be cold in this weather?" Marty asked.

"Not enough," Dexter replied. "LNG has to be stored at minus-162 degrees Celsius. That's minus-260 degrees Fahrenheit."

"Feels like that's what it is out here now," Marty grumbled.

"Not quite," Dexter said. "If LNG hits a tank that's too warm—and this is way too warm—you get a vapor cloud. You don't want to be around when that happens."

"Why is that?" Marty asked.

"'Cause you won't be around after."

"It blows up?"

"Kaboom, baby."

Dexter's badge allowed them into the plain brick building, and they walked to the facility's control room. He was relieved to find Leo Caesare, the long-time supervisor, at a computer.

"I thought you'd retired by now," Dexter said as they shook hands.

"Almost," Leo said. "I'm out January 1 with the rest of our crew. And I can't wait. Those assholes have got me working nights and holidays."

"Glad you're here," Dexter said. "We've got a shipment coming in tomorrow morning."

"So I heard."

"Can you handle it?"

"We're running through our protocols now," Leo said, before explaining the preparations that had just begun. "We're purging oxygen from the tanks, loading arms, and manifold pipes. Once that's done, I've got just enough LNG in reserve to cool the tanks.

"Any worries?"

"I need a bigger crew."

"Jeanette's on the case. What else?"

Leo nodded toward the river. "Whitecaps on the river concern me. I'm not sure we can keep the ship stable enough to unload it."

Dexter nodded. "I'll call for tugboats to assist. Anything else?"

"These computers are acting up," Leo said. "Not sure what's going on, but they need to be running when the ship arrives, or we'll be locked out. If you could have somebody troubleshoot it, that would help."

Lindsey said, "I'll call our tech team to check it out."

"One other worry bead," Leo said.

"What's that?"

"If the fanatics who run this place find out we're bringing in LNG, they'll go bananas. Boyd, Betty, and Felicity Redfeather are running this place into the ground. It almost looks like it's on purpose."

"It might be," Lindsey said.

"The good news is, we've worked with both ships you've ordered," Leo said. "If all goes well, we can get the gas flowing quickly."

Dexter looked him in the eye. "Will you stay with us?"

Leo frowned. "C'mon, Dex. You know I don't leave until the job's done."

"I love you, man," Dexter said, clapping him on the shoulder.

By midnight, the temperature outside had plunged to single digits, top wind speeds reached fifty miles per hour, and eight inches of snow were on the ground in Queens. Dexter led Lindsey and Marty out of the LNG Annex back to the docks, where turbulent waves were loudly slapping the breakwater. One worker struggled to keep his balance in the gusty wind as he shoveled snow and another spread salt along the shoreline in a futile effort to keep a path clear. Dexter looked up at the sky, then dropped to his haunches to study the wave depths.

"Leo's right," Dexter said. "Unloading a ship in this chop may be too risky. If we lose a connection while we're unloading and LNG mixes with oxygen, we'll have a big problem."

"What happens then?" Lindsey asked.

"Kaboom?" Marty suggested.

Dexter nodded. "Nobody within a half-mile of this plant would have to wonder what they're getting for Christmas."

"Great," Marty muttered.

"The good news is these crews know what they're doing," Dexter said. "If Leo senses a problem, he can probably stop the loading in time."

"Probably?" Lindsey asked.

"What can I say? LNG is dangerous stuff in the best of conditions," Dex said. He looked around him. "This is less than ideal."

"Anything I can do?" she asked.

Dexter looked at her blankly and shrugged.

Lindsey understood what Dexter couldn't say. "Gotcha," she said. "I'm going to get out of your way and let you do your job."

"Don't go far," Dexter said. "I'll need you if Felicity shows up."

47. BREAK POINT

Lindsey and Marty headed to the employee break room to thaw out. There they found a wall of vending machines and a microwave oven, where two custodial workers in jumpsuits warmed up burritos. The TV was showing a telenovela, but they weren't watching.

"Should I ask if we can turn it to the news?" Marty asked Lindsey.

"If you don't mind," Lindsey replied, "I'd rather not see it right now."

"I hear you."

They grabbed cups of coffee and took a table in a dark corner of the room, away from the TV, where they could talk quietly.

"How did we get here, Marty?" she asked. "All this talk about an existential threat turned out to be true. It's just not the one that Felicity Redfeather and her fellow travelers warned us about." She shook her head in dismay. "This is a disaster they created themselves."

Marty shrugged. "Felicity's a bit player in this drama," he said. "She is to the Climate Industrial Complex what a button man is to the mob: an enforcer."

"Enforcer for what?"

"To get people in line."

"People like me?" Lindsey asked.

"Like you. Like me. Like all of us."

"In line for what?"

"To pick up the tab for their so-called solutions," Marty said. He pushed back on his chair so that it was resting on its back two legs. "She demonizes fossil fuel energy and prosecutes the people who provide it. That leaves the public no option but to buy whatever 'clean' scheme her backers want to shove down our throats. It doesn't matter how many rare minerals you need to pull out of the earth to make them. It doesn't matter how much slave labor is involved. It doesn't even matter whether it makes any difference on climate. We have to buy their solutions or else."

"Or else what?"

He nodded toward her. "They ruin you."

"They try to anyway," she conceded. "But I think there's something else."

"Like what?"

"A lot of people out there are genuinely scared. They've heard the prediction about a climate catastrophe so often, they think it must be true. They don't have access like we do to climate scientists who say this is all overblown. Sensible voices are rarely heard. It's a virtual blackout in journalism, entertainment, education, and international organizations like the UN. Everyone says the same thing. The science is supposedly settled. So let's act, whether it does anything or not. You know what that tells me?"

"What?"

She leaned across the table. "The prize is huge," she said. "The next big thing in energy—I'm talking the real deal, not this wind/solar placebo—will be bigger than information technology. Bigger than oil and gas. Bigger than autos, AI, or pharma. That's because energy undergirds everything. All this money funneled into tamping down demand for fossil fuels is aimed at clearing a path."

"For what? Fusion?"

"Down the road, perhaps. We're getting there slowly," she said. "But we have pressing needs in the more immediate future that will have to be met soon. The only sensible option aside from fossil fuels has to be a different form of nuclear energy. Not the big scary reactors that freak out the activists, but small, modular reactors. Build them either on the grounds of military facilities or a mile below the surface of the earth. That reduces public resistance and still gets the job done."

"You think that can happen?"

"It better," Lindsey said. "The nation that fails to procure enough power in an energy-intensive world will lose its wealth, its freedom, and maybe its sovereignty. There are plenty of others out there who are more than willing to take our place."

They heard a click of the door and turned to see Dexter entering the room looking grim. He paused at the bulletin board, covered with fliers promoting the Big Green Deal Marketplace website, a rally to support "Clean Energy as a Human Right," and a festive Ujamaa Pajama Party on New Year's Eve to celebrate Marxist economics at a hall near St. Mark's Place in Lower Manhattan. Dexter glanced over all of it, shaking his head, then rapidly ripped it all down.

"Enough of this shit," he grumbled.

He gathered all the paper and crumpled it as he walked over to the table where Lindsey and Marty were sitting.

"What are you doing with that?" Lindsey asked.

Dexter looked at the paper he was balling up in his hands. "I'm gonna burn it. We might need the heat."

"Uh-oh," Lindsey said.

Dexter tossed the ball of paper at a trash can, where it dropped in with a dull thud. "We're down to one ship," he said. "The tanker out of Gloucester turned back."

Lindsey sat up with a start. "What happened?"

"Swells were so deep the captain worried the ship might roll over."

"What about the other ship?"

"It's still coming, as far as we know. Communications are spotty."

Lindsey reached over and squeezed his hand.

Dexter sucked in his breath. "Say a prayer. We need it."

48. NEW YORK AFTER DARK

Marty woke up slumped against a humming ice machine, dreaming he was driving a dogsled down Broadway. Lindsey was gone but his gallbladder was still around, and it was making its ugly presence felt. *Note to self: a dinner of Spicy Queso Funyuns and KitKat bars doesn't age well.* He sipped from a can of flat Coke to wash away the aftertaste and picked up one of the two empty bags of Funyuns from the tabletop to check the ingredients. Enriched corn meal. Vegetable oil. Corn starch, buttermilk, maltodextrin, salt, onion mix, cheddar cheese... Well, he thought, at least it claimed to contain "natural" flavors. *Gotta be a little healthy, right?*

He pushed away from the table and walked over to the TV, which was reporting on the mounting death toll across the country from Winter Storm Ivan, including eighteen people killed in New York. Overnight blackouts had caused panic, discomfort, and confusion among residents. Extensive looting occurred in SoHo after the lights went out, attributed by Congressperson Evita Manolo to the need for disenfranchised people to swath themselves in Gucci apparel to ward off the bitter cold. National Guard troop carriers were cruising Fifth Avenue to dissuade looting there, traffic was snarled at the icy exits out of Manhattan, and the lights were turned off on all city landmarks. Vast portions of the city were completely dark overnight. Yet New Jersey Governor Wertheimer warned New Yorkers to stay home, or they would face long delays at the exits from tunnels and bridges into his state. His Christmas message was, "There's no room at the inn."

Especially hard-hit were the housing projects in Brooklyn and Queens, which the city had neglected for years. Residents could see their breath in their frigid apartments. Toilets wouldn't flush, which sent sewage cascading down stairwells. Hypothermia had caused all eighteen storm-related deaths in the city, including one family attempting to leave the city in an electric car that ran out of power near the Henry Hudson Bridge. They froze to death as they huddled together in the back seat of their vehicle. The city offered residents bus rides to shelters for warmth, but it was unclear whether the overcrowded shelters could take in more people, or whether people were even getting the message in the blackouts. The forecast called for temperatures to fall to zero by noon and remain there for the rest of the day.

The time in the corner of the TV screen said it was seven-forty-five, which was a few minutes after sunrise on one of the shortest days of the year. Marty peered out the window to see snow drifts covering cars in the lot and the ground strewn with broken tree branches. The weather was not likely to save them if their ship didn't come in. He headed downstairs to the control room, hoping for good news.

He found Lindsey standing with Dexter, who looked every bit like a man who had been up all night. Dexter sagged sullenly against a desk and his eyes were heavy. His former boss, the supercilious Boyd Meriwether, stood across from him, his arms folded across his chest. Marty noted as he approached that Boyd's shoulders were covered in white, indicating he'd either just arrived or suffered from world-class dandruff.

"I'm the one who cancelled that LNG shipment last summer," Boyd barked at Dexter. "You have no authority to override my order."

"Well, here's the thing, Boyd," Dexter said. "I did."

Boyd seethed. "Felicity Redfeather will have something to say about that when she arrives. I can tell you she does not approve."

Dexter, suddenly very much awake, bolted upright. He mockingly slapped his palms on his cheeks. "Oh, no! Felicity doesn't approve?" He dropped his hands and his expression turned deadly serious. "You need to understand something, Boyd. I don't give a shit whether Felicity approves or not. She's not my boss and neither are you. My orders are to do whatever it takes to power this city and save lives. And that's what I'm going to do."

"Don't try claiming the high ground with me," Boyd sneered. "You don't save lives by killing the planet."

"Alright. You know what? I don't need this right now, Boyd," Dexter growled, stepping toward him. "You need to get the fuck outta here before somebody hurts you. And do you know who that somebody is?" He reached behind him toward his waistband and Marty thought for a moment Dexter might shoot Boyd. Instead, he simply pulled out his phone from his back pocket.

Boyd pointed his finger at Dexter. "You touch me, and you'll be charged with assault."

Dexter grabbed Boyd's finger and twisted it, causing him to yelp in pain. "Whatever charges I face might depend on your next of kin."

Boyd jerked his finger away, turned on his heel, and marched off in a huff.

Dexter gathered himself and turned to Lindsey. "Alright. Back to business." He ticked off his tasks on his fingers. "Our crews are ready. Tanks are prepared. Water's calmed a bit. *Methane Princess II* is scheduled to arrive at ten-thirty." He grimaced. "That's a little later than I'd hoped."

Lindsey asked, "Does that give us enough time?"

Dexter winced. "It will if everything goes right."

As he said it, the wall of monitors went blank as did all the computers at the smaller desks.

Lindsey, startled, asked, "We're not subject to the blackouts, are we?"

"Oh, hell no!" Dexter exclaimed.

Margaret came running over. "The computer system's down."

Lindsey thought back to her briefing on Chinese hackers targeting pipeline companies. Were they coming after the powerhouse when it was most vulnerable? "Where's Faraz?"

Margaret nodded. "He's on it. Upstairs."

"We can't do this without our computer system," Dexter said.

"I know," Lindsey said. "Let me see what's going on."

Lindsey and Marty hurriedly followed Margaret to the computer room, where they found Faraz shaking his head. A team of his techs were working on computers nearby.

"What happened?" Lindsey asked.

"We had to take the system down to stop the hack," Faraz said.

"Who hacked us?"

"Same MO as the Chinese, so we assume it's them," Faraz said. "We've disconnected from the internet and backed up the system. Now we've got to reboot, reload our software, and get new passwords for everybody who needs access."

"How long will that take?"

"A couple hours," Faraz said.

"I don't know if we have that long," Lindsey fretted.

Faraz sighed. "Sorry. We're working it as fast as we can."

Lindsey sucked in her breath. "Why would the Chinese hit us now?"

Marty said, "A report on TV said China was sending warships to Taiwan. New York City's collapse could serve as a useful distraction if they decide to invade."

Lindsey took a deep breath. "I can't worry about that right now. I'm worried about this." She patted Faraz's shoulder. "Do the best you can… but hurry."

49. FELICITY'S POWER TRIP

The massive *Methane Princess II* entered New York Harbor under the Verrazzano-Narrows Bridge, carrying the fate of the city in its cargo hold. Ten stories tall and a hundred feet longer than the Titanic, the ship was designed for one purpose: to transport natural gas supercooled to a liquid, reducing its volume to one six-hundredth of its natural state. The ship's four spherical tanks protruded through the topside, giving it a distinctive look, and its double-hulled structure added a level of protection in the event of a collision or an attack.

Dexter had spread word among first responders that the arrival of the *Methane Princess II* was critical to New York City's health and safety, and it must not face any obstructions as it sailed up the East River. In response, the ship was met by a convoy of escorting boats from the Coast Guard, the New York Police Department, the New York Fire Department, and the Port Authority, as well as a half-dozen tugboats.

As rumors spread that the East River Powerhouse was importing LNG, resistance to the shipment was gathering on land and sea. The very idea of importing more fossil fuels to the powerhouse now controlled by "the People" was repugnant to the coalition of climate activists that had defeated Crowe Power in court. They had bad old energy on the run, and they weren't going to let it come back. The Planetistas organized a protest outside the powerhouse grounds, while the Climate Rangers chartered a boat of their own to block the dock.

Felicity's black SUV arrived at the powerhouse, escorted by two blue State Police cruisers along with her usual convoy of TV news trucks, ever ready to chronicle her planetary heroics. Her vehicle had barely rolled to a stop before the enraged governor-elect barreled out of the back seat to join Boyd, who stood outside huddled in the doorway of the powerhouse smoking a cigarette, emitting carbon monoxide as well as carbon dioxide and other gases into the atmosphere. After reporting to Felicity about the shenanigans inside the plant, Boyd flicked his cigarette in the snow and tramped through the wind and snow over to the dock, where workers were preparing for the arrival of the *Methane Princess II.*

Powerhouse security personnel prevented the TV crews from entering the property, forcing them to set up their cameras on the uncleared sidewalk just outside the gates. They were soon treated to a special holiday performance by Ernesto and the Planetistas, who attached their "LNG=Death" and "No Fracking Way!" banners to the cyclone fence and offered theatrical chants for the cameras.

Lindsey looked out the window with disbelief at the gathering crowd. "Why would anyone oppose what we're doing?"

Marty peered out. "You may as well ask, 'why do they lay down in traffic? Why do they throw food at priceless art? Why do they throw fake blood on buildings?'"

Lindsey shook her head. "You tell me."

"Because they're nuts." Marty nodded toward another vehicle pulling into the parking lot. Frank Cardini emerged from its back seat and hurriedly rushed over to Felicity and Boyd. "Looks like your calvary has arrived without any horses."

"Just one lame duck," Lindsey said. "We'd better get down there." They hustled over to the conference room to retrieve their coats, hardhats, and boots, then clambered down the metal staircase to the control room, where Dexter was putting on his coat.

"Can you get the TV crews out of here?" Lindsey asked.

"Not if they're on public property."

"Can you at least block their view?" she pressed. "Things could get ugly."

Dexter nodded and picked up his phone. "Yo, Leo. Your guys have the keys to those panel trucks in the lot?"

By the time Lindsey and Marty had bundled up and made their way outside, Leo's people had parked three trucks along the fence to block the TV cameras from capturing anything happening on the powerhouse grounds. That did not prevent reporters from telling their audiences that, according to highly credible sources inside the climate movement, a bitter Lindsey Harper Crowe had stormed the compound with her henchmen, attempting to retake her former property. Fortunately, Felicity Redfeather had arrived to hold the fort.

Marty followed Lindsey and Dexter to the docks, where Frank Cardini was engaged in a heated exchange with Felicity and Boyd as the snow swirled around them. In the distance, Marty could make out the shadow of the hulking *Methane Princess II* and the faint lights of its escorting boats as they made the turn around Halletts Point toward the Robert F. Kennedy Bridge.

"You have no authority here, Frank," Felicity yelled into the howling winds.

"I'm still the governor," Frank shot back.

"Not for long," she replied as a quartet of cops gathered behind her.

Frank pointed a gloved finger at her. "Back off, Felicity."

Lindsey and Marty approached the gathering, kicking Felicity's rage into a higher gear. "What do you think you're doing here?"

Lindsey held her palms up to catch the snow. "I'm helping Dexter deal with all this global warming."

"Get out of here right now, or I will have you thrown in jail." Felicity turned toward Sergeant Harold Washington of the State Police and pointed to four workers clearing away snow and ice from the dock. "Sergeant, I want you to tell those workers to stand down. No LNG ships are docking here today, tomorrow, or ever."

Frank held up his hands. "Don't do it, Sergeant." Behind him, the activists' boat, a dinner cruiser called *Lost Empire*, pulled into the dock, blocking the path of the *Methane Princess II*. A half-dozen activists stood on the bow, holding a banner: NO LNG IN NYC!

Frank turned to Dexter and asked quietly, "Can you get that boat out of here?"

"Yes, I can," Dexter said.

Dexter got on the phone and walked away. At his request, a pair of tugboats pulled into the dock, facing the *Lost Empire*. A call could be heard over a loudspeaker from one of the tugboats. "*Lost Empire*: move away from the dock." The activists' boat held its position, bobbing up and down.

A tugboat issued a second warning as the Methane Princess II closed in. "*Lost Empire*: you are directed to move away from the dock immediately, or *we will move you!*"

The pilot of the *Lost Empire* issued his response through a loudspeaker. "Fuck off." The activists on the bow gave a rousing cheer.

Dexter looked over his shoulder at the approaching *Methane Princess II*, which was a hundred yards away. He barked into his phone. "Move 'em out."

The pair of tugboats moved in unison, converging on the hull of the *Lost Empire*. They revved their engines, producing a roar, and began their push. The *Lost Empire* revved its own engines to fight back, but the dinner cruiser was no match for the powerful tugs. It gave way quickly and was pushed backward, as the activists shook their fists and shouted epithets.

Dexter issued another order into his phone. "Get that boat as far away as you can and hold it until we're through." He turned to Lindsey, who was on the phone with Faraz. "Are the computers back up?"

Lindsey pulled her phone away from her ear. "They're finishing the rebuild," she said. "Hold on..." She listened intently for Faraz's go-ahead. At last, she turned to Dexter and gave him the thumbs up. "Good to go."

Dexter radioed Leo. "Ready to unload this lady?"

"Yes, we are," Leo said.

Dexter yelled to his workers on the dock who were clearing snow. "Let's get this done!"

Felicity walked over to the workers, who continued to clear snow and ice off the docks. "You there!" she shouted. "Stop what you're doing!"

The workers looked at Dexter, who shook his head.

A dock worker nodded and turned back to Felicity with a shrug. *"No comprendo."*

The workers resumed their preparations for the ship's arrival, prompting Felicity to call out to the state troopers. "Arrest all these people. Now!"

The troopers moved toward the dock, but Lindsey rushed over and stepped in their way. She stood toe-to-toe with Sergeant Washington and looked up into his face. "Please, Sergeant. I beg you. Don't listen to her," she said. She pointed to the *Methane Princess II*. "That ship has to land here. We're in a desperate situation."

"So am I." The sergeant nodded toward Felicity. "She's my boss."

Frank stepped in. "No, she's not," he insisted. "I am. Let that ship come in."

Lindsey looked over at Felicity, then back to Sergeant Washington. "Felicity Redfeather is a dangerous nut with a grudge against a lot of people, including me. She also happens to hate cops. Residents of New York are dying right now because they don't have heat or electricity. If that ship doesn't dock, you'll have a disaster like none this city's ever seen."

"She's absolutely right," Frank said. "You've got to help us."

Dexter appeared at Lindsey's shoulder. "That's no bullshit, brother," Dexter said to the policeman. "We've got one shot at this. And we've got to move fast."

Felicity walked over. "Sergeant!" she said, heatedly. "Are you *slow?*"

Behind them, the hulking *Methane Princess II* was moving toward the dock whether it was ready or not. Four tugboats maneuvered around it to carefully push it closer to the platform, while a crane slowly approached, bearing four massive unloading arms.

"Stop this *now!*" Felicity shrieked at the sergeant. "Can't you follow simple directions?"

Sergeant Washington, bristling, turned to his three troopers, who were awaiting his command. "We have a public safety emergency. Clear this area so that the workers can do their jobs without interference." He called more loudly for all to hear. "Anyone who is not essential to the landing and unloading of this ship needs to move off the docks immediately."

Felicity shrieked. "How dare you ignore my command!"

Sergeant Washington glared at her. "My order includes you. Back off now, or you will be arrested."

Felicity was in full hysteria. "Step aside!" she commanded. As she took a stride toward the approaching ship, Lindsey stepped into her path.

"I see you, ShaNeeNah," Lindsey said.

That stopped Felicity in her tracks. "What did you call me?"

"I know who you are," Lindsey continued. "You're still a Wannabe."

Felicity sneered. "And you still wear your privilege on your sleeve."

"This isn't about me," Lindsey said. "And it's not about you either. Hundreds of people have already been killed in this storm. How many more have to die for you to prove a point?"

Felicity glared at Lindsey, who was still standing in her path. "Out of my way!" Felicity yelled.

Lindsey folded her arms across her chest and stood her ground, just a few feet from the river's edge. "Absolutely not," she said firmly. "We're going to unload this ship whether you like it or not."

Felicity made a move to run past Lindsey, who blocked her way. Felicity shoved Lindsey with all her might, causing her to stumble. Lindsey recovered, using her kickboxing skills to execute a pirouette and a side kick to Felicity's midsection. Felicity's heavy coat cushioned the blow, and she charged back at Lindsey harder.

Lindsey deftly ducked out of the way and Felicity's momentum carried her forward onto a patch of ice that would have been cleared had she not interfered with the workers. The ice sent her slipping and sliding to the edge of the dock. As she tried to stop, her boot hooked on a cleat, sending her careening into arriving *Methane Princess II*. Her head smacked against the hull, knocking her out and pasting a bloody smear on its white-painted bow. She tumbled over headfirst and splashed into the water below.

"Oh my God!" Lindsey shrieked. "Felicity!"

Careful not to make the same mistake Felicity made, Lindsey and Marty trod carefully toward the edge and looked into the churning water, searching for a sign of her. A pair of troopers looked at each other and shrugged hopelessly, while Sergeant Washington called on his radio to ask police and fireboats to commence a search and rescue. It was quickly apparent that Felicity's odds of surviving the plunge into the frigid water were practically nil.

A hysterical Boyd pointed at Lindsey. "You did this!"

"She tripped," Lindsey protested.

"After you kicked her!" Boyd said.

"I was defending myself," Lindsey said. "That didn't cause her to fall in the water."

Sergeant Washington concurred. "She slipped on the ice."

"I'm taking this to the FBI," Boyd said, tearing up. "And I'm telling them you killed her."

As workers secured the ship to the dock, Dexter approached Boyd from behind and put his arm around his shoulder, gently guiding him out of sight from the others. "Don't call the FBI, Boyd."

Boyd said bitterly, "Just watch me."

Dexter pressed his pistol to Boyd's temple. "You feel me?"

"I think so," Boyd said nervously.

"You make any more moves against Lindsey and I'll make sure you never have to worry about climate change again."

Boyd thought it over.

"Do you understand what I'm saying?" Dexter asked.

"Yep. I think it's, um, pretty clear."

"Good." Dexter put his gun back in his coat and patted Boyd on the back. "Go home, Boyd. We've got work to do here."

As Boyd hustled off to his car, Dexter returned to the dock and called out to the workers. "Let's get this done."

50. SHIP SHAPE

Lindsey and Marty stepped away from the dock to get out of the way of Dexter's crews tending to the *Methane Princess II*. Ferries helped block the whitecapped waves in the river from beating against its frame, and four tugboats helped to steady her.

The bloody residue on the hull from Felicity's mad dash soon washed away, and protesters on the *Lost Empire* could only look on from a distance in dismay as the LNG poured through the loading arms to the annex, where it was vaporized and sent through the gas lines to homes and businesses throughout the city.

By early afternoon, New York City's energy situation had stabilized. Pressure in gas lines was no longer a threat, blackouts ended, subway and train service resumed, and lights came on across the city. Christmas festivities could resume for those who celebrated the holiday, but a somber mood prevailed over the city as Ivan's terrible impact was measured by first responders and reported by the media.

The death toll in New York stood at 182 people and was destined to climb still higher with hundreds more hospitalized from hypothermia, smoke inhalation, carbon monoxide poisoning, injuries from tumbles on icy steps and sidewalks, and concussions from falling tree branches. Health officials reported that most of the deaths would have been prevented had the power never gone out.

Another casualty was residents' faith that their leaders knew how to run things. Few people knew or cared about LNG, electric loads, or pipeline pressure, but they did know their lights were off, their heat was out, and the loss of power was more than an inconvenience and a damper on the "hap-happiest season of all." It was life-threatening. It was scary. And it had been eminently avoidable.

"So unnecessary," Lindsey said with a sigh as she watched the news. "What a waste."

Marty found that the last coal-fired pizza shop in Queens had reopened and ordered a dozen pies for Dexter and his crews working in the powerhouse, the dock, the ship, and the annex. He dug his car out of the snow drifts and drove through tunnels of snow to pick them up. Back at the powerhouse, he laid out the pies and a large salad in the break room, and the workers were invited to toast their success with Dr Pepper and coffee. They came in groups of three or four and gladly scarfed down a bite or two before returning to work.

Frank Cardini, ever the campaigner, instinctively worked the break room, thanking the red-cheeked workers in Carhartt gear and steel-toed boots for their labors and wishing them a happy holiday. In the back of his mind was the thought that he would need their votes sooner rather than later.

Frank's hunch was confirmed in the late afternoon when the body of a white woman was found along the shore of the United Nations building. Early indications were that it was the remains of governor-elect Felicity Redfeather, AKA Felicity O'Leary, AKA Two Blue Eyes, AKA ShaNeeNah. When her identity was confirmed shortly afterward, New York's Secretary of State announced that a special election would be held in the coming months to identify a successor.

Marty tended the break room buffet until all of the plant's workers had come through, then grabbed a slice for himself. Sidling up to Lindsey, he asked, "Do you think it's safe to leave?"

Lindsey took a deep breath and nodded. "Dexter says he'll stick around through New Years'. Beyond that, I guess it's up to the People." She looked at her watch. "Frank promised me a police escort and snowplow to get me to Teterboro. I plan to take him up on that."

"Let's go."

51. AS THE CROWE FLIES

The escort for Lindsey and Marty to Teterboro proved unnecessary. Between the storm and Christmas Eve, there was little traffic other than that of snowplows, salt spreaders, police cars, and ambulances. The major thoroughfares were clear, as was the tarmac where Crowe Bird I waited.

As they strapped into their seats, Lindsey marveled at Marty's attire. "You know what I like about that shirt?"

"Let me guess," he replied. "Nothing?"

"No," she said, pointing to an area near the breast pocket. "You can't tell a splotch of tomato sauce from the design."

Marty looked down. "I think that's a parrot."

"Maybe," Lindsey said uncertainly.

"I do have other shirts in my luggage, you know."

"That's a relief."

"Oh?"

"Feel free to put one on," she needled.

"Thank you," he said tartly. "I will when we get there. Is that okay with you?"

"Of course," she said with a smile. She kissed her fingertip, leaned over, and planted it on the tip of Marty's nose. "Feel better?"

"I'll survive."

As the pilot, Captain Mike, and the flight attendant, Charles, made their last preparations for departure, Lindsey flipped through a copy of the *Daily Reaper* while Marty scrolled through his phone for news.

"Here's one for you," Marty said. "'The FBI raided the office of the Center for Unity and Cooperation and issued an arrest warrant for Li Zhang. Federal officials said the Chinese national, accused of spying on U.S. energy companies, is believed to have fled the country.'"

Lindsey chuckled. "Of course Robbie was in bed with her. Makes total sense."

"Here's another interesting nugget," Marty said. "Chinese warships withdrew across the Straits of Taiwan today, characterizing their incursion yesterday as merely an exercise."

Lindsey folded her paper shut. "When did that happen?"

Marty flipped through the story. "It looks like—hmm. Just a few hours ago."

"Around the time our lights came back on."

Marty nodded. "You think there's a connection?"

"I doubt it's a coincidence." She settled back into her seat and picked up another paper, glanced over it and put it down. "I don't know why I bother to read a newspaper anymore. The news is old by the time I get it. I'm old school, I guess."

"You are definitely that," Marty said. He looked up from his phone. "A story just broke saying California has filed suit against seven energy companies over climate change."

Lindsey scoffed. "You're kidding."

Marty shook his head.

"Are we named?" Lindsey asked.

Marty turned off his phone and placed it face down on the table. "Let's not worry about that for the next twenty-four hours."

"You're not going to tell me?"

He shook his head. "No."

She patted his knee and smiled, then leaned into the aisle and called up to the cockpit. "Wheels up!"

ABOUT THE AUTHOR

Jon Pepper is a novelist and consultant based in New York City. He was previously an executive for two Fortune 100 companies, a business columnist and national writer for *The Detroit News*, a reporter for the *Detroit Free Press*, a magazine publisher, a radio talk show host, and advertising copywriter. He and his wife, Diane, who designed the cover, reside in Manhattan.

Jon's Fossil Feuds series is comprised of five books:
A Turn in Fortune (2018)
Heirs on Fire (2020)
Green Goddess (2022)
Missy's Twitch (2023)
Hostile Climate (2024)

More about Jon and his novels is available at www.jonpepperbooks.com

You can learn about Jon's consulting firm at www.indelable.com

Printed in the USA
CPSIA information can be obtained
at www.ICGtesting.com
LVHW090014111224
798766LV00007B/181